Using

Microsoft® Plus!

Jerry Honeycutt

with

Chris Hughes
Lori Kern
Brad Phillips

Using Microsoft Plus!

Copyright© 1995 by Que® Corporation

Library of Congress Catalog No.: 95-71444

ISBN: 0-7897-0626-1

97 96 95   6 5 4 3 2 1

Interpretation of the printing code: the rightmost double-digit number is the year of the book's printing; the rightmost single-digit number, the number of the book's printing. For example, a printing code of 95-1 shows that the first printing of the book occurred in 1995.

Screen reproductions in this book were created using Collage Plus from Inner Media, Inc., Hollis, NH.

Composed in *ITC Century*, *ITC Highlander*, and *MCPdigital* by Que Corporation.

Credits

President
Roland Elgey

Publisher
Stacy Hiquet

Publishing Director
Brad R. Koch

Editorial Services Director
Elizabeth Keaffaber

Managing Editor
Sandy Doell

Director of Marketing
Lynn E. Zingraf

Senior Series Editor
Chris Nelson

Publishing Manager
Jim Minatel

Acquisitions Editor
Cheryl D. Willoughby

Product Director
Benjamin Milstead

Senior Editor
Nancy Sixsmith

Production Editor
Susan Christophersen

Assistant Product Marketing Manager
Kim Margolius

Technical Editor
Don Funk

Technical Specialist
Cari Skaggs

Acquisitions Coordinator
Ruth Slates

Operations Coordinator
Patty Brooks

Editorial Assistant
Andrea Duvall

Book Designer
Ruth Harvey

Cover Designer
Dan Armstrong

Production Team
Angela D. Bannan
Brian Buschkill
Bryan Flores
DiMonique Ford
Mike Henry
Darren Jackson
Damon Jordan
Bobbi Satterfield
Jody York

Indexer
Mary Jane Frisby

This book is for Becky. Becky was there when my hours grew long, and sometimes she would sleep in my office so that I would not work alone. She provided an endless supply of encouragement, support, and love. Oh, and lots of coffee, too. This book would not have been possible without Becky. Thank you.

About the Authors

 **Jerry Honeycutt** is a business-oriented technical manager with broad experience in software development. He has served companies such as The Travelers, IBM, Nielsen North America, and most recently, Information Retrieval Methods as Director of Windows Application Development. Jerry has participated in the industry since before the days of Microsoft Windows 1.0, and believes that Windows 95 puts real power in the hands of regular folks.

Jerry was a contributing author on *Special Edition Using Windows 95* for Que. He has also been published in *Computer Language Magazine* and is a regular speaker at the Windows World and Comdex trade shows on topics related to software development and corporate solutions for Windows 95.

Jerry graduated from the University of Texas at Dallas in 1992 with a B.S. in Computer Science. He currently lives in the Dallas suburb of Frisco, Texas with his wife, Becky; two Westies, Corky and Turbo; and two cats, Scratches and Chew-Chew. You can reach Jerry on the Internet at **jerry@honeycutt.com**, Compuserve at **76477,2751**, or the Microsoft Network at **Honeycutt**.

Chris Hughes is the Director of Globalization for Micrografx in Richardson, Texas. Previously, he spent ten years at Nielsen North America where he pioneered the use of full-color digital images to assist retailers in achieving higher product sales through more efficient merchandising tactics. When Chris is not up to his eyeballs in work, he can usually be found either training for his next marathon or talking about running on the Internet. Chris lives with his wife, Fran, his daughter, Marissa, and two cats, Oliver and Callie. He can be reached at **chris@onramp.net**.

Lori Kern is an independent computer consultant specializing in Web page development. She has been in the computing industry for more than 10 years. Lori graduated from the University of Texas at Austin in 1985 with a B.B.A. in data processing. She shares her home with her husband, Fred, a cat named Maggie, and a dog named Schotzy. She can be reached at **lpkern@onramp.net**.

Brad Phillips is a project leader at Rapp Collins Worldwide. He graduated from Southern Methodist University in 1984 with a degree in M.I.S. He is also a musician who uses the computer to compose and play music. He can be reached at **brdp@onramp.net**.

Acknowledgments

This book came into being very quickly. A lot of people contributed their very special talents to make it happen. At the top of my list is Cheryl Willoughby, Acquisitions Editor at Que. Cheryl had the faith in me and provided the encouragement to get this project done. Thanks.

I'd also like to thank Benjamin Milstead for the "go get 'em" attitude that made sure you got a top-notch book; Susan Christophersen for her tireless editing and handy common sense; and Don Funk for checking those technical details. Thanks are also due Alec Saunders at Microsoft for getting me up to speed as quickly as possible on some of the more cryptic bits of Microsoft Plus!.

And thanks to the contributing authors Chris Hughes, Lori Kern, and Brad Phillips, who I worked very, very hard. But they'll all tell you that it was worth it. (Won't they?)

We'd Like to Hear from You!

As part of our continuing effort to produce books of the highest possible quality, Que would like to hear your comments. To stay competitive, we *really* want you, as a computer book reader and user, to let us know what you like or dislike most about this book or other Que products.

You can mail comments, ideas, or suggestions for improving future editions to the address below, or send us a fax at (317) 581-4663. For the online inclined, Macmillan Computer Publishing has a forum on CompuServe (type **GO QUEBOOKS** at any prompt) through which our staff and authors are available for questions and comments. The address of our Internet site is **http://www.mcp.com** (World Wide Web).

In addition to exploring our forum, please feel free to contact me personally to discuss your opinions of this book: I'm **Benjamin Milstead, 102121,1324** on CompuServe, and **bmilstead@mail.msp.com** on the Internet.

Thanks in advance—your comments will help us to continue publishing the best books available on computer topics in today's market.

Benjamin Milstead
Product Development Specialist
Que Corporation
201 W. 103rd Street
Indianapolis, Indiana 46290
USA

Contents at a Glance

Table of Contents

Deselect features you don't want to install

see page 5

Part II: Having Fun on Your Windows 95 Desktop   29

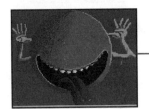

See page 38 for resizing your wallpaper

Scoring
Summary

see page 102

Jumping to a linked Web page

see page 140

Sound Surfing

see page 162

What is a home page?

see page 166

Go see the
White House!

see page 204

How do I get on a mailing list?

see page 215

Scripting commands

see page 250

*How to back up
when you're
not using your
computer*

see page 316

Introduction

Windows 95 is a major leap forward in computing. It makes your computer easier and more fun to use with many user interface and performance enhancements. You'll get more done in less time.

What's missing, however, is the glitz and glamour. Of course, Windows 95 provides a handful of animated cursors, basic screen savers, and wallpaper. But they don't sparkle. Windows 95 also provides Dial-Up Networking, DriveSpace disk compression, and a few games. But they don't go far enough. Windows 95 lets you connect to the Internet, too. But it doesn't let you browse the Web or exchange e-mail with other Internet users. This is where Microsoft Plus! takes over. If you'd consider Windows 95 a '57 Chevy, then Microsoft Plus! would be the chrome wheels, fins, and leather trim—not to mention that big-block engine under the hood.

This book is for people like you who want to have more fun with Windows 95 and get more power out of it. You're going to live with Windows 95 for a long time; you should fix it up just the way you want.

I've assumed that you already have Windows 95 installed and have learned how to get around in it. You should know about shortcuts, how to start a program from the Start button, how to use Explorer, and so on. For in-depth coverage of Windows 95, get *Using Windows 95* or *Special Edition Using Windows 95*, both from Que.

What makes this book different

This book presents some pretty technical topics in terms that you can understand and use. Of course, avoiding technical terms altogether, when discussing disk compression or Dial-Up Networking, is impossible. This book, however, presents everything in plain English so that you'll be sure to get it.

You'll find that you won't be swamped with more details than you need. You want to get the job done. So, this book recommends the one best way to get the job done.

Also, you'll find the information you need laid out so that you can use it. For example, before choosing a desktop theme, look in Chapter 5, "Themes Included with Microsoft Plus!," to compare the themes side by side. Chapter 10, "Finding Your Way Around the Web," shows you a lot of exciting World Wide Web pages that you might want to give a whirl.

How do I use this book?

You don't have to read this book front to back. You can jump around all you like. The table of contents is a great place to look for a place to dive into this book. Also, look at the Action Index in the back of the book if you've got a particular question or problem.

You'll pick up a lot of information just by browsing the book. There are a lot of special elements in this book that will jump out at you as you thumb through it.

How this book is put together

This book is divided into five major parts to help you find exactly what you're looking for. These parts are described in the following sections.

Part I: Getting Started with Microsoft Plus! for Windows 95

Chapters 1 and 2 introduce you to Microsoft Plus!. You'll learn about all the new features Plus! adds to Windows 95. You'll be shown the contrast with Windows 95, and you'll also learn how to install Microsoft Plus!. Because many different areas of Windows 95 are changed when you install Plus!, you'll learn where all these features get hidden.

Part II: Having Fun on Your Windows 95 Desktop

Chapters 3 through 6 describe the lighter side of Microsoft Plus!. You'll find visual enhancements to make your desktop really cool, themes that make every visual aspect of Windows 95 consistent with the theme you choose, and a game of pinball that's so real, you'll think you are in an arcade.

Part III: Surfing the Internet with Internet Jumpstart

This may very well be your first opportunity to get on the Internet. Microsoft Plus! makes it easy. Chapters 7 through 12 include everything you need to know about getting started. You'll learn how to set up your account using Exchange with the Internet, and you'll learn to use Internet Explorer. You'll also find a handy reference to some of the most exciting spots on the World Wide Web and how to find some of your own.

Part IV: Connecting Remotely with Dial-Up Networking

Dial-Up Networking is a Windows 95 feature. But Microsoft Plus! adds a few of its own twists. In Chapters 13 through 15, you'll learn how to set up a dial-up connection, use the new scripting tool, and set up a dial-up server so that you can access your computer or network remotely.

Part V: Using the Microsoft Plus! Power Tools

Windows 95 comes with disk compression and a few other handy disk tools. You get real power, however, with Microsoft Plus!. In Chapters 16 through 19, you'll learn how to use DriveSpace 3, Compression Agent, and System Agent. As a bonus, you'll also learn how to use the Windows 95 backup tool effectively with System Agent.

Indexes

That's right. Not just one index, but two. Besides the good old standard index of keywords, you'll find an index for troubleshooting tips and other common questions to help you get the job done fast.

Information that's easy to understand

You'll find a number of special elements and conventions in this book that will jump right off the page. These elements will provide timely information.

TIP   **Tips point out things that you can do to get the most out of** Microsoft Plus!. These are often not found in the text or online help, and come from personal experience.

CAUTION   **Cautions warn you of possible trouble. They warn you about** things you should avoid or things that you need to do to protect your computer.

Q&A   ***What are Q&A notes?***
These elements anticipate your questions and provide advice on how to solve problems or avoid bad situations.

 Plain English, Please!
These notes explain technical terms in a manner that you can understand.

I also use different typefaces in this book:

- New terms are in **bold** letters.

- In a series of steps, text that you should type is put in **bold** letters.

- Commas are used to separate a string of menu selections, and the hotkeys are underlined. For example, you'll see File, Properties when I want you to open the File menu and choose the Properties command.

- If you see two keys separated by a plus sign, such as Alt+F, it's a key combination. Press and hold the first key. Press the second key. Then, let go of both.

Sidebars are oh-by-the-ways

Sidebars provide useful and interesting informa-
tion that doesn't really fit in the text. You'll find more technical information or interesting war stories.

Part I: Getting Started with Microsoft Plus! for Windows 95

1

What Does Microsoft Plus! Add to Windows 95?

● **In this chapter:**

● Plus! isn't just a bunch of screen savers

● How does Plus! expand Windows 95's functionality?

● Here are some examples of how you can use it

Microsoft Plus! is more than just a pretty face. It adds real power to Windows 95 . . . . ➤

I was in one of those computer superstores recently, when I over-heard a salesperson telling a customer that Microsoft Plus! wasn't worth the money—it was nothing more than a bunch of pretty wallpapers and screen savers. He was obviously not on commission. Otherwise, he would install Microsoft Plus! and discover that what he was saying couldn't be further from the truth.

Microsoft Plus! adds real value to Windows 95. It adds more support for mobile computer users and launches you onto the Internet. It gives more control over your computer. And yes, it has a bunch of incredibly pretty wallpapers and screen savers. Not convinced yet? Read on. This chapter introduces you to Microsoft Plus! and describes how it adds value to Windows 95.

Plus! keeps you connected

More and more users are doing their thing on the road. Some work at home. Some have busy travel schedules. Either way, their needs are similar: stay connected to the information and people they need to do their job. This means that they need to be able to connect their computer to the network while they're away. Other users also find that they need to connect to their own desktop computers while they're traveling.

Windows 95 does provide the capability to connect to a network or another computer with Dial-Up Networking. It requires a compatible server on the other end of the phone line such as Windows NT RAS or NetWare Connect because Windows 95 doesn't provide a dial-up server. Therefore, you can't connect two Windows 95 computers via the phone line—unless, of course, you've purchased Microsoft Plus!

Dial-Up Server

Plus! provides two tools that enhance Dial-Up Networking. First, the Dial-Up Server, shown in figure 1.1, allows you to configure a Windows 95 computer to accept calls from Dial-Up Networking. A real-world example might help you understand the power of Dial-Up Networking and Dial-Up Server (shown in figure 1.1). Here's how I've used them:

- As I was running out of the office to catch a flight, an associate told me that I didn't have the latest copy of my presentation. I asked her to put it in my network user directory because I was pressed for time. Later that evening, I connected to my desktop computer with Dial-Up Networking, logged on to the network, and copied the file onto my notebook computer.

- While working on this book, the other contributors connected their computers to my desktop computer to create a workgroup network. We were able to share files and send messages back and forth. I was also able to use the connection to fix any problems that arose on their computers.

Fig. 1.1

For more information about the Dial-Up Server, read chapter 15, "Accessing Your Computer Remotely with Dial-Up Server."

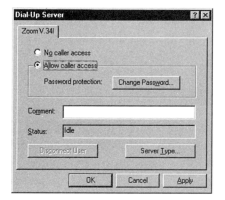

Possibly the best part about Dial-Up Networking and Dial-Up Server is their simplicity. You can answer as few as two questions to create a Dial-Up Networking connection. Setting up a Dial-Up Server is even easier. And, what about actually dialing up and connecting? A couple of mouse clicks is all it takes.

Dial-Up Scripting

The next Plus! feature that expands Windows 95's dial-up capabilities is a tool called Dial-Up Scripting (shown in figure 1.2). It lets you script the logon process so that you can log on automatically.

Fig. 1.2
For more information about Dial-Up Scripting, read chapter 14, "Using the Scripting Tool."

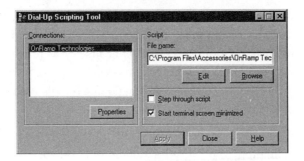

For example, my Internet service provider doesn't allow me to automatically log on to the host. I have to type my user name and password, select PPP from a menu, and continue the automatic process from there. I've completely automated this process using Dial-Up Scripting. Likewise, you can use Dial-Up Scripting to automate your connection to your Internet service provider, your school, or any other network that speaks TCP/IP, IPX/SPX, or NetBEUI.

Connect to the Internet

The Internet has always been a bit intimidating for a lot of people. Rightfully so. Figuring out what you need to do to get on the Internet is confusing. How do you select a provider? What software do you need to buy? Do you need any special equipment? Can you access the Internet through a service such as CompuServe or America Online? The questions are endless.

You may have considered one of those one-stop shops for your connection. These companies give you the software and connection. All you have to do is install the software and log on to the Internet. Sounds easy, right? But snags often occur that make these companies less attractive. For example, some companies use a proprietary protocol that prevents you from being able to use any other software product but their own to access the Internet. Other services may not provide full access, either. Or, you may not be able to send file attachments with your e-mail. How are you supposed to wade through all this?

I thought Windows 95 gave me Internet access

Windows 95, by itself, provides only part of the solution. You can use it to connect to a service provider with Dial-Up Networking. It also comes with a few tools such as FTP and Telnet. But these don't get you very far on the Internet, and they certainly won't get you onto the World Wide Web.

Plus! expands Windows 95's Internet capabilities with the Internet Jumpstart kit. This kit includes a wizard to help you set up your connection, Internet Explorer so that you can browse the World Wide Web, and Internet mail services for Microsoft Exchange. This is all that you need to be fully productive on the Internet. And, the tools included with Microsoft Plus! will allow you to connect to virtually all Internet service providers—except those with proprietary protocols. Therefore, you're not stuck with one software package and one provider. You can add other Internet tools to your arsenal as your needs vary.

Tell me more about the Plus! Internet tools

The Internet Jumpstart kit provides all the tools that you need to take full advantage of the Internet. Here's what they are:

- **Internet Setup Wizard** walks you through the process of configuring your computer to connect to the Internet. If you don't yet have an Internet provider, you can use the Microsoft Network as your connection. The Microsoft Network provides full PPP access to the Internet with no restrictions on what you can do. To learn how to use the wizard to set up your Internet connection, see chapter 7, "The Internet—The Easy Way."

- **Internet Explorer** is your browser for the World Wide Web. The Web is the fastest growing segment of the Internet. It's where all the action is. Internet Explorer, which is shown in figure 1.3 is enhanced to make your visits to the Web both productive and fun.

- **Internet Mail Service** enables Microsoft Exchange to check your Internet mail. Imagine getting your Microsoft Mail, CompuServe mail, and Internet mail all in this same mail box. And, you won't notice a difference between them because you'll use the same program to check all of them. This is easy to configure to because the Internet Setup Wizard does it all for you. Chapter 12, "Using Exchange to Send and Receive Internet Mail," describes how to get the most of e-mail on the Internet.

Fig. 1.3
Read chapter 8, "Browsing the World Wide Web with Internet Explorer," for information about using Explorer, and chapters 9 through 11 for information about navigating the Web.

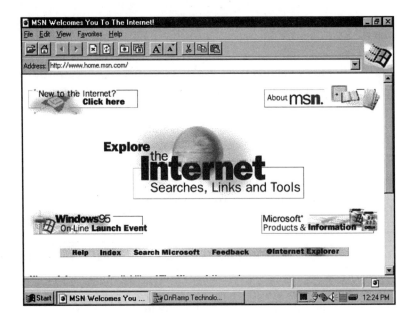

Rev-up Windows 95

Windows 95 provides a healthy set of disk tools: DriveSpace, Disk Defragmenter, and ScanDisk. DriveSpace is basically the same old disk compression that you've grown fond of, however. And Windows 95 doesn't give you a way to schedule your computer maintenance tasks such as ScanDisk to happen automatically when it won't impact your work. As a result, important tasks such as these usually don't get done at all. Right?

Plus! installs additional tools that give you a lot of power and control over your computer. These include System Agent and DriveSpace 3. It also installs a few other tools to be used with System Agent, such as Compression Agent and Low Disk Space Notification.

System Agent

You can use System Agent, shown in figure 1.4, to schedule programs to run at specific times. The scheduling is quite flexible. For example, you can schedule a program to run every week, every day, every hour, and so on. You also have a lot of control over how the program behaves when it's run by the System Agent, and control over what happens when you start using your computer while the program is running.

Fig. 1.4

For more information about System Agent, read chapter 18, "Using System Agent to Maintain Your Computer."

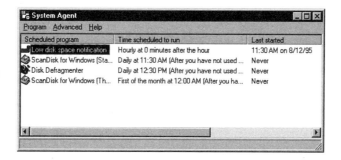

Plus! comes with additional tools that were specifically designed for the System Agent. These include Compression Agent, Low Disk Space Notification, ScanDisk, and Disk Defragmenter. Here's a description of what they do:

- **Compression Agent** compresses your drive while you're not looking. When you're using your computer, your files are written to the drive uncompressed. Then, Compression Agent will run at the scheduled time and compress your files. Chapter 17, "Getting More Disk Space with Compression Agent," will help you create your own compression strategy.

- **Low Disk Space Notification** warns you when you're getting low on space. You can schedule it to run every 15 minutes to keep a watchful eye on your space situation. You'll never be surprised with one of those out-of-space error messages again. For more information about Low Disk Space Notification, read chapter 18.

Other Windows 95 tools are useful with System Agent:

- **ScanDisk for Windows** was designed to be run by System Agent. It scans your hard drive for errors. If it finds any, it will notify you and optionally automatically fix them.

- **Disk Defragmenter** was also designed to be run by System Agent. It makes your drive faster by making sure that each file is not scattered all over your drive.

- **Backup** was not written for System Agent. It works with the agent just fine, however. It is definitely worth your time to make sure that your computer is backed up regularly. To learn more, see chapter 19, "Using Microsoft Backup with System Agent."

DriveSpace 3

DriveSpace 3 is about 20 percent faster than DriveSpace. You get tasks done quicker. Also, it gives you much more control over how your drive is compressed. It provides different levels of compression: None, Standard, HiPack, and UltraPack. These compression levels allows you to control how much performance is traded for drive space. Figure 1.5 shows DriveSpace 3.

Fig. 1.5
For more information about DriveSpace 3, see chapter 16, "Upgrading to DriveSpace 3."

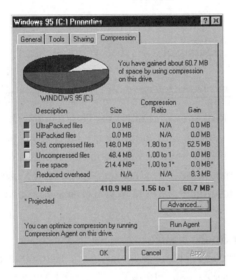

For example, if you want all the drive space that you can get without regard for performance, use UltraPack. On the other hand, if you don't want to impact your computer's performance, use None and tell DriveSpace 3 to compress files only when you're running out of disk space. I use DriveSpace 3 with Compression Agent to get the most drive space possible without significantly impacting my computer's performance. Here's how I've set it up:

- I told DriveSpace 3 not to compress my files unless my computer has only about 10 percent of its drive space left.

- I have Compression Agent compress my files using HiPack compression while I'm not using my computer. Instead of waiting on files to be compressed when I'm trying to use them, I have them compressed later.

- I told Compression Agent not to compress any of my documents, spreadsheets, or other data files. They load faster because I'm not waiting for them to be decompressed.

Most important, DriveSpace 3 is safe to use. Unlike its predecessors, there's not a large risk of losing your files if your machine crashes or there is a power failure. In fact, I turned my computer completely off while DriveSpace 3 was initially compressing my drive. When I turned my machine back on, DriveSpace 3 picked up where it left off—without a hitch. I didn't lose a single file.

It's fun, too

Windows 95 does come with a few screen savers, mouse cursors, and wallpapers. But there's really nothing too special about them. Microsoft Plus!, however, lets you put some razzle-dazzle on your desktop. First, the Visual Enhancements let you sharpen those desktop icons and smoothen your on-screen fonts so that they don't have jagged edges. You'll learn all about these enhancements in chapter 3, "Make Your Desktop Sparkle with Visual Enhancements."

Second, you'll be able to create a consistent theme for all of the Windows 95 desktop elements. Desktop Themes are a set of related wallpapers, screen savers, fonts, window colors, mouse pointers, icons, and desktop icons. For example, the sports theme's mouse pointers, wallpapers, and desktop icons are all related to sports. The graphics aren't plain Jane, either. Themes include high-quality, rendered graphics that will impress and amaze you. Chapter 4, "Make Windows 95 Your Own with Desktop Themes," shows you how to personalize your desktop to your own tastes. And if you want to see all the desktop themes side by side before you pick one, see chapter 5, "Themes Included with Microsoft Plus!."

The folks at Microsoft didn't forget the game enthusiast in all of us. They've included an impressive pinball game in Microsoft Plus!. Space Cadet Pinball is a high-quality pinball game with three-dimensional graphics and realistic sound effects. The action is so real that you'll think you're in the arcade. Chapter 6, "Take a Break, Play Space Cadet Pinball," will help you play to win.

Getting Started with Microsoft Plus!

● In this chapter:

- Installing Microsoft Plus!

- Do I have to install the whole thing?

- Plus! adds features to many parts of Windows 95

Installing Microsoft Plus! is easy. You'll need a few hints to find everything, however . . . . ⊳

It's easy to install Microsoft Plus!. If you're installing Plus! from disk, you can do it from the Control Panel. If you're installing Plus! from CD-ROM, all you have to do is insert the disk in the drive, and the setup program will run automatically; Microsoft calls this "Spin-n-Grin."

In this chapter, you'll learn how to install Microsoft Plus!. You'll also learn which features you should install. And, because Plus! expands a lot of Windows 95's functionality, you'll learn where all those features were installed and how to get to them.

Installing all or part of Microsoft Plus!

You can install all or part of Plus!. Which features you choose depends largely on your needs. To determine whether you need to install a particular Plus! feature, use the following list:

- **DriveSpace 3.** If you have a compressed drive or intend to compress your drive, you need to install this feature. For example, if you have fewer than 50 megabytes free on your drive, you need disk compression.

- **System Agent.** Go ahead and install System Agent. It's a great tool. If you're concerned with performing routine computer maintenance while you're not using your computer, you need it.

- **Internet Jumpstart Kit.** If you have an Internet account or want to get on the Internet, install the Jumpstart Kit. You can use it to connect to your current account or you can use The Microsoft Network as your Internet provider.

- **Desktop Themes.** Install the desktop themes if you have a newer computer that displays at least 256 colors. To get the most benefit from themes, you need to have a super VGA display. Also, you may want to install only the themes that you're interested in, as shown in chapter 5, "Themes Included with Microsoft Plus!," so that you can conserve drive space.

- **Dial-Up Networking Server.** Do you intend to connect to your computer remotely, or do you need to get access to a network using your computer? If so, install the server. Otherwise, you don't need it.

- **Space Cadet Pinball.** Why not? Space Cadet Pinball is an entertaining game. You'll need at least a VGA monitor to play it, however. If you're installing Plus! on an office computer, you may want to consider leaving this one out.

- **Visual Enhancements.** Most of the visual enhancements require a super VGA display configured for high color. If you're not limited to 256 colors, you'll want to install it. Also, full-window drag requires a pretty quick machine. But it's worth it if your computer is at least a 486 running at 50 MHz and you're using at least 256 colors.

After you've decided what features to install, doing it is easy. First, you need to run the setup program. If you're installing from CD-ROM, insert the disk in the drive. After you close the drive, Windows automatically will display the window shown in figure 2.1. Click on Install Plus!.

Fig. 2.1
Click on Install Plus! to start the setup program. You can also see other product offerings from Microsoft by clicking on Multimedia Catalog.

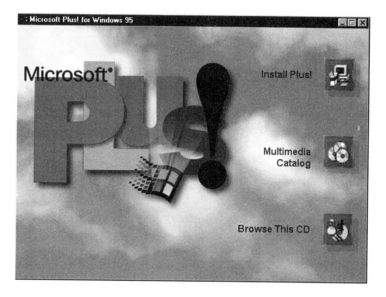

If you're installing from floppy disk, insert the first disk in drive A, double-click on Add/Remove Programs in the Control Panel, click on Install, and click on Next when the Install Program wizard pops up. After the wizard has found SETUP.EXE on your disk, click on Finish to run the setup program.

In either case, use the following steps to install Plus! after you've run the setup program.

1 Make sure that you have closed any applications open on your desktop. The Plus! setup may fail if you're running programs that are accessing files that Plus! needs to update. Then, click on Continue.

2 Type your name and company name in the spaces provided. The company name is not required. Then, click on OK. Click on OK again to confirm your entries. Setup displays the dialog box shown in figure 2.2.

Fig. 2.2
You must type your CD Key if you're installing from CD-ROM.

3 Type your ten-digit CD key, found on the back of the CD-ROM case, if you're installing from CD-ROM. Then, click on OK. When Setup displays your product ID, click on OK to continue.

4 Click on OK if you're happy installing Plus! in C:\Program Files\Plus!. Otherwise, click on Change Folder, select another path, and click on OK. Setup displays the dialog box shown in figure 2.3.

Fig. 2.3
Click on Typical and follow Setup's instructions if you're not exactly sure which features you want to install. Setup will install the features that are most commonly used.

5 Click on Custom. Setup displays the dialog box shown in figure 2.4.

Fig. 2.4

Solid check boxes indicate that the entire feature is being installed. Gray check boxes indicate that only a portion of the feature is being installed.

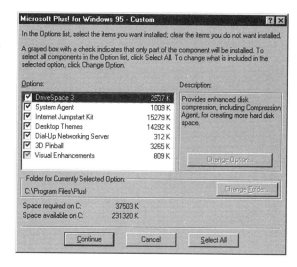

6 Deselect all of the features that you don't want to install, as I discussed earlier in this section. For example, if you don't need drive compression, deselect DriveSpace 3.

7 If you're installing Desktop Themes, select Desktop Themes from the list and click on Change Option. Setup displays the dialog box shown in figure 2.5. Deselect any of the themes that you don't want to install, and click on OK.

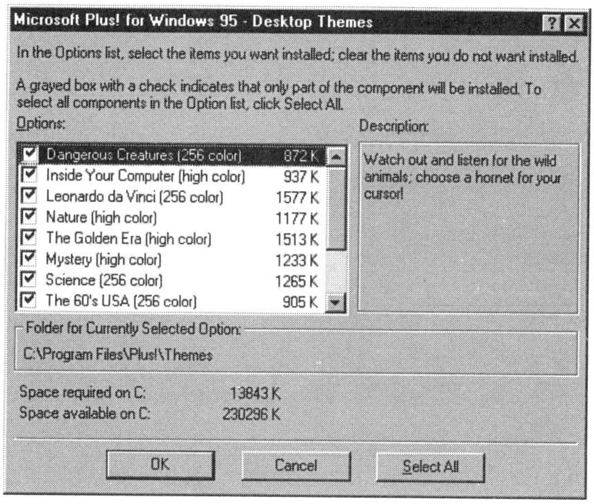

Fig. 2.5

Select the themes that you want to install. If you're unsure what is included in each theme, see chapter 5.

8 If you're installing Visual Enhancements, select Visual Enhancements from the list and click on Change Option. Setup displays the dialog box shown in figure 2.6. Deselect any of the enhancements that you don't want to install, and click on OK.

Fig. 2.6
If you're using 256 colors, deselect high-color icons and font smoothing.

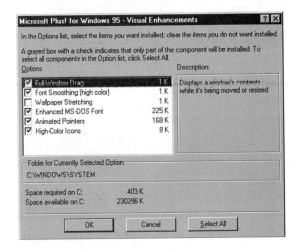

9 Click on Continue to install Microsoft Plus!. If you're installing System Agent, Setup displays the dialog box shown in figure 2.7. Click on Yes if you want to schedule the default tasks at night. Otherwise, click on No to schedule them during the day.

Fig. 2.7
If you're using a notebook computer, you'll want to schedule these programs during the day—maybe your lunch hour—instead of at night, because you'll be charging your batteries at night.

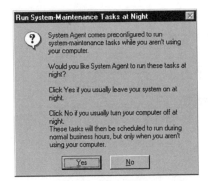

10 If you're installing Desktop Themes and your display is configured for 256 colors or fewer, Setup will ask you whether you want to go ahead and install the high-color themes. Click on Yes if you will be changing to high color; click on No if you're keeping your computer at 256 colors.

After you've completed these steps, Setup will copy all of your files onto your drive. Now it will run the Internet Setup Wizard. For detailed instructions on using this wizard, see chapter 7, "The Internet—the Easy Way." After you've completed the wizard, Setup will open Desktop Themes so that you can choose a theme. See chapter 4, "Make Windows 95 Your Own with Desktop Themes," for detailed instructions on selecting a theme.

TIP **Your experience with the Plus! Install wizard is typical in Windows 95.** In most cases, you'll find it much easier to install new hardware and software than previously possible.

Where did everything go?

Plus! enhances a lot of Windows 95 features. It adds capabilities to Dial-Up Networking. It enhances your desktop and provides you with Internet tools. It also provides new computer maintenance tools. These program are installed in a number of different places on your computer, however.

This handy guide will help you quickly locate the Plus! programs in the Control Panel, Display Properties, Dial-Up Networking folder, Start menu, icon tray, and Microsoft Exchange.

The Control Panel

A lot of the features that Microsoft Plus! installed on your computer can be configured in the Control Panel. Here, you can change your desktop theme, display properties, the Internet connection for use with Internet Explorer, and more, as shown in figure 2.8.

Double-click to configure
your Internet connection
for Internet Explorer.

Double-click to select a
Desktop Theme.

Double-click to load the Display
property sheet. You can change
your background wallpaper,
screen saver, desktop appearance, and visual enhancements
on this property sheet.

Fig. 2.8
To load the Control
Panel, select Settings,
Control Panel from the
Start menu.

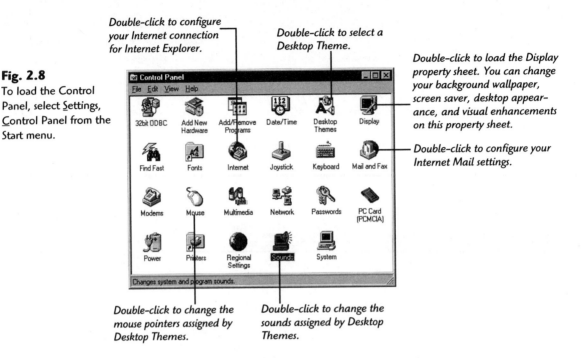

Double-click to configure your
Internet Mail settings.

Double-click to change the
mouse pointers assigned by
Desktop Themes.

Double-click to change the
sounds assigned by Desktop
Themes.

Display Properties

Most of the display's characteristics are configured in the Display property
sheet. This includes everything from the desktop background and icons to
the size, color, and font used for all your windows. Figure 2.9 describes each
tab available on the Display property sheet and what you'll be able to change
in that tab.

Click to change the wallpaper assigned by Desktop Themes.

Click to change the screen saver assigned by Desktop Themes.

Click to change the appearance of your desktop and windows as assigned by Desktop Themes.

Fig. 2.9
Right-click on your desktop to show Display Properties.

Click to change your color palette and display resolution.

Click to select which Visual Enhancements you'll use. You can also change your desktop icons here.

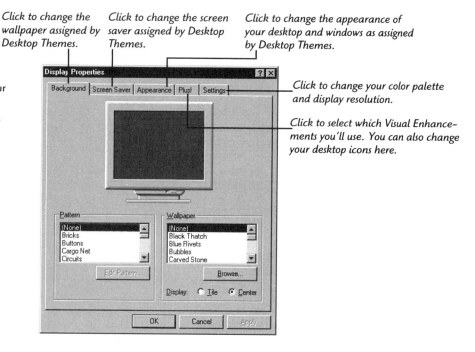

Dial-Up Networking

The Dial-Up Networking folder, shown in figure 2.10, is in the Start menu. In this folder, you'll find all your connections and an icon that starts the New Connection wizard when you double-click on it. You can also configure how Dial-Up Networking and Dial-Up Server work by selecting Configure from the main menu.

Double-click to create a new Dial-Up Networking connection.

Select to change your Dial-Up Networking Settings or configure your Dial-Up Server.

Fig. 2.10
Select Programs, Accessories, Dial-Up Networking to load the Dial-Up Networking folder.

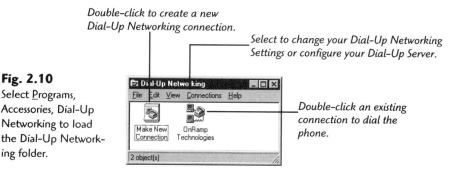

Double-click an existing connection to dial the phone.

Start Menu

There are many shortcuts to some of the features in Plus!. But if you have difficulty remembering them all, you can rely on the Start menu for most. All of the Plus! shortcuts are within the Accessories folder as shown in figure 2.11.

Fig. 2.11
Many of the Plus! programs can be accessed through the Start menu.

Select to play Space Cadet Pinball.

Select to run Internet Explorer or the Internet Setup Wizard.

Select to run Compression Agent or System Agent.

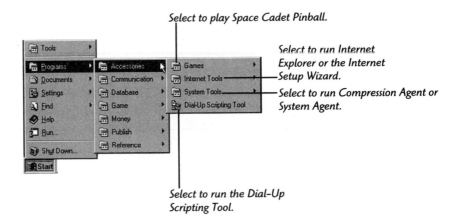

Select to run the Dial-Up Scripting Tool.

Icon Tray

A handful of programs and devices have an icon in the icon tray portion of the taskbar—located at the lower-right corner of your display. These represent the status of that program or device. For example, System Agent has an icon in the tray. If you position your mouse over it for a second, you'll see the current status of System Agent, such as whether it's idle or currently running a program. Figure 2.12 shows the taskbar with System Agent in the icon tray. To start the System Agent from the taskbar, double-click on its icon.

Fig. 2.12
Many programs and devices put an icon in the tray that indicates their status. You can put your mouse pointer over the icon to get more information, or right-click on the icon to select an action from a menu.

Double-click to open the System Agent.

Microsoft Exchange

Figure 2.13 shows Microsoft Exchange with the Tools menu open. You can configure your Internet Mail Service by selecting Services from this menu. Then, select Internet Mail Service from the list and click on Properties.

Fig. 2.13
Select Services to change your Internet mail configuration.

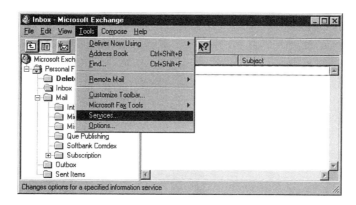

Part II: Having Fun on Your Windows 95 Desktop

Make Your Desktop Sparkle with Visual Enhancements

● In this chapter:

- See the whole window while you drag it

- Get rid of those jaggy fonts

- Dress up your desktop icons

- Stretch your wallpaper to fit your desktop

- Jazz up that mouse while you're at it

Visual enhancements give Windows 95 a touch of class . .

Remember your first car? I remember mine. It was a dependable work horse, but not too glamorous. I washed it. Buffed it. Put chrome wheels and custom plates on it. And I even hung fuzzy dice from the mirror. Wow! It was the envy of the neighborhood.

The Microsoft Plus! visual enhancements are chrome wheels and fuzzy dice for Windows 95. They add a bit of excitement and class: fonts are smoother, windows are cooler, and your desktop sparkles just like the chrome on that old car. Read on to find out how to make your desktop the envy of the neighborhood.

Drag the whole window—not just an empty box

When you move or resize a window in Windows 95, you don't get much feedback on what you're going to end up with. Well, you do see an outline of the window, but that's about it. Figure 3.1 shows Notepad being moved across the desktop. Notice the outline of the window.

Fig. 3.1
When you move or resize a window in Windows 95, all you see is an outline. What a help!

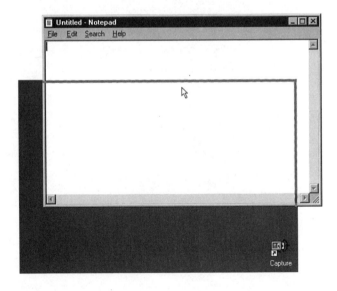

See a window's contents while you move or size it

Have you ever tried to get a window in just the right spot? First, you click on the title bar and move the window. But all you see is an outline. So, you drop it onto the desktop to see what it looks like in its new home. Oops! You want to adjust it a bit. So, you pick it up and move it some more. You could keep adjusting the darn thing all day.

And what about sizing a window? All you see is the outline. If the window has stuff in it, such as the Control Panel or Notepad, you can size the window many times before you get it to fit the contents just right. For example, you might want to size the Control Panel so that it displays 15 icons arranged in three rows of five columns. So, you size it using the outline. But when you're done, you've cut off some of the icons. You size it again, but the window is too big now. Finally, you either give up or manage to nudge it into just the right spot.

 TIP **If you really want to see what a window is going to look like while** you're resizing it with full-window drag, turn on Auto Arrange. In most windows, select <u>V</u>iew, Arrange <u>I</u>cons, <u>A</u>uto Arrange.

Plus! gives you more feedback when you move or size a window. If you're moving a window, you can see what it's going to look like in its new home before you drop it onto the desktop. You move it only once. And if you're sizing a window, you can see how its contents are going to be arranged before you let go of the window. For example, figure 3.2 shows the Control Panel being sized. The icons in the Control Panel arrange themselves automatically as the window is sized—you don't have to wait until you drop the window on the desktop to see what you've got. Now, it's easy to arrange the icons three by five.

Fig. 3.2
When you size the
Control Panel, the
icons arrange them-
selves automatically.

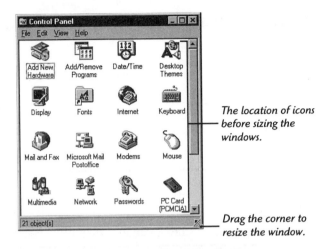

*The location of icons
before sizing the
windows.*

*Drag the corner to
resize the window.*

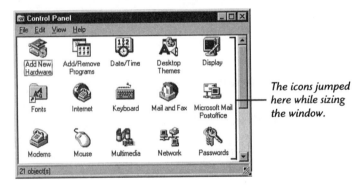

*The icons jumped
here while sizing
the window.*

Are you convinced? Good. If you haven't installed Microsoft Plus! Visual
Enhancements, you'll need to do so now. When you install it, the setup
program turns on full-window drag. You can use the following steps, however, if it's not enabled:

1 Right-click on your desktop and select P**r**operties.

2 Click on the Plus! tab in the display property sheet.

3 Select **S**how Window Contents While Dragging and click on OK.

Slow computer? You're better off with the box

As always, there is some fine print. If you have a slower computer, such as a
486 DX/2 50 megahertz, you may not be happy with Windows 95 updating the

window as you move or size it. And a slow display adapter won't be very satisfying, either. Windows 95 can't update the screen fast enough to make it look attractive. What you end up with is window trails. You'll see many copies of the window as you drag it across the desktop. Figure 3.3 shows the trails left behind while Notepad is being moved on a slower computer.

Fig. 3.3
Windows 95 can't update the screen fast enough on a slower computer. The result: window trails.

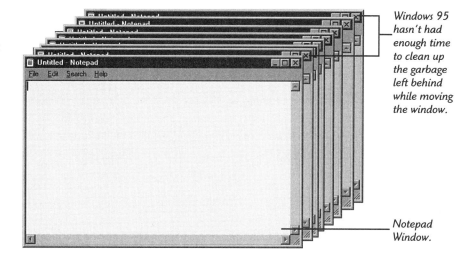

Windows 95 hasn't had enough time to clean up the garbage left behind while moving the window.

Notepad Window.

PowerToys from Microsoft

As time goes by, you'll discover plenty of great enhancements that you can drop into Windows 95. One of my favorites is PowerToys from the engineers at Microsoft. PowerToys is a collection of desktop enhancements that adds features to the desktop's **context menu** (right-click menu) and lets you change your display properties on the fly.

You won't find PowerToys on your Windows 95 disk, though. It's available only online. That's good, too, because the engineers at Microsoft have promised to keep adding goodies to this collection of enhancements as they come up with great ideas.

To get your own copy of PowerToys, log onto The Microsoft Network and use the Go word Win-dows. Double-click on Free Software to go to the Free Software forum. Then, double-click on Windows 95 Power Toys to download and unzip the PowerToys file all in one step. Follow the instructions included with PowerToys for installing each enhancement you want.

Give up the jaggies—these fonts are smooth

Try this. Open Wordpad, select a really large font such as 72 point, and type some text. Do you like what you see? The jagged edges around the curves of the font are called **jaggies**—a technical term. Microsoft Plus! helps you get rid of the jaggies with font smoothing.

Why do fonts get the jaggies?

A font displayed on the screen is nothing more than a bunch of blocks arranged to form characters. When you're looking at a small font, you don't really notice the blocks. But the blocks start to appear larger and more pronounced as the font gets larger. Thus, the font appears jagged around the edges.

Imagine that you have a big bucket of blocks and you're going to use them to spell out the word *Plus!*. You'd put the blocks together to form characters and arrange the characters together to form the word. My attempt at it is shown in figure 3.4. Are your characters smooth? Not unless the blocks you used were very tiny.

Fig. 3.4
The word *Plus!* created using blocks. Notice how jaggy it is around the curves.

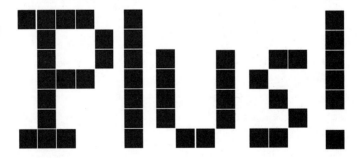

Why? Because no matter how hard you try, you just can't make a smooth curve out of blocks. And pretty much every character in a font has one of those nasty curves in it.

Font smoothing makes them go away

Microsoft Plus! will make those jaggies go away. How? It tricks the eye into believing that the curves are smooth.

Font smoothing softens the edges of a font by shading in all the curves with a much lighter shade of the color that you used for the font. Remember, the curves are where the blocks are more pronounced. And you can barely notice it—unless you blow up the font really big as I did in figure 3.5.

On the top of the figure, you'll notice a font without smoothing. On the bottom, you'll notice the same font with smoothing. Notice how the edges around curves are fuzzy.

Fig. 3.5
A smoothed font almost appears to be blurred around the edges. This makes the jaggies go away.

Jaggy edges without smoothing.

Using Microsoft Plus!

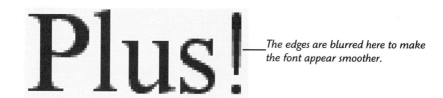

The edges are blurred here to make the font appear smoother.

Using Microsoft Plus!

To turn on font smoothing, use the following steps:

1 Right-click on the desktop and select P̲roperties.

2 Click on the Plus! tab of the display property sheet.

3 Select Smooth Edges of Screen F̲onts and click on OK.

Q&A *I turn on font smoothing and get an error that says, "Your display is currently configured for 256 colors or less."*

Font smoothing works only with high-color or true-color display modes. To change video modes, right-click on the desktop and select Properties. Click on the Settings tab, change Color Palette to high-color or true-color, and click on OK.

Note that some games and other graphics programs work only with the 256-color palette. You can use the QuickRes utility, included with PowerToys described earlier in this chapter, to quickly change between the 256 palette and high-color palette without requiring you to restart Windows 95.

Some of my fonts still have the jaggies.

Font smoothing works only with TrueType fonts. Make sure that the font you've selected has the TrueType icon next to it.

How do I make my wallpaper fill my desktop?

Does your wallpaper fill only the center portion of your desktop? If you're not happy with this, you have two choices:

- **Tiling**. You can tile your desktop wallpaper so that it is duplicated side by side and top to bottom on your desktop until it fills the entire area.

- **Stretching**. You can stretch your wallpaper so that it fills the entire desktop area.

Figure 3.6 shows a normally sized wallpaper and the same wallpaper after it's stretched to fill the desktop.

Here's how to stretch your wallpaper to fit the entire desktop:

1 Right-click on the desktop and select Properties.

2 Click on the Plus! tab in the display property sheet.

3 Select Stretch Desktop Wallpaper to Fit the Screen, and click on OK.

Fig. 3.6
Stretching your
wallpaper makes it fill
the entire area. But if
the wallpaper was
originally pretty small,
it'll be chunky when
it's stretched to fill the
desktop.

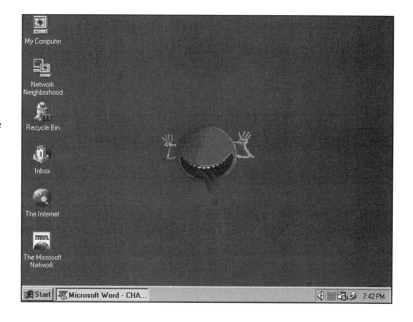

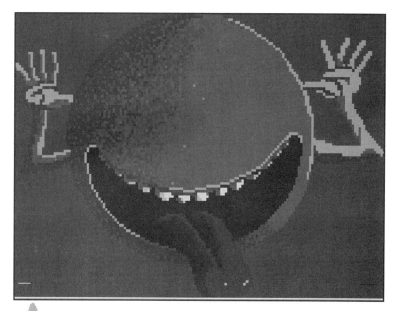

 TIP **If you have a small picture that you'd like to put at a specific place** on your desktop, create a bitmap that is the same size as your desktop (for example, 640 by 480 or 800 by 600). Then, fill the bitmap with the same color as your desktop background so that the captions of your desktop icons blend nicely with the wallpaper. Paste the picture into the bitmap at the specific place you want it to display.

If you don't already have a desktop wallpaper, create one with Microsoft Paint or use one of the wallpapers supplied with Windows 95. Then, use the following steps to select it:

1 Right-click on the desktop and select Properties.

2 Click on Browse in Wallpaper and select your new picture file. Alternatively, you can select one of the wallpapers in the Wallpaper list.

3 Click on OK.

Desktop icons just the way you want them

Windows 95 desktop icons are pretty exciting compared to previous versions of Windows. They can still use a bit of sprucing up, however. For example, Windows 95 desktop icons use only 16 colors, they come in only one size, and you just might want to use your own anyway. In this section, I explore some of the things you can do to customize your desktop icons.

Can't see your desktop icons? Make 'em bigger

Your desktop icons are shrinking. That's because your display resolution is getting larger, but your icons haven't changed size.

Think of it this way. Imagine a floor plan of your home on a regular piece of paper. If you doubled the size of your home and put the floor plan on the same piece of paper, the doors would appear much smaller than in the original plan.

66 *Plain English, please!*

A **pixel** (picture element) is a dot on your screen. Pixels are combined to form windows, text, and graphics. The amount of information that you can display on your screen is called the screen's **resolution**. An 800–by–600 resolution display is 800 pixels high by 600 pixels wide. 99

Likewise, your desktop icons look great on a display set to 640 by 480. But if you put more information on the same screen by setting your resolution to

800 by 600—or higher—your icons get smaller. Fortunately, Microsoft Plus! lets you double the size of the icons on your desktop. Here's how:

1 Right-click on the desktop and select Properties.

2 Click on the Plus! tab in the display property sheet.

3 Select Use Large Icons and click on OK.

Table 3.1 that follows shows the difference between the normal desktop icons and the enlarged icons. In some cases, the quality is not as good. But on a larger display resolution, you won't notice the difference and you'll finally be able to see the icons.

Table 3.1 Original versus enlarged desktop icons

Original	Enlarged
My Computer	My Computer
Network Neighborhood	Network Neighborhood
Inbox	Inbox
The Microsoft Network	The Microsoft Network
Recycle Bin	Recycle Bin

I've got my own icons—can I use them?

Yes! You can use your own icons. While you're at it, why don't you check out some of the alternative icons that Windows 95 provides. Here's how:

1 Right-click on your desktop and select P**r**operties.

2 Click on the Plus! tab of the display property sheet. The current desktop icons are at the top of the property sheet, as shown in figure 3.7.

Fig. 3.7
Check out the current desktop icons. If you don't like them, change them by clicking on **C**hange Icon.

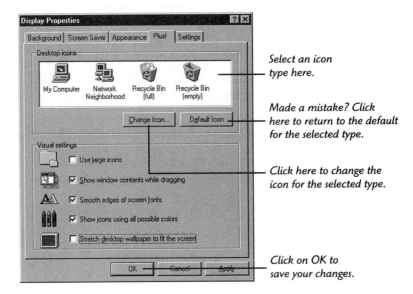

Select an icon type here.

Made a mistake? Click here to return to the default for the selected type.

Click here to change the icon for the selected type.

Click on OK to save your changes.

3 Select one of the icons. Then, click on **C**hange Icon and select one of the icons shown in the **C**urrent Icon list.

4 Alternatively, click on **B**rowse to choose another file, such as a program file or icon file, which you can use to find more icons. Then, select an icon.

5 Click on OK and repeat steps 3 and 4 for any other icons that you want to change.

6 Click on OK to save your changes.

TIP **The file MORICONS.DLL in your Windows 95 folder has more** cool icons to choose from. Make sure that you're showing hidden files by selecting **V**iew, **O**ptions in the Explorer window, and select **S**how All Files.

Get your full-color icons here

You can make your desktop icons really sparkle. If you're using the high-color display mode, you can use full-color icons. These icons use more than 16 colors, so you get more detail and shading. Here's how:

1 Right-click on your desktop and select Properties.

2 Click on the Plus! tab of the display property sheet.

3 Select Show Icons Using All Possible Colors.

Figure 3.8 shows the difference between a desktop without full-color icons and with full-color icons. Take a close look at the Explorer window. You'll notice that its icons have changed, too. Full-color icons brighten up more than just the desktop icons.

Fig. 3.8
Full-color icons really enhance your desktop. Notice that the Explorer icons have changed, too.

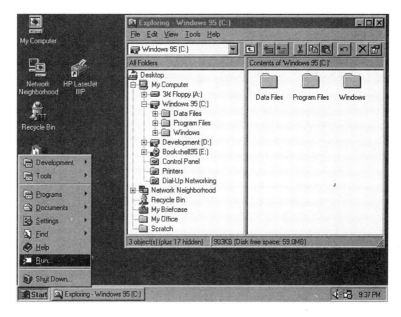

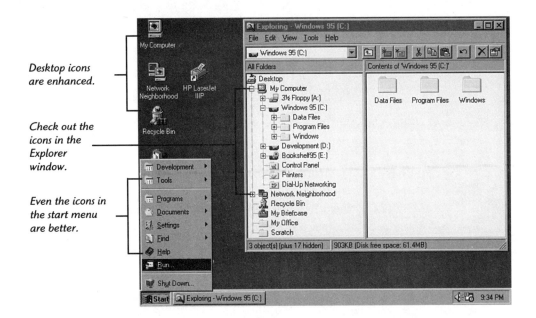

Desktop icons are enhanced.

Check out the icons in the Explorer window.

Even the icons in the start menu are better.

Jazz up that mouse pointer with animated pointers

Your mouse pointer doesn't do much. You can point with it, drag a window with it, and more. But the pointer itself just kind of sits there—no entertainment value at all.

Wouldn't it be great if the mouse pointer would entertain you while the computer was busy? It will. Microsoft Plus! installs a bunch of animated mouse pointers in your Windows\Cursors directory. Table 3.2 shows you what the pointers look like.

Table 3.2 These animated cursors will keep you entertained while the computer is busy

Pointer	Name	Description
Apple	Apple	The leaves on the apple move
Banana	Banana	This banana peels itself
Coffee	Coffee	Be careful not to spill the coffee
Coin	Coin	The coin turns around while you wait
Dinosaur	Dinosaur	The dino walks
Hand	Hand	The hand taps on the desktop
Horse	Horse	The horse runs across your desktop
Piano	Piano	I bet you didn't know you could play
Tv	Tv	This TV has really bad reception
Winflag	Winflag	The Windows flag flaps in the wind

To change your mouse pointer, use the following steps:

Mouse

1 Double-click on the mouse icon in the Control Panel.

2 Click on the Pointers tab on the mouse property sheet. Figure 3.9 shows the Pointers tab of the mouse property sheet.

Fig. 3.9
Select a predefined pointer scheme or choose your own pointers.

Choose the pointer that you want to change in this list.

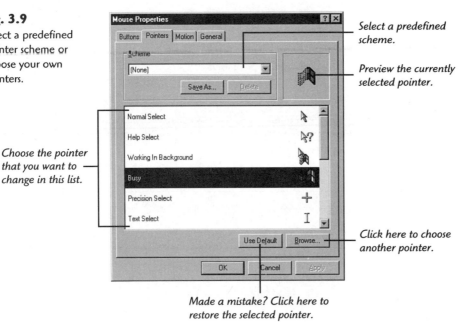

Select a predefined scheme.

Preview the currently selected pointer.

Click here to choose another pointer.

Made a mistake? Click here to restore the selected pointer.

3 Select either the Working in Background or Busy pointer. I recommend that you use only animated mouse pointers with these two types.

4 Click Browse and select one of the mouse pointers described in table 3.2, shown previously.

5 Repeat steps 3 and 4 for the other mouse pointer.

6 Click on OK to save your changes.

Make Windows 95 Your Own with Desk- top Themes

● In this chapter:

● How much do themes affect my desktop?

● I like a particular theme, except for the wallpaper

● Can I create my own themes?

● Do I need any special equipment to use themes?

Break out from the crowd. Personalize your computer with
Desktop Themes . . . . ⏵

The default Windows 95 desktop looks pretty good. But it's rather plain. The background is solid green. The desktop icons aren't very special. And the Windows are standard issue, too. Because everyone who installs Windows 95 gets the same desktop, it's not very personal.

You can personalize your desktop yourself. Change the wallpaper. Change the appearance of your windows and icons. Even choose one of the simple screen savers. You can put a lot of effort into the whole thing and still not end up with a dazzling desktop that has a consistent theme, however.

Microsoft Plus! helps you personalize your desktop just the way you want it. You can choose a Desktop Theme that is consistent across the board. For example, if you choose the Sports theme, your mouse pointers, desktop icons, background, and other elements will all be related to that theme. And you won't be disappointed with the graphics.

 TIP If you're using user profiles, each user's desktop can have a different theme. To turn on user profiles, double-click on the Passwords icon in the Control Panel, click on the User Profiles tab, and select Users Can <u>C</u>ustomize their Preferences. Then, click on OK to save your changes.

What's included in a Desktop Theme?

Every visible desktop element is included in a theme. Sounds are included as well. When you select a theme, Plus! changes the appearance of those items. Note that for each item that a Desktop Theme changes, there is usually an alternative way to change that item yourself. This is how you'll customize themes later. Here are the elements that are affected by Desktop Themes:

- **Screen saver.** The screen saver takes over your screen after you haven't used your computer for a while. Each theme has its own screen saver. You can also change the screen saver in Display Properties.

Sounds

- **Sound events.** Windows 95 will play different sounds when different things happen on your computer. For example, it'll play one sound when you maximize a window, and another sound when you minimize a window. Different themes have different types of sounds. In the Nature theme, you'll hear birds, monkeys, crickets, and more. And if you don't

Chapter 4 Make Windows 95 Your Own with Desktop Themes **49**

like a particular sound, you can change it with the Sounds icon in the Control Panel.

Mouse

- **Mouse pointers.** You'll see different mouse pointers at different times. Any of the pointers can be changed to animated pointers. Desktop Themes, however, will usually animate only the Busy and Working in Background pointers. The other pointers are related, but not animated. Like Sounds, you can change the mouse pointers with the Mouse icon in the Control Panel.

- **Desktop wallpaper.** The wallpaper is a bitmap image that is displayed on your desktop. A Desktop Theme makes its greatest impact on your desktop with its wallpaper. Some have astounding high-color images. But if you've created the ultimate wallpaper and want to use it instead of a theme's, you can change it in Display Properties.

- **Icons.** The desktop icons include the My Computer, Network Neighborhood, Full Recycle Bin, and Empty Recycle Bin icons. Desktop Themes make another large impact on your desktop with these icons. You can change the icons in Display Properties.

- **Colors.** Desktop Themes will change the colors used for your windows and desktop so that they coordinate well. The colors it chooses will be appropriate for that particular theme. For example, the Harvest theme uses earth tones, whereas the 60s USA theme uses psychedelic colors. You'll find the colors in Display Properties.

- **Font names and styles.** It's hard to say whether one font belongs with a particular theme more than any other. But the fonts were carefully chosen to look good with each theme. Like many of the other settings, you can change fonts in Display Properties.

- **Font and window sizes.** Aside from the chosen font, Desktop Themes also sets the size of the fonts and the size of each portion of a window so that they are appropriate for the theme. You'll change these in Display Properties.

TIP **You can apply portions of multiple themes to your desktop.** For example, you can apply the sounds from the Science theme and the mouse pointers from the Sports theme.

As you can see, Desktop Themes have covered just about all the bases. But how do you choose one theme over another? Look in chapter 5, "Themes

Included with Microsoft Plus!." This chapter will help you choose a theme by laying out all the choices for you to compare. You'll see what the wallpaper, icons, windows, and other elements look like. Also, you can preview a particular theme in Desktop Themes before applying it to your computer.

What do I need to use desktop themes?

First, you'll want a well-tuned computer before using one of the Desktop Themes. For example, you won't be happy with the performance of your computer if you try to use Desktop Themes with a 486 SX 33 MHz and 4M of memory. There's not a definitive answer, however. You're the one true test. If you're happy with the performance of your computer while using Desktop Themes, that's all that matters.

As for the display, if you've configured it for at least 256 colors, you're in good shape. If you want to use the high-color themes, however, you'll need to configure your display for high color or true color. Here's how:

1 Right-click anywhere on your desktop and select Properties.

2 Click on the Settings tab. Windows 95 displays the tab shown in figure 4.1.

Fig. 4.1
If your display is capable of displaying more than 256 colors, you'll see High Color in the Color Palette list.

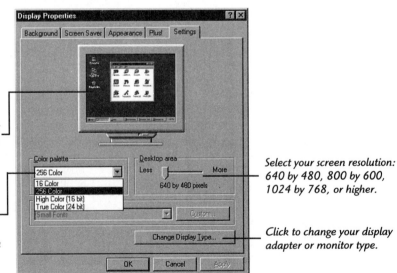

Preview your current display settings here.

Select one of the available color palettes. If you get an error message after you restart Windows 95, you may have selected a palette that your adapter can't handle.

Select your screen resolution: 640 by 480, 800 by 600, 1024 by 768, or higher.

Click to change your display adapter or monitor type.

3 Select High Color from the Color palette list and click on OK.

4 Click on Yes to let Windows 95 restart your computer if it asks you to restart.

If you're just now changing over to high color, you might want to consider using some of the Visual Enhancements that require high color. For example, the font-smoothing and high-color icons make a dramatic impact on your desktop. See chapter 3, "Make Your Desktop Sparkle with Visual Enhancements," for more information.

I want to use the whole theme

The simplest way to use Desktop Themes is to select a theme and live with all its settings. Each theme will change all of the desktop elements discussed earlier. It's easy. Here's how to do it:

Desktop
Themes

1 Open the Control Panel and double-click on the Desktop Themes icon. Desktop Themes is shown in figure 4.2.

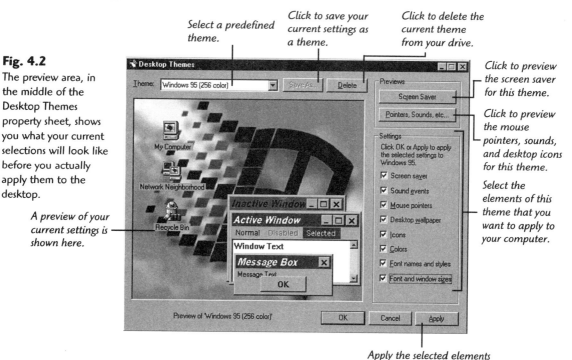

Select a predefined theme.

Click to save your current settings as a theme.

Click to delete the current theme from your drive.

Click to preview the screen saver for this theme.

Click to preview the mouse pointers, sounds, and desktop icons for this theme.

Select the elements of this theme that you want to apply to your computer.

Apply the selected elements to your computer.

Fig. 4.2
The preview area, in the middle of the Desktop Themes property sheet, shows you what your current selections will look like before you actually apply them to the desktop.

A preview of your current settings is shown here.

2 Select a theme from the Theme drop-down list. You can use chapter 5 as a handy reference to help you choose which theme to use.

3 Click on OK to save your changes. Or, if you don't like what you see in the preview area, you can select another theme or click on Cancel.

I want to apply only a part of a theme

Why would you want to do such a thing? Because you're likely to find a theme that, in general, you really like, but you hate its wallpaper. Don't throw out the paste with the wallpaper—apply the best parts of the theme to your desktop. Then, apply your own wallpaper.

I'm personally very fond of the default Windows 95 desktop. I like the Windows 95 Desktop Theme's screen saver, sound events, mouse pointers, and icons, however. So, I've applied only those parts of the theme to my desktop. Otherwise, I kept the default elements. Figure 4.3 shows my Desktop Theme property sheet—contrast this to figure 4.2.

Fig. 4.3
You don't have to apply the entire theme. Apply only those elements that appeal to you. Click on Pointers, Sounds, Etc. to see elements that aren't in the preview area.

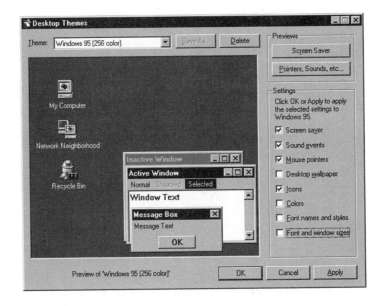

Here's how you can apply a portion of a theme

To apply only specific portions of a theme, use the following steps:

Sounds

1 Double-click on Desktop Themes in the Control Panel. You'll see the Desktop Themes property sheet, as shown in figure 4.2.

2 Select one of the themes available from the Theme drop-down list. The preview area will change to reflect the theme.

3 Select the settings that you want to apply, or deselect the settings that you don't want to apply, in the Settings area. For example, if you want to use only the Theme's mouse pointers, deselect everything except Mouse pointers in the Settings area.

4 Click on OK to save your changes.

And here's how you can preview a theme

Only the elements that you selected in the Settings area are applied to your computer. This is convenient. You can apply all of the default Windows 95 settings first. Then, apply specific portions of a particular theme. You'll get the default desktop with some specific personalization.

You probably want to see each element before you decide whether you want to apply it to your computer. Not all of the elements are shown in the preview area, however. Clicking on Pointers, Sounds, Etc. and Desktop Themes will display the Preview Current Window Settings dialog box. This dialog box lets you preview the mouse pointers, sounds, and desktop icons for that particular theme. Figure 4.4 shows the Pointers tab of the preview dialog box. Select any mouse pointer in the list to see the pointer. If it's animated, you'll see that, too.

Click on the Sounds tab to display the tab shown in figure 4.5. If an event has a check mark beside it, a sound is attached to it. Select a sound, then click on the play button to preview it.

Fig. 4.4

Double-click on the
Mouse icon in the
Control Panel and
customize the specific
pointers that you want
to change.

Fig. 4.5

A question mark
indicates a missing file.
Double-click on the
Sound icon in the
Control Panel to assign
a sound to these
events.

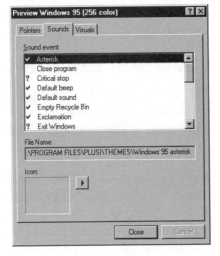

The last tab on the preview dialog box is the Visuals tab shown in figure 4.6.
This tab shows the icons, wallpaper, and screen saver used for this theme.
You can preview the icons at the bottom of the dialog box. It will show only
the file names for the wallpaper and screen saver, though.

Fig. 4.6

You can't change the desktop icons here. Right–click anywhere on the desktop and click on the Plus! tab to change the desktop icons.

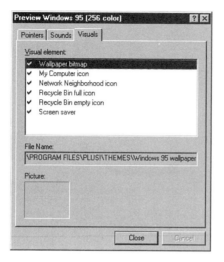

I want to make my own Desktop Theme

So, you don't like any of the themes that came with Microsoft Plus!. Or maybe you just want to create a theme that contains the best of all the elements in Microsoft Plus! Creating your own theme is simple. Set up your desktop just the way you want it, then save it as a theme. You've got to track down all those settings, however.

 TIP **If you want to start off with one of the desktop themes, apply it** to your computer first. Then, use the steps in this section to change the theme and save it with a different name.

Remember the Desktop Theme elements that I discussed earlier in this chapter (screen saver, sound events, mouse pointers, desktop wallpaper, icons, colors, font names and styles, and font and window sizes)? Each of these elements has a property sheet somewhere in Windows 95. The first step in creating your own theme is to visit each property sheet and change it to reflect your own taste. Here's how:

1 Right-click anywhere on your desktop and select Properties. Display Properties is shown in figure 4.7. Select a wallpaper from the list or click on Browse to set any other picture as your wallpaper.

Fig. 4.7

If you've got a smaller wallpaper, like the ones in the list, you might want to click on Tile to have it repeated on the display horizontally and vertically.

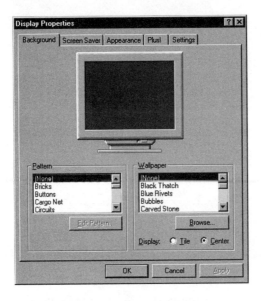

2 Click on the Screen Saver tab to display the tab shown in figure 4.8. Select and configure your screen saver.

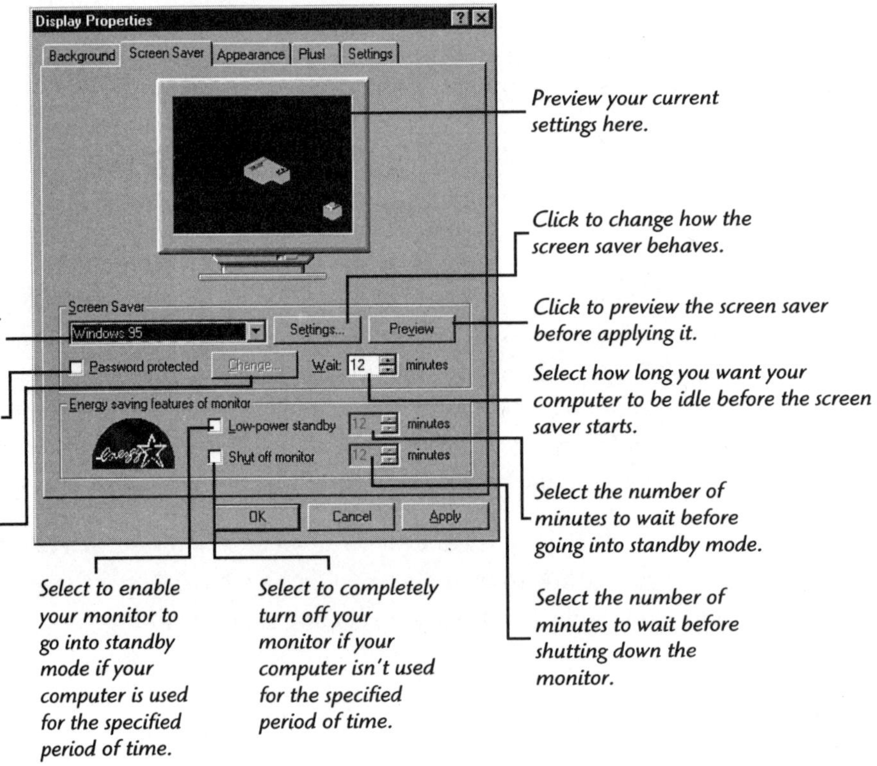

Fig. 4.8

Screen savers that are installed on your computer will be in the Screen Saver drop-down list. If you didn't install all of the themes, you won't have all of the screen savers.

Select a screen saver from this list.

Select to password protect your screen saver.

Click to change your password.

Preview your current settings here.

Click to change how the screen saver behaves.

Click to preview the screen saver before applying it.

Select how long you want your computer to be idle before the screen saver starts.

Select the number of minutes to wait before going into standby mode.

Select the number of minutes to wait before shutting down the monitor.

Select to enable your monitor to go into standby mode if your computer is used for the specified period of time.

Select to completely turn off your monitor if your computer isn't used for the specified period of time.

3 Click on the Appearance tab to display the tab shown in figure 4.9. Configure the size, color, font, font size, font color, and font style for each of the items in the Item drop-down list.

Fig. 4.9

If you don't want to configure each item by hand, select a scheme from the Scheme list. Then, change individual items to suit your taste.

Preview your current settings here.

Select a predefined scheme from this list.

Select the item on your desktop that you want to change.

Click to save your current scheme.

Click to delete the current scheme.

Select the color for the current item.

Select the size for the current item.

Select the font for the current item.

Select the font size for the current item.

Select the font style, bold or italic, for the current item.

Select the font color for the current item.

Display Properties

Background | Screen Saver | Appearance | Plus! | Settings

Inactive Window

Active Window

Normal | Disabled | Selected

Window Text

Message Box ×

Message Text

OK

Scheme:

Save As... | Delete

Item:

Desktop

Size: | Color:

Font:

Size: | Color: | B | I

OK | Cancel | Apply

4 Click on the Plus! tab. The property sheet should look similar to figure 4.10. Select an icon that you want to change and click on Change Icon. Select an icon from the list or click on Browse to grab an icon from another program.

 TIP **You can steal icons from other programs, DLLs, and .ICO files.** The file MORICONS.DLL in your Windows directory contains a bunch of icons that you can use.

5 Click on OK to save your changes to the Display Properties.

6 Double-click on the Mouse icon in the Control Panel. Figure 4.11 shows the Mouse Properties. Click on the Pointers tab and select a pointer for each item in the list. Click on OK to save your changes.

Fig. 4.10

If you regret changing your icons, click on Default Icons.

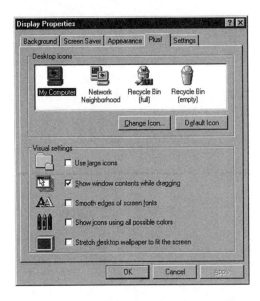

Fig. 4.11

If you don't want to select all your pointers by hand, choose a scheme from the Scheme list. Then, individually change any pointers, such as Working in Background and Busy, to your taste.

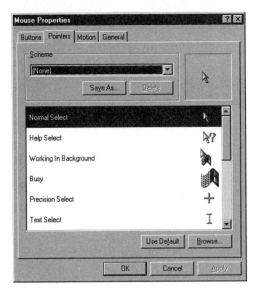

7 Double-click on the Sounds icon in the Control Panel. Figure 4.12 shows the Sounds Properties. Select a sound for each item in the Events list.

Fig. 4.12
If you don't want to select all your sounds by hand, choose a scheme from the Schemes list. You can preview each sound with the play button (the one with the > symbol).

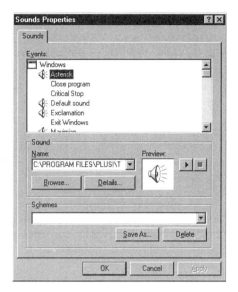

 TIP **The sounds attached to events are plain ol' .WAV files. Thus, you** can create your own sound files with the sound recorder or clip sounds from other files.

8 Double-click on the Desktop Themes icon in the Control Panel. Select Current Windows settings from the Theme list and click on Save As. Type a meaningful name in the space provided and click on Save.

Why do my Windows 3.1 programs look bad with themes?

Many Windows 3.1 programs don't allow the user to control the colors used within the window. For example, some products use gray buttons and gray backgrounds. When you change the color of 3D Objects in Display Properties, however, the program's buttons change colors, but its background doesn't. For example, figure 4.13 shows Quicken for Windows. The buttons correctly changed colors, but the background didn't. This makes for a funny-looking window.

Fig. 4.13
Quicken's background is permanent. It doesn't matter what you set in Display Properties. So, this application looks a bit funny using themes.

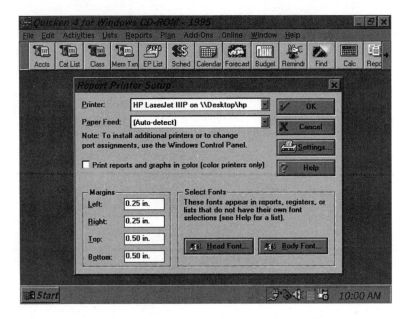

What can you do about this? You can't do anything to the program. If it doesn't check with Windows about the colors it's going to use, it may look funny with Desktop Themes. You can, however, select themes whose 3D Object color matches the color of your Windows 3.1 programs. Light-gray is generally a good choice. If you do want to use a theme that doesn't match and you still want your programs to look good, try selecting the theme and overriding the color of 3D Objects in Display Properties.

Themes Included with Microsoft Plus!

● **In this chapter:**

- **What does the wallpaper look like for each theme?**

- **Different mouse pointers for different occasions**

- **Each theme has different desktop icons, too**

- **Don't forget the screen savers**

Microsoft Plus! comes with a bunch of desktop themes. This handy-dandy reference will help you pick which theme you want to use . . . .➤

Themes are like entrées on a menu.

The last time I went to the local diner, I had a bit of trouble making up my mind. Hmm. Chicken fried steak or Mom's meatloaf? If only I could actually see a sample of each. Anyway, by the time I had read the descriptions of all the entrées available, I had forgotten most of them.

Just like the entrées on the diner's menu, it's hard to choose a particular theme just by its description. And, previewing the themes in the Control Panel doesn't help you compare them because, by the time you've previewed the last theme on the list, you've probably already forgotten what was in the first theme.

This chapter will help you choose a theme by laying out all the details of each one. You can flip back and forth between different themes to find the one that's just right for you.

Dangerous Creatures (256 Color)

Fig. 5.1
The wallpaper for
Dangerous Creatures.

Fig. 5.2
A window using
Dangerous Creatures.

Table 5.1   Mouse pointers for Dangerous Creatures

Pointer	Description
	Normal Select
	Text Select
	Busy
	Precision Select
	Help Select
	Move

continues

Table 5.1 Continued

Pointer	Description
	Unavailable
	Handwriting
	Diagonal Resize 2
	Vertical Resize
	Diagonal Resize 1
	Horizontal Resize
	Alternate Select
	Working in Background

Table 5.2 Desktop icons for Dangerous Creatures

Pointer	Description
	My Computer
	Network Neighborhood
	Recycle Bin Empty
	Recycle Bin Full

Fig. 5.3
The screen saver for Dangerous Creatures with moving sea animals

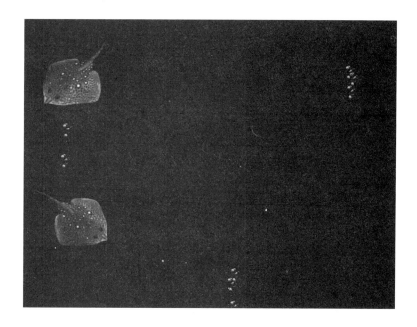

Inside Your Computer (High Color)

Fig. 5.4
The wallpaper for Inside Your Computer.

Fig. 5.5
A window using Inside
Your Computer.

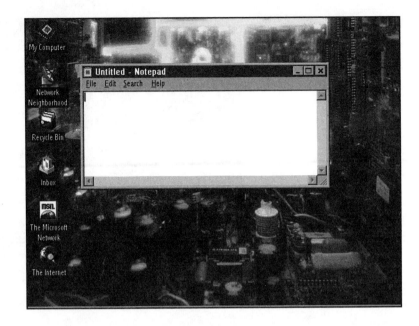

Table 5.3 Mouse pointers for Inside Your Computer

Pointer	Description
![Normal Select pointer]	Normal Select
![Text Select pointer]	Text Select
![Busy pointer]	Busy
![Precision Select pointer]	Precision Select
![Help Select pointer]	Help Select
![Move pointer]	Move
![Unavailable pointer]	Unavailable

Pointer	Description
	Handwriting
	Diagonal Resize 2
	Vertical Resize
	Diagonal Resize 1
	Horizontal Resize
	Alternate Select
	Working in Background

Table 5.4   Desktop icons for Inside Your Computer

Pointer	Description
	My Computer
	Network Neighborhood
	Recycle Bin Empty
	Recycle Bin Full

Fig. 5.6
The screen saver for
Inside Your Computer
with floating transistors.

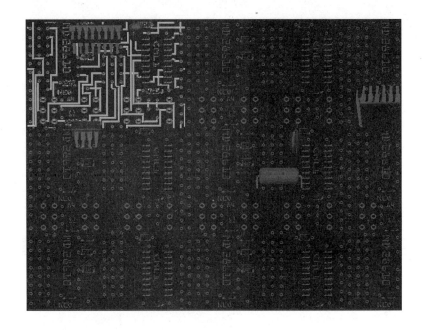

Leonardo Da Vinci (256 Color)

Fig. 5.7
The wallpaper for
Leonardo Da Vinci.

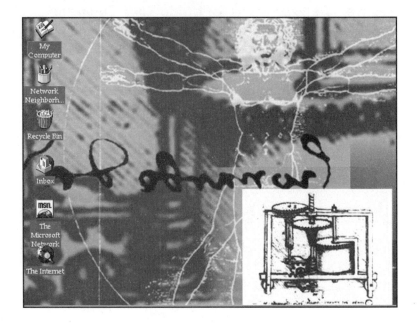

Fig. 5.8
A window using
Leonardo Da Vinci.

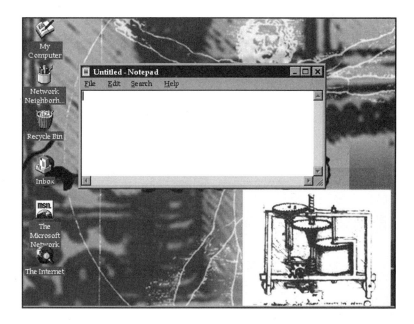

Table 5.5 Mouse pointers for Leonardo Da Vinci

Pointer	Description
	Normal Select
I	Text Select
	Busy
+	Precision Select
	Help Select
	Move
⊘	Unavailable

continues

Table 5.5 Continued

Pointer	Description
	Handwriting
	Diagonal Resize 2
	Vertical Resize
	Diagonal Resize 1
	Horizontal Resize
	Alternate Select
	Working in Background

Table 5.6 Desktop icons for Leonardo Da Vinci

Pointer	Description
	My Computer
	Network Neighborhood
	Recycle Bin Empty
	Recycle Bin Full

Fig. 5.9
The screen saver for
Leonardo Da Vinci with
various moving
inventions.

More Windows (High Color)

Fig. 5.10
The wallpaper for
More Windows.

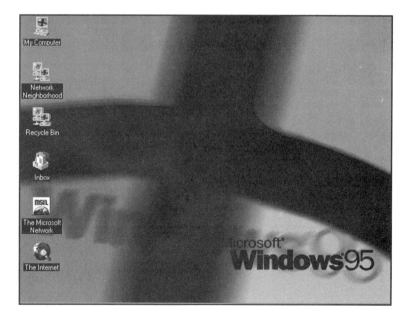

Fig. 5.11
A window using
More Windows.

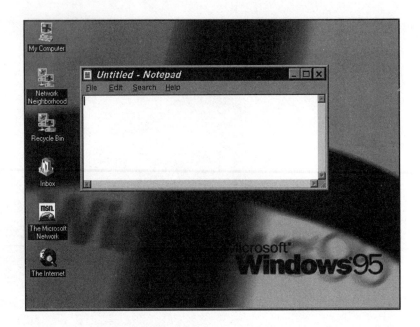

Table 5.7   Mouse pointers for More Windows

Pointer	Description
	Normal Select
	Text Select
	Busy
	Precision Select
	Help Select
	Move
	Unavailable

Pointer	Description
	Handwriting
	Diagonal Resize 2
	Vertical Resize
	Diagonal Resize 1
	Horizontal Resize
	Alternate Select
	Working in Background

Table 5.8   Desktop icons for More Windows

Pointer	Description
	My Computer
	Network Neighborhood
	Recycle Bin Empty
	Recycle Bin Full

Fig. 5.12
The screen saver for
More Windows with
moving 3-D blocks.

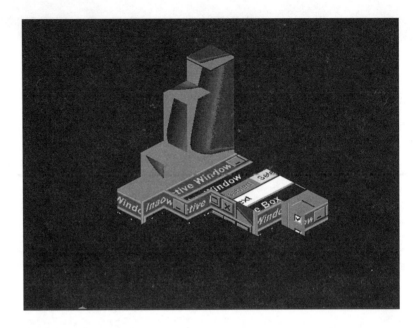

Mystery (High Color)

Fig. 5.13
The wallpaper for
Mystery.

Fig. 5.14
A window using
Mystery.

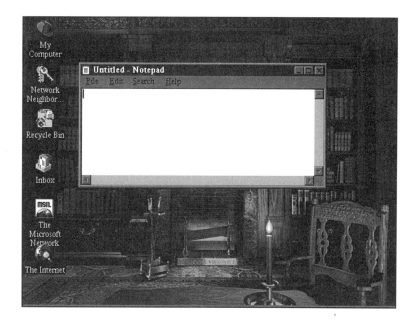

Table 5.9   Mouse pointers for Mystery

Pointer	Description
	Normal Select
	Text Select
	Busy
	Precision Select
	Help Select
	Move
	Unavailable

continues

Table 5.9 Continued

Pointer	Description
	Handwriting
	Diagonal Resize 2
	Vertical Resize
	Diagonal Resize 1
	Horizontal Resize
	Alternate Select
	Working in Background

Table 5.10 Desktop icons for Mystery

Pointer	Description
	My Computer
	Network Neighborhood
	Recycle Bin Empty
	Recycle Bin Full

Fig. 5.15
The screen saver for Mystery with flying animals and sound effects.

Nature (High Color)

Fig. 5.16
The wallpaper for Nature.

Fig. 5.17
A window using
Nature.

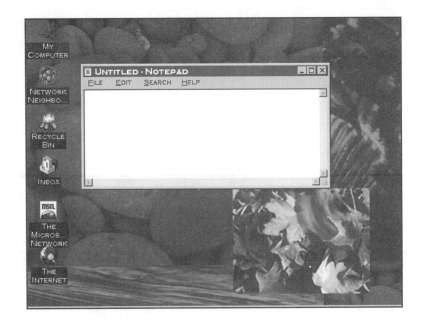

Table 5.11   Mouse pointers for Nature

Pointer	Description
↖	Normal Select
I	Text Select
🐝	Busy
+	Precision Select
↖?	Help Select
✥	Move
⊘	Unavailable

Pointer	Description
	Handwriting
	Diagonal Resize 2
	Vertical Resize
	Diagonal Resize 1
	Horizontal Resize
	Alternate Select
	Working in Background

Table 5.12   Desktop icons for Nature

Pointer	Description
	My Computer
	Network Neighborhood
	Recycle Bin Empty
	Recycle Bin Full

Fig. 5.18
The screen saver for
Nature with crawling
caterpillars.

Science (256 Color)

Fig. 5.19
The wallpaper for
Science.

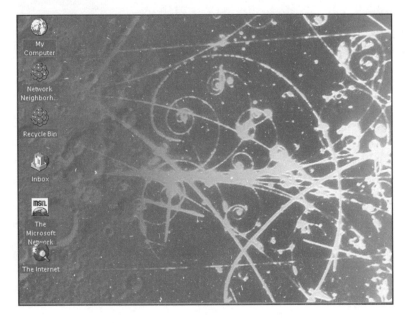

Fig. 5.20
A window using
Science.

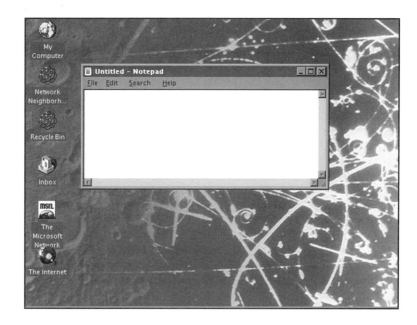

Table 5.13   Mouse pointers for Science

Pointer	Description
	Normal Select
	Text Select
	Busy
	Precision Select
	Help Select
	Move
	Unavailable

continues

Table 5.13   Continued

Pointer	Description
	Handwriting
	Diagonal Resize 2
	Vertical Resize
	Diagonal Resize 1
	Horizontal Resize
	Alternate Select
	Working in Background

Table 5.14   Desktop icons for Science

Pointer	Description
	My Computer
	Network Neighborhood
	Recycle Bin Empty
	Recycle Bin Full

Fig. 5.21
The screen saver for
Science with moving
"warp field."

Sports (256 Color)

Fig. 5.22
The wallpaper for
Sports.

Fig. 5.23
A window using Sports.

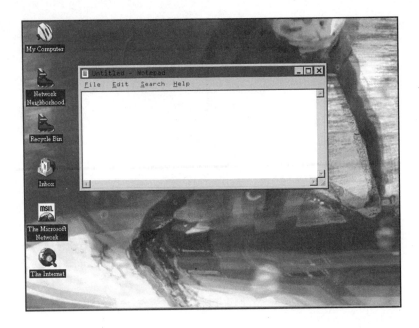

Table 5.15 Mouse pointers for Sports

Pointer	Description
	Normal Select
	Text Select
	Busy
	Precision Select
	Help Select
	Move
	Unavailable

Pointer	Description
	Handwriting
	Diagonal Resize 2
	Vertical Resize
	Diagonal Resize 1
	Horizontal Resize
	Alternate Select
	Working in Background

Table 5.16   Desktop icons for Sports

Pointer	Description
	My Computer
	Network Neighborhood
	Recycle Bin Empty
	Recycle Bin Full

Fig. 5.24
The screen saver for Sports with animated chalkboard and sound effects.

The 60's USA (256 Color)

Fig. 5.25
The wallpaper for The 60's USA.

Fig. 5.26
A window using The
60's USA.

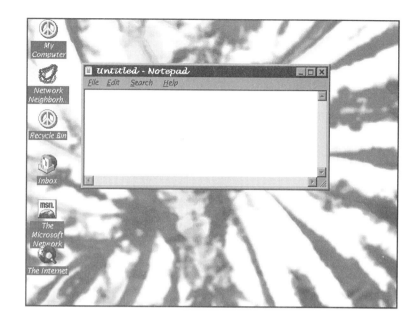

Table 5.17   Mouse pointers for The 60's USA

Pointer	Description
	Normal Select
	Text Select
	Busy
	Precision Select
	Help Select
	Move
	Unavailable

continues

Table 5.17   Continued

Pointer	Description
	Handwriting
	Diagonal Resize 2
	Vertical Resize
	Diagonal Resize 1
	Horizontal Resize
	Alternate Select
	Working in Background

Table 5.18   Desktop icons for The 60's USA

Pointer	Description
	My Computer
	Network Neighborhood
	Recycle Bin Empty
	Recycle Bin Full

Fig. 5.27
The screen saver for
The 60's USA with
moving "spiro lens."

The Golden Era (High Color)

Fig. 5.28
The wallpaper for The
Golden Era.

Fig. 5.29
A window using The
Golden Era.

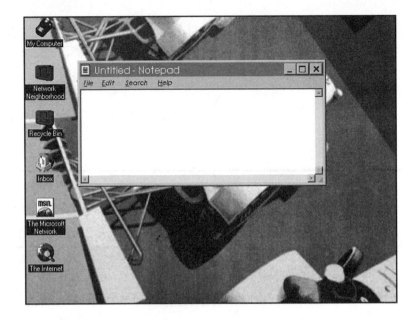

Table 5.19   Mouse pointers for The Golden Era

Pointer	Description
	Normal Select
I	Text Select
	Busy
+	Precision Select
	Help Select
	Move
	Unavailable

Pointer	Description
	Handwriting
	Diagonal Resize 2
	Vertical Resize
	Diagonal Resize 1
	Horizontal Resize
	Alternate Select
	Working in Background

Table 5.20 Desktop icons for The Golden Era

Pointer	Description
	My Computer
	Network Neighborhood
	Recycle Bin Empty
	Recycle Bin Full

Fig. 5.30
The screen saver for
The Golden Era with
tapping foot and
sound effects.

Travel (High Color)

Fig. 5.31
The wallpaper for
Travel.

Fig. 5.32
A window using Travel.

Table 5.21 Mouse pointers for Travel

Pointer	Description
	Normal Select
I	Text Select
	Busy
+	Precision Select
	Help Select
	Move
⦰	Unavailable

continues

Table 5.21 Continued

Pointer	Description
	Handwriting
	Diagonal Resize 2
	Vertical Resize
	Diagonal Resize 1
	Horizontal Resize
	Alternate Select
	Working in Background

Table 5.22 Desktop icons for Travel

Pointer	Description
	My Computer
	Network Neighborhood
	Recycle Bin Empty
	Recycle Bin Full

Fig. 5.33
The screen saver for Travel with moving airplanes.

Windows 95 (256 Color)

Fig. 5.34
The wallpaper for Windows 95.

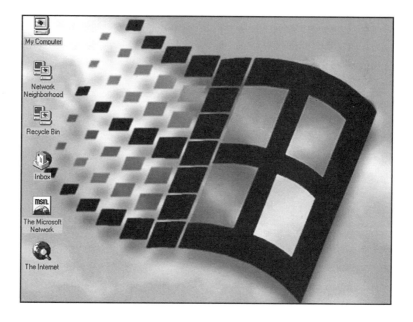

Fig. 5.35
A window using
Windows 95.

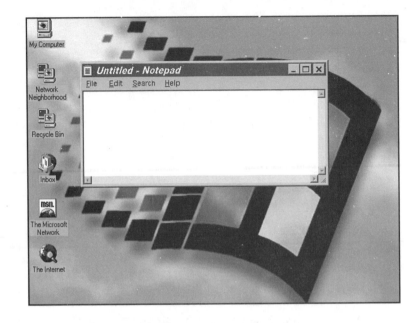

Table 5.23   Mouse pointers for Windows 95

Pointer	Description
	Normal Select
I	Text Select
	Busy
+	Precision Select
	Help Select
	Move
⃠	Unavailable

Pointer	Description
	Handwriting
	Diagonal Resize 2
	Vertical Resize
	Diagonal Resize 1
	Horizontal Resize
	Alternate Select
	Working in Background

Table 5.24   Desktop icons for Windows 95

Pointer	Description
	My Computer
	Network Neighborhood
	Recycle Bin Empty
	Recycle Bin Full

Fig. 5.36
The screen saver for
Windows 95 with
moving 3-D blocks.

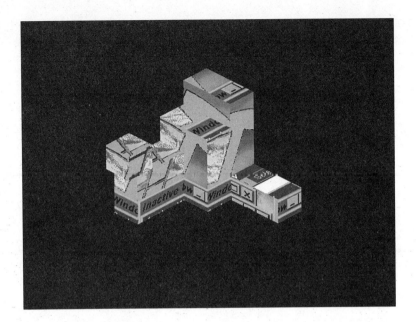

Take a Break, Play Space Cadet Pinball

● **In this chapter:**

- ● **I want to play—now!**

- ● **There's a lot of stuff on the table**

- ● **Where are the BIG points?**

- ● **How do I become The Pinball Wizard?**

Attention, Space Cadets. Your mission is to reconnoiter hyperspace, make a clean reentry, and advance your rank to Fleet Admiral . . . . ▶

Space Cadet Pinball is as close as you're going to get to the real thing. It turns Windows 95 into a private arcade. Space Cadet Pinball comes complete with Ramps, Chutes, Targets, and Bumpers. And, just like the real thing, it has the sounds to match the visuals. Points are awarded for simply picking off targets; big points are awarded for nailing down targets in specific sequences for the truly pinball crazed.

Quick Start—I Just Want to Play!

The Microsoft Plus! install will set up a shortcut to Space Cadet Pinball in your Start menu. Select Programs, Accessories, Games, 3D Pinball, Space Cadet Table from the Start menu.

Press F2 to start your space voyage. You can launch the ball with the Spacebar, or, from the main menu, select Game, Launch. Table 6.1 shows the default keys necessary to play the game. Enjoy!

TIP   **To launch the ball with the Spacebar, hold the Spacebar down** until the plunger is pulled back far enough to launch the ball. Game, Launch will launch the ball instantly. You can control how far and fast the ball goes by letting go of the spacebar before the plunger is pulled all the way back.

Table 6.1   Space Cadet Pinball keyboard guide

Key	Function
Z	Left Flipper
X	Left Table Bump
.>	Right Table Bump
/?	Right Flipper
Spacebar	Plunger
Up Arrow	Bottom Table Bump

A visual guide to the Space Cadet Pinball table

The Space Cadet Pinball table is similar to the pinball tables you find in arcades everywhere. On the bottom-right side of the table is the plunger that you use to start the game. The ball will travel up the deployment chute and drop on the table through the Reentry Lanes. Chances are, the ball will then encounter the bank of Attack Bumpers that are located at the top and center of the table. At the bottom of the table are your flippers, which are used to control the ball. There are a couple of targets that you'll want to keep in mind. The purple ramp on the left side of the table is the Launch Ramp. You'll use the Launch Ramp to select your mission. Underneath the Launch Ramp is the Fuel Chute. When your fuel is low, you will need to send the ball up this chute. Figure 6.1 shows the layout of the Space Cadet table with its major points of interest noted. Table 6.2 provides a scoring summary of the major game features listed by their location on the table.

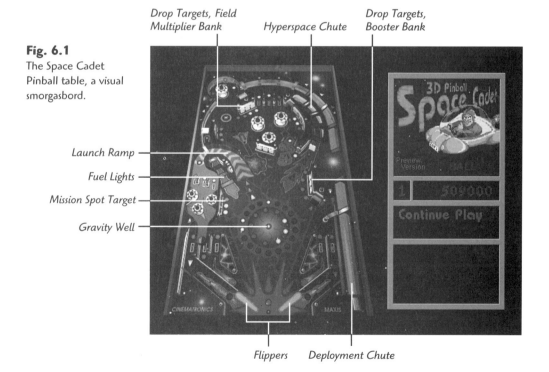

Fig. 6.1
The Space Cadet Pinball table, a visual smorgasbord.

Drop Targets, Field Multiplier Bank

Hyperspace Chute

Drop Targets, Booster Bank

Launch Ramp

Fuel Lights

Mission Spot Target

Gravity Well

Flippers   Deployment Chute

Table 6.2 Space Cadet Pinball scoring summary

Zone	Features	Points
Lower Left	Left Kicker & Lights	
	Left Rebound	500
	Replay Light	
	Return Lane	5,000
	Return Light	10,000
	Bonus Lane	10,000
	Bonus Light	Bonus
	Out Lane	20,000
	Extra Ball Light	Extra Ball
Lower Center	Center Post & Light	
	Gravity Well	2,000,000
	Rank Lights (9)	
	Rank Progress Lights (18)	
Lower Right	Attack Bumpers (4)	500–2000
	Right Kicker & Lights	
	Right Rebound	500
	Plunger	
	Shoot Again Light	
	Return Lane	5,000
	Return Light	10,000
	Out Lane	20,000
	Extra Ball Light	Extra Ball
Left Center	Launch Bumpers (3)	1500–4500
	Launch Ramp	5,000
	Reflex Light	25,000
	Time Warp Light	Gain One Rank
	Mission Light	25,000–100,000
	Launch Lanes (3)	500
	Mission Target (3)	1,000
	Fuel Chute	
	Black Hole Kickout	5,000
	Flag	500/Turn
	Flag	500/Turn
	Flag Light	2,500/Turn

Zone	Features	Points
Right Center	Wormhole	1,000–5,000
	Booster Drop Target (3)	500
	Hyperspace Chute	
	Hyperspace Kickout	5,000–150,000
	Reflex Light	25,000
	Time Warp Light	Lose One Rank
	Maelstrom Light	10,000,000
	Space Warp Target	750
	Flag	500/Turn
	Flag Light	2,500/Turn
Upper Center	Wormhole	1,000–5,000
	Right Hazard Target (3)	750
	Attack Bumper (3)	500-2000
	Rebounds (2)	500
	Field Multiplier Target (3)	500
	Field Multiplier Light	1,500
	Re-Entry Lane (3)	500
Upper Left	Attack Bumper	500–2000
	Wormhole	1,000–5,000
	Space Warp Rollover	10,000
	Left Hazard Target (3)	750
	Fuel Target (3)	750
	Medal Target (3)	1,500
	Medal Target Light	10,000–50,000
	Extra Ball	

TIP   **Space Cadet Pinball comes with a picture that describes every** object on the table. You'll find this picture in \Program Files\Plus!\ Pinball\Table.bmp.

Customizing Space Cadet Pinball

To fully enjoy the comfort of your space voyage, you may want to customize some of the features of the game. Space Cadet Pinball will allow you to change the keyboard controls and its audio and visual presentation. As any space cadet will tell you, to be most effective in space battle, the cockpit needs to be adjusted to fit the comfort of the cadet. The seat needs to be placed in the proper position, and the controls need to be set to accommodate the cadet. When you play Space Cadet Pinball, you should make sure that the game is configured to your style of play.

Changing the key controls

The thing that I find most annoying about the default key layout is that the Bump From Bottom function is attached to the up-arrow key. I don't know about you, but on my keyboard I can't even reach the up-arrow key when I have my middle and index fingers on the ? and > keys. I recommend that you move the Bump From Bottom to the Spacebar and move the Plunger to the up-arrow. Here's how:

1 Select Options, Player Controls from the main menu. Figure 6.2 shows the dialog box that allows you to remap the game controls on your keyboard.

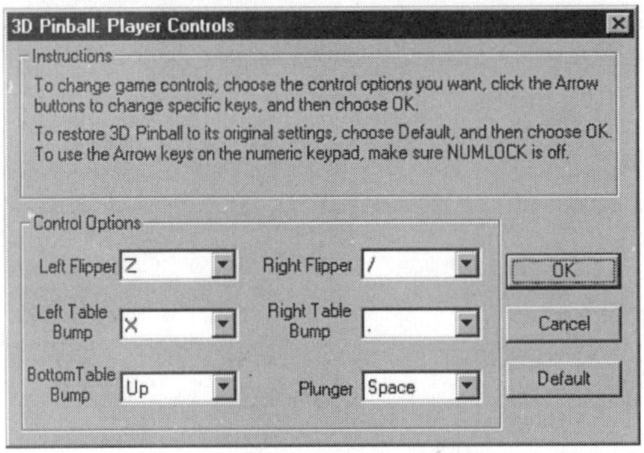

Fig. 6.2
Space Cadet Pinball can be set to use almost all of the keys on your keyboard, but don't try to use the Shift key!

2 Select Space from the Bump Table Bottom drop-down list.

3 Select Up from the Plunger drop-down list.

4 Click OK to save your changes.

Running Space Cadet Pinball full screen

When you're getting ready to blast off, the last thing you need is to be distracted by the earthly remnants of your desktop laying about. Select Options, Full Screen or press F4, and Space Cadet Pinball will fully take over your desktop.

Selecting how many players will play

Have you selected a crew to accompany you on your mission? Select Options, Select Players, 1 through 4 from the main menu.

Configuring the Sound

For the true arcade effect—and to drive everyone around you nuts—make sure to select <u>S</u>ounds and <u>M</u>usic from <u>O</u>ptions menu. On the other hand, if you're playing at work, you'll want to deselect these, and keep an eye out for the boss.

 TIP **If the game audio is not up to par, execute the Sound Mixing** Configuration program. From the Start menu, Choose <u>R</u>un, and type:

C:\Program Files\Plus!\Pinball\Wmconfig.exe

You can then manually select from a list of available sound cards, and test them out. There are several configurations for many cards, so test them all to get the best one.

Basic strategy

Beginners will want to acquire points by simply learning to hit targets and keep the ball alive. Familiarize yourself with the target values listed in table 6.2, and try to go after the most lucrative values. The message box will guide you to appropriate targets, too, so keep an eye on it!

As you become more familiar with the flippers, you'll want to start learning how to bump and nudge the table. A good bump can help you get the ball to fall down a particular chute. Or, a nudge against a bumper can cause the ball to rebound several times, racking up valuable points. But be careful! If you bump the table too hard, you'll tilt the machine and all functions will stop, including the flippers, until the ball drains. The Tilt Light is the big red X to the left of the Gravity Well.

Intermediate strategy

So, you're an intermediate player. You'll want to complete simple sequences of shots to accumulate higher scores and initiate new modes of play.

The following list consists of simple sequences that should be mastered before taking on a Space Cadet Mission:

- **Skill Shots.** Launch the ball only part way up the Deployment Chute and let it fall back down onto the table. For maximum points, try to light only two of the lights. One light lit is worth 15,000; two lights, 30,000; three, 5,000; four, 30,000; five 15,000; six 7,500.

- **Reflex Shot**. When the Reflex Shot Light is on for either the Launch Ramp or the Hyperspace Chute, a Reflex award of 25,000 points is awarded when you send the ball up the chute or ramp that is lit. Turn on the Hyperspace Reflex Shot Light by landing the ball in the Hyperspace Kickout. The Launch Ramp Reflex Shot Light is turned on when the ball drains from the Launch Ramp. You had better act quickly, though; the lights stay lit for only five seconds.

- **Bonus**. A bonus of 25,000 points is available by knocking down the targets of the Booster Bank three times. The bonus is awarded when the ball drains or when the ball drops through the Bonus Lane when the Bonus Light is lit.

- **Jackpot**. To activate the Jackpot, knock down all the targets in the Booster Bank twice. Collect the Jackpot of 20,000 points by shooting the ball into the Hyperspace Chute twice.

- **Gravity Well**. The Gravity Well is located in the center of the table. It is activated by shooting the ball into the Hyperspace Kickout five times in a row. If the ball gets sucked into the Gravity Well, the player is awarded 50,000 points.

Advanced strategy

As a cadet in the Space Academy, your goal is to move up through the ranks to Fleet Admiral. To accomplish your goal, you'll need to complete missions and receive accommodations. After you complete each mission, you will light one or more Rank Progress Lights in the center of the table. Your promotion is secured by lighting all 18 of these lights, and is indicated by lighting one of the 9 Rank Lights in the center of the table. These lights are the prominent feature displayed in the lower-center section of the table (refer to figure 6.1 shown previously).

Ranks

Moving through the ranks is the essence of being a Space Cadet. Table 6.3 shows the rank associated with each level in the game.

Table 6.3 Ranks in Space Cadet Pinball

Lights	Rank
1	Cadet
2	Ensign
3	Lieutenant
4	Captain
5	Lt. Commander
6	Commander
7	Commodore
8	Admiral
9	Fleet Admiral

Completing missions

The only way for a lowly space cadet to move up in rank is to complete a difficult mission. To select a mission, you need to hit the Mission Targets. Table 6.4 lists the missions available for a given rank.

Table 6.4 Missions available in Space Cadet Pinball by rank

Rank	Light	Mission
Cadet	First Light	Re-Entry Training
	Second Light	Launch Training
	Third Light	Target Practice
	All Lights	Science Mission

continues

Table 6.4 Continued

Rank	Light	Mission
Ensign Lieutenant	First Light Second Light Third Light All Lights	Bug Hunt Rescue Mission Alien Menace Secret Mission
Captain Lt. Commander	First Light Second Light Third Light All Lights	Stray Comet Space Radiation Black Hole Threat Cosmic Plague
Commander Commodore	First Light Second Light Third Light All Lights	Satellite Retrieval Recon Mission Doomsday Machine Time Warp
Admiral Fleet Admiral	First Light Second Light Third Light All Lights	Secret Mission Cosmic Plague Time Warp Maelstrom

Once a mission is selected, the player must send the ball up the Launch Ramp to activate the mission. The mission sequences must be completed to collect the mission award and light up the Rank Progress Lights. Table 6.5 lists the sequences required to complete each mission, along with the number of points awarded and the number of Rank Progress Lights Awarded for each completion.

Table 6.5 Mission Completion Sequences in Space Cadet Pinball

Mission	Requirement	Points	Progress Lights
Target Practice	8 Attack Bumpers	500,000	6
Launch Training	3 Launch Ramps	500,000	6
Re-Entry Training	3 Re-Entry Lanes	500,000	6
Science Mission	9 Drop Targets	750,000	9
Bug Hunt	15 Targets	750,000	7

Mission	Requirement	Points	Progress Lights
Alien Menace	Upgrade Attack Bumpers 12 Attack Bumpers	750,000	7
Rescue Mission	Upgrade Flags, then Hyperspace Kickout	750,000	7
Secret Mission	Yellow Wormhole, then Red Wormhole, then Green Wormhole	1,500,000	10
Stray Comet	Light Rt. Hazard Bank, then Hyperspace Kickout	1,000,000	8
Black Hole Threat	Upgrade Launch Bumpers, then Black Hole Kickout	1,000,000	8
Space Radiation	Light Lt. Hazard Bank, then Any Wormhole	1,000,000	8
Cosmic Plague	75 flags, then Space Warp Rollover	1,750,000	11
Satellite Retrieval	5 Remote Attack Bumpers	1,250,000	9
Recon Mission	15 Lanes	1,250,000	9
Doomsday Machine	3 Out Lanes	1,250,000	9
Time Warp	25 Rebounds, then Launch Ramp (which will increase rank by one) or, Hyperspace Kickout (which will decrease rank by one)	2,000,000	12
Maelstrom	Any Drop Target 3 times, then any spot target 3 times, then any lane 5 times, then up the Fuel Chute, then up the Launch Ramp, then any flag, then any Wormhole, then Hyperspace Kickout. (Turns on all the table lights.)	5,000,000	18

Fuel

It's critical to keep track of your fuel. A Space Cadet can never advance in rank if he or she can't manage the fuel supplies. There are five Rollover lights in the Fuel Chute. When the last light goes dim, you're out of fuel and your mission is aborted. To refuel, send the ball up the Fuel Chute.

Part III: Surfing the Internet with Internet Jumpstart

7

The Internet—the Easy Way

● In this chapter:

- Internet terms

- What is an Independent Service Provider?

- The wizard makes it easy

- You have everything you need on your desktop

- How do you secure your computer while you're connected?

Hooking up to the Internet doesn't have to be intimidating. The Internet Setup Wizard makes it easy . . . . ▶

Time Magazine. USA Today. Newsweek. Rolling Stone. **And even your local news broadcast. What do all these have in** common? They are all talking about the Internet. In fact, everyone is talking about the Internet.

You can think of the Internet as a huge library. And, like a library, the Internet provides a bunch of books that contain information you want. But unlike a library, the Internet has an infinite number of books.

You can become part of the action. The Internet Setup Wizard makes it easy. You can drop in on the White House, explore the newest galaxies discovered by the Hubble space telescope, exchange e-mail with friends and colleagues, and much more.

What can I do on the Internet?

The Internet is your source for information and communication. It provides the infrastructure so that you can send and receive information.

Before Windows 95, if you wanted to get connected to the Internet, you had to collect and install software from a variety of sources and hope that everything played well together.

Now, everything you need to connect to the Internet is right on your desktop. All you have to do is click. Here are some of the things you can do:

- **Surf the World Wide Web.** Each Web page will appear like a page from a book. You'll find text, graphics, sounds, movies, and more. You can use the Web to check out services from companies or the menu at your local restaurant. You can even set up your own personal Web page to which anyone in the world can connect. Your page might contain photos of you, your family, and even Fido.

- **Exchange e-mail.** Does your mother tell you that you don't call enough? Mine does. But we've solved that problem. I hooked Mom up on Internet e-mail, and now we communicate much more frequently. Internet e-mail also can be used to keep in touch with any number of topics that interest you. Not unlike a magazine subscription, and usually free, a **mailing list** delivers ongoing "threads" or group discussions on a particular topic right to your mailbox, with one extra benefit: you get to post your own opinions whenever you want. If you're interested in running, for example, you might subscribe to the Dead Runners Society (DRS) mailing list. The DRS list is dedicated to talking about issues that concern runners and running. There are mailing lists for all interests.

- **Exchange files.** Does your family complain that you spend more of the family budget on software than you do on them? Those days are over once you tap the Internet for your habit. The Internet contains a vast amount of shareware and freeware programs for the picking. Windows 95 comes with a tool called **FTP**, which you can use to download these remote files.

- **Obtain instant information.** How would you like to have a panel of experts available to answer any question that you have on any subject at any time? That's exactly what the USENET news groups are. They're also good for expressing your opinions to a group of like-minded individuals.

- **Connect to other computers.** Windows 95 comes with an Internet utility program called Telnet, which allows you to log on as a terminal to a remote computer. You may want to telnet to the University of Minnesota and use its Gopher system, for example, which allows you to perform text searches for files on other computers connected to the Internet.

 Plain English, please!

Shareware programs are programs that you can download and try out free of charge for a time. The author expects you to pay for it, however, if you find it useful. **Freeware** programs are programs that you can download without ever incurring a charge.

 After you've created your dial-up connection, you might want to experiment with **Telnet** or **FTP**. To use Telnet or FTP, select Run from the Start menu, type **Telnet** or **FTP**, and click on OK.

Gee, what are all these buzzwords?

One thing that you have probably learned by now is that computer "nerds" have their own lingo. I call it Technobabble. Don't let this intimidate you. The lingo is easy to learn. So, hold on while I explore the language of the Internet:

- **TCP/IP** stands for Transmission Control Protocol/Internet Protocol. Simply put, these are electronic communications standards or protocols that are used for sending information on the Internet. For more information about network protocols, see chapter 13, "Dial-Up Networking—Anywhere, Anytime."

- An **IP Address** is how your computer is identified on the Internet using the TCP/IP protocol. In reality, it's a 32-bit number. You'll see this number represented as four small sets of numbers joined by periods (for example, 250.1.128.137).

- **Domain** names save you the trouble of using IP addresses. Can you imagine remembering your friend's e-mail address if it were **chris@119.12.11.217** instead of **chris@onramp.net**? **net** is the highest-level domain in this name and represents the set of all computers on the Internet that are service providers. **onramp** is a lower-level domain that represents a computer within the **net** domain. And **chris** is a particular account in the **onramp.net** domain.

- **PPP, SLIP, and CSLIP** are connection protocols that your computer uses to talk to the Internet server. For more information about these connection protocols, see chapter 13.

Common high-level domain names

COM—A commercial institution.
Microsoft Corporation: microsoft.com

EDU—An educational institution.
The University of Vermont: uvm.edu

GOV—A government site.
The office of the President of the United States: whitehouse.gov

MIL—A military location.
The United States Air Force: aimhigh.mil

Net—An Internet service provider.
On-Ramp Technologies: onramp.net

ORG—A private organization.
The Dead Runners Society: drs.org

- **PAP** stands for Password Authentication Protocol. It's another protocol that is used so that a network provider and a client (your computer) can authenticate your password without you having to type your password too many times.

- **Packets** contain information that is sent between computers on the Internet. These packets are like envelopes that you would use to send a letter through the U.S. mail, but they are addressed with IP addresses instead of street addresses.

What's the easiest way to hook up? Use MSN

If you don't already have an Internet account with an independent service provider, you may want to consider using MSN as your connection. Why? First, it's simpler than using an independent provider. You don't have to answer as many questions.

Also, it's available now. Windows 95 and Microsoft Plus! installed everything you need to use MSN to hook up to the Internet. And, if you have an account set up on MSN, you already have Internet connection available to you.

 Using the Internet Setup Wizard to configure your Internet connection for MSN is a breeze. To keep things simple, I'm assuming that you already have an account on MSN. If you don't, double-click on the MSN icon on your desktop.

The Microsoft Network

The Microsoft Network (MSN) is an online service included in Windows 95. With MSN, you can exchange messages with people around the world. You have access to the latest news wire services, sports information, weather forecasts, and financial information. You can find answers to your technical questions on Windows 95, Microsoft Plus!, and any other product represented on The Microsoft Network. You can download files including software, pictures, and sound. You can also use The Microsoft Network to connect to the Internet.

First, create your connection

Make sure that you have Internet Jumpstart installed from your Microsoft Plus! disk. To set up your computer to use MSN as your Internet connection, use the following steps:

1 Start the Internet Setup Wizard. You'll find it in the Start menu under Programs, Accessories, Internet Tools.

2 Click on Next to display the dialog box shown in figure 7.1.

Fig. 7.1

Select Connect Using My Local Area Network only after consulting with your network administrator.

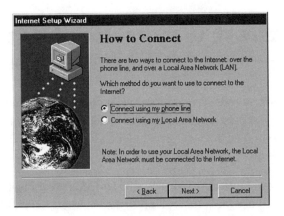

3 Select Connect Using My Phone Line and click on Next.

4 Select Use The Microsoft Network and click on Next. If the wizard asks for the Windows 95 or Microsoft Plus! disks, insert them as requested.

5 Click on Yes to indicate that you are already a member. Then, click on Next.

6 Click on OK after the wizard loads MSN. MSN displays the dialog box shown in figure 7.2.

7 Type your area code and the first three digits of your phone number. Then, click on OK.

8 Click on Connect and log on to MSN as you normally do. The MSN software will connect you to MSN to get the latest list of Internet phone numbers.

Fig. 7.2
MSN will use these to determine the closest MSN phone number for you. The numbers that MSN finds will be different than the regular MSN phone numbers.

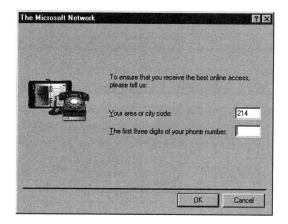

Q&A *MSN reports that no phone numbers were found for my location.*

You may need to pick a number in a different area code or even a different state. Note that you'll add up a pretty good phone bill if you connect to MSN long distance.

9 Click on OK.

Then, connect

Wow! Now you have an Internet connection. It's time to use it. There are a few different ways to connect.

- If you double-click on the Internet Explorer icon, which is on your desktop, it will display the MSN Sign In dialog box. Click on Connect to dial the connection. Figure 7.3 shows the MSN Sign In dialog box. Notice that when you connect this way, you are connected to both the Internet and MSN. Therefore, you can browse the World Wide Web using Internet Explorer, and you can browse MSN using the MSN software. When you disconnect from MSN, you are disconnected from both.

Fig. 7.3
When you connect using the MSN Sign In dialog box, you're connecting to both the Internet and MSN. You can browse both at the same time.

- You can connect by opening the Dial-Up Networking folder and double-clicking on The Microsoft Network. Figure 7.4 shows the Dial-Up Networking connection for accessing the Internet through MSN. (For more information about using Dial-Up Networking, see chapter 13.) Click on Connect. When you're connected using Dial-Up Networking, you're connected only to the Internet. If you want to browse MSN, you need to double-click on the MSN icon on the desktop.

Fig. 7.4
You can connect to just the Internet, or double-click on the MSN icon to connect to MSN, too.

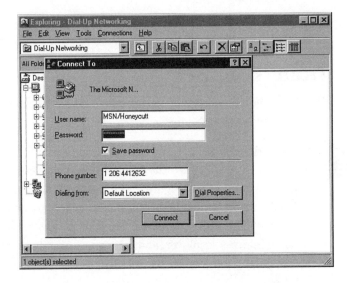

What about Independent Service Providers?

You've decided to use the Internet Setup Wizard to configure your Internet Access through a local Internet service provider. Before you can get started, you'll need an account with an ISP and some information from the administrator:

 Plain English, please!

An **Independent Service Provider** (ISP) maintains a computer system to which you can connect for Internet access. As the name implies, this type of provider is not usually associated with any other organization, but is in business to sell Internet access.

- **PPP, SLIP, or CSLIP user name/password.** Your user name is used to connect to the server. See chapter 13 for more information about PPP and dial-up connections. If you're using SLIP or CSLIP, read chapter 14 to learn how to use a Dial-Up Script with your connection.

- **Mail name/password.** Your mail name is used to check your e-mail and log on to the server using Telnet. Sometimes, your PPP name and mail name will be the same.

- **Phone number**.

- **Mail server name.** This is the domain name of the server that handles your mail.

- **IP address.** Most PPP connections automatically assign you an IP address when you connect. If they don't, however, you'll need the permanent address.

- **Gateway IP address.** Your provider may require you to configure your system to use a gateway.

- **DNS addresses.** Your provider will give you a DNS address and an alternate DNS address.

TIP   **Make sure that you have not bound File and Printer Sharing for** Microsoft Networks to the TCP/IP Protocol. If they are bound together, other people on the Internet will have access to your computer. To double check, right-click on Network Neighborhood and select Properties. Select TCP/IP->Dial-Up Adapter from the list and click on Properties. Click on the Bindings tab of the TCP/IP Properties dialog and make sure that File and Printer Sharing for Microsoft Networks is not selected. Click on OK twice to save your changes.

First, make your connection

Make sure that you have Internet JumpStart installed from your Microsoft Plus! disk. To set up your computer to use an ISP, use the following steps:

1 Start the Internet Setup Wizard. You'll find it in the Start menu under Programs, Accessories, Internet Tools.

2 Click on Next.

3 Select Connect Using My Phone Line and click on Next.

4 Select I Already Have an Account with a Different Service Provider and click on Next. The wizard displays the dialog box shown in figure 7.5.

Fig. 7.5
You can use an existing dial-up connection or use the wizard to create a new connection.

5 Type the name of your service provider or select an existing dial-up connection from the list. Click on Next.

6 Type the phone number of your provider in the fields provided. If you must manually log in to the server (that is, your provider doesn't support PAP or CHAP), select Bring Up Terminal Window After Dialing.

7 Type your PPP name and PPP password in the fields provided. Click on Next. Figure 7.6 shows the IP address configuration dialog that is currently displayed.

Fig 7.6

In the rare circumstance in which the provider doesn't automatically assign you an IP address, click on Always Use the Following and fill in your individual IP address.

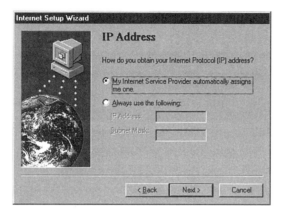

8 Select My Internet Service Provider Automatically Assigns Me One if your IP address is assigned automatically. Otherwise, select Always Use the Following and type your IP address and subnet mask in the fields provided. Click on Next and the wizard displays the DNS dialog box shown in figure 7.7.

Fig. 7.7

You must provide a DNS server to log on to the Internet.

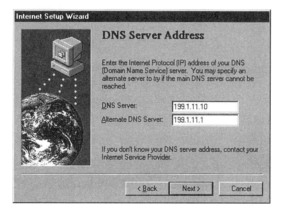

9 Type your DNS and alternate DNS servers in the fields provided. Click on Next.

10 Select <u>U</u>se Internet Mail if you want to get your e-mail through Microsoft Exchange. Type your e-mail address (for example, **chris@onramp.net**) and the name of your mail server (for example, **mailhost.onramp.net**) in the fields provided. Click on Next.

TIP **Registering your own domain with the InterNIC gives you a more** personal e-mail address. It also makes it easier to change service providers because your e-mail address will be the same regardless of which provider you use. Contact your service provider for help registering and setting up your own domain name.

If you've set up your own domain name with a service provider, make sure that you use it for your e-mail address (for example, **chris@hughes.com**). This will ensure that when people reply to your e-mail or add your address to their address book, they'll be using your domain name.

11 Click on Next to accept the default exchange profile.

12 Click on Finish.

Q&A *How do I connect to a SLIP or CSLIP account?*

Create your dial-up connection as described previously. Open the connection in the Dial-Up Networking folder, right-click on the connection, and select P<u>r</u>operties. Change the server type by clicking on Server <u>T</u>ype and selecting SLIP or CSLIP from Type of Dial-Up <u>S</u>erver.

Then, connect

Congratulations! Your Internet dial-up connection is done. There are a couple of ways to use your new connection.

• If you double-click on the Internet Explorer icon on your desktop, it will display the dial-up connection dialog box shown in figure 7.8. Click on Connect.

Fig. 7.8
Click on Connect to
dial your service
provider. If you want
Dial-Up Networking to
remember your
password, select Save
Password.

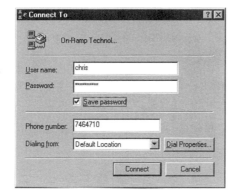

- You can connect by opening the Dial-Up Networking folder and double-clicking on your new connection. Click on Connect. For more information about using dial-up networking, see chapter 13.

The connection dials OK, but it never connects.

Your provider may not support PAP or CHAP. Make sure that you select Bring Up Terminal Window After Dialing in step 6. Then, you can log on to the server manually. Click on Continue after your session has started.

Browsing the World Wide Web with Internet Explorer

In this chapter:

- **What is the World Wide Web?**

- **Internet Explorer is your window on the Web**

- **What is a home page?**

- **What are HTTP, HTML, and URL?**

- **You don't have to wait for all those pictures**

- **You can get there quickly next time**

Internet Explorer is a great board for surfing the Internet.
This chapter will show you how to surf like a pro . . . . ⊖

By now, you've probably used Windows 95's online help. Some of the words and phrases on each help screen are highlighted to indicate that they are links. If you click on one of the links, you'll jump to another help topic—possibly in another file. This way, you can follow the links in a help file until you find information for which you're looking.

The World Wide Web is similar to the help files on your computer. It contains a large number of documents, or Web pages, and each Web page contains links to others. Just like the help files, you can jump to another document by clicking on a link until you find what you're looking for.

Internet Explorer is your window on the world

Internet Explorer is a tool that you can use with Windows 95 to explore the World Wide Web on the Internet. Simply put, the Web consists of millions of documents, or Web pages, all linked together to create a vast network of information. A Web page may contain text, graphics, sounds, or video. A growing number of pages are experimenting with animation, radio, and virtual reality (see chapter 9 to learn about the Virtual Reality Modeling Language, or VRML). A Web page may also contain a link, or shortcut, to another Web page. You navigate, or *surf*, the Web by clicking on these links. When you click on a link, Explorer loads that page.

Some examples might help you visualize the types of information available for people with different interests. In the rest of this section, you'll find examples of Web sites for professionals, users in need of product support, students, and folks looking for entertainment on the Web. Keep in mind, though, that there are a countless number of Web pages available on the Internet for virtually every interest you can imagine. For example, you'll also find Web pages for shopping, playing games, checking the stock market, looking up words in a dictionary, downloading shareware programs, reading the daily news, listening to clips from your favorite soundtracks, and much more.

I'm a professional—what can the Internet do for me?

The Web is an unlimited source of information. You'll find news, employment information, stock information, and business tips all over the Web. To perform research, you'll want to save some shortcuts to Web search tools as described in chapter 10, "Finding Your Way Around the Web." For example, I used the search tool called WebCrawler, at **www.webcrawler.com**, to search for employment opportunities. Figure 8.1 shows the results of this search. The search resulted in producing links to more than 1,600 job listings on the Web.

Fig. 8.1
**www.webcrawler
.com**—The Web-
Crawler search will
return a list of links
that you can use to
research topics that
interest you.

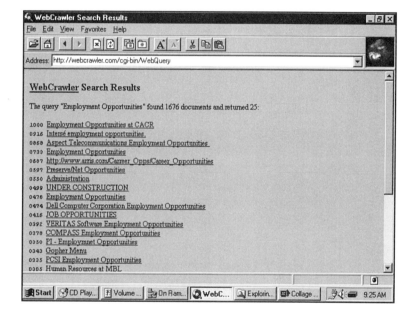

As a busy professional, you need access to the latest news and business information. Internet Explorer can link you to *USA Today* (**www.usatoday.com**) as shown in figure 8.2, instantly. No more searching for a newsstand. Note that if you want the full online edition of *USA Today*, you'll have to subscribe to it.

TIP **Subscription services provide valuable information such as news,** stock reports, and encyclopedias for a fee. Most of the services available on the Web, such as *USA Today*, allow you to preview their product. Then, you'll have access to the full service after you've subscribed. The cost of these services ranges anywhere from a few dollars a month to more than thirty dollars a month.

Fig. 8.2
www.usatoday.com—
USA Today will provide you access to the latest news and information—online.

Help! I need product support and information

You've bravely decided to install a new hard drive in your computer to give Windows 95 more space. It's not hard—really. You've found, however, that you need more information about the drive before you can finish installing it. And, trying to get through to the manufacturer can take a long time—not to mention, it's your dime.

Many companies are providing technical support on the Web now. So, it's very likely that you'll find the information you need online. For example, figure 8.3 shows the Compaq Web Server Search, at **www.compaq.com/cgi-bin/ice/cpq-formg.pl**, where you can find more information about Compaq hardware.

Fig. 8.3
www.compaq.com/ cgi-bin/ice/cpq- formg.pl—Obtain product support online from Compaq.

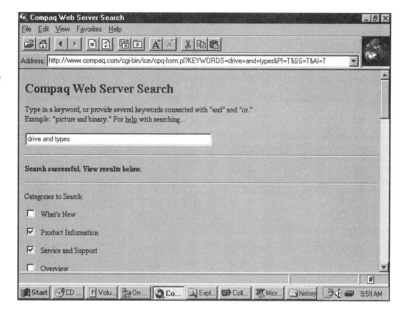

I'm a student and need reference material

"Man, I'll tell ya, this calculus course is really killing me." Does that sound familiar? Well, the Internet has just the formula. You just need a little help, courtesy of the Ohio State Math Department. Figure 8.4 shows how you can check out its home study materials on Calculus and Mathematica at **www-cm.math.uiuc.edu/get/download.html**.

Fig. 8.4
www–cm.math.
uiuc.edu/get/
download.html—You
can use Internet
Explorer to locate
supplemental course
information.

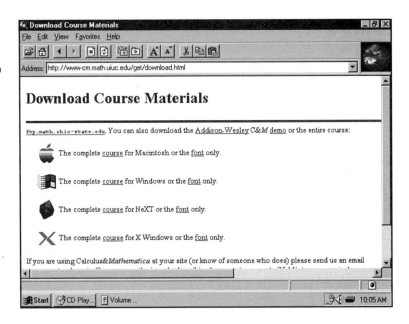

As a student, you can use the Web as a handy way to access traditional
reference material. For example, figure 8.5 shows the *Encyclopedia*
Britannica at **www-pf.eb.com:88/cgi-bin/splash**.

Fig. 8.5
www-pf.eb.com:88/
cgi-bin/splash—The
Encyclopedia
Britannica is truly
information at your
fingertips.

I just wanna have fun

How about creating a personal Web page like the one shown in Figure 8.6, which is at **www.crl.com/~hinkmond**. You can create links to people and places that interest you, and you can have other folks create links to your page. How many visits do you think you can generate in a week? For more information about HTML and creating your own home page, read *Using HTML*, published by Que.

Fig. 8.6
**www.crl.com/
~hinkmond**—With an
HTML editor, you can
create your own home
page.

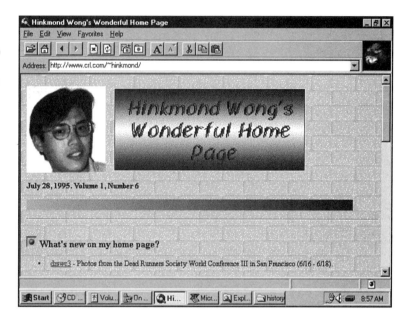

Or, say that you had planned for a trip to Orlando and were interested in playing some golf. You could connect to the Golf Web and search for a course, review player comments, and even hook up with a partner. The Golf Web (**www.golfweb.com/gws/tgws.html**), shown in figure 8.7, allows you to do just that. When you get to Florida, you'll be having the time of your life, out on the links, while your spouse is enjoying Disneyworld with the kids.

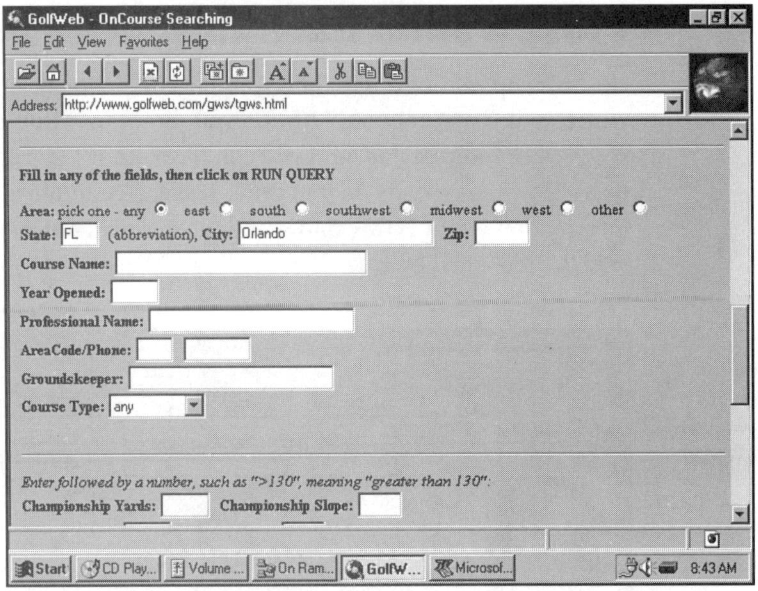

Fig. 8.7
www.golfweb.com/
gws/tgws.html—
Many Web pages have
advanced search and
retrieval engines.

Are you interested in science fiction? If you've ever read *The Hitchhiker's Guide to the Galaxy* by Douglas Adams, you'll enjoy the page shown in figure 8.8, which is at **www.galcit.caltech.edu/~jdavis/hhgttg.html**.

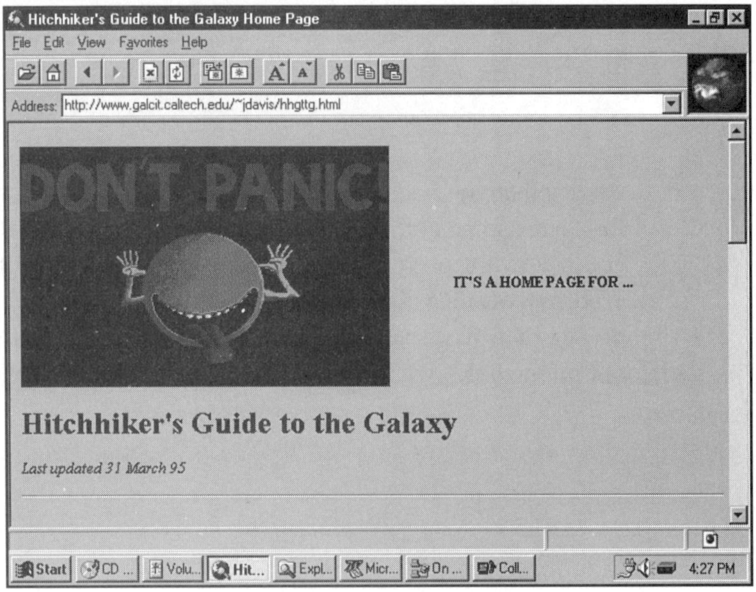

Fig. 8.8
www.galcit.caltech
.edu/~jdavis/
hhgttg.html—
You can use the
Hitchhiker's Guide
home page to explore
Douglas Adams trivia.

First things first—Let's learn some new buzzwords

You learned some new terminology in chapter 7. The Web has terminology that you need to learn, too, so that you can better understand how it works. Here are some useful terms you should know before continuing in this chapter:

- **FTP.** File Transfer Protocol defines how Internet Explorer browses file sites on the Web and how files are downloaded from those sites.

- **Gopher.** Gopher sites provide useful information in a structured or outlined manner. Internet Explorer has the capability to display these sites by using the Gopher protocol.

- **HTTP.** HyperText Transport Protocol defines how Web pages are sent from a server to Internet Explorer.

- **HTML.** HyperText Mark-Up Language is a formatting language that describes how a Web page appears in Internet Explorer. In practical terms, HTML is a collection of styles (indicated by mark-up tags) that define the various components of a Web page. HTML was invented by Tim Berners-Lee. When you look at a page on the Web, you are looking at an HTML (sometimes pronounced *hot metal*) document.

- **Link.** The real power of HTML comes from its capability to link regions of text (and also images) to other documents. The browser highlights these regions to indicate that they are hypertext links, or shortcuts. When you click on a link, Internet Explorer displays the page referred to by that link.

❝ Plain English, please!

In Windows 95, a **shortcut** is an alias for a file somewhere on your computer. When using Internet Explorer, you'll also hear the term *shortcut* referring to a link in a Web page. These two terms are interchangable. In this chapter, however, I tend toward the word *link*. ❞

- **URL.** Uniform Resource Locators specify the location of files on other servers. A URL includes the type of resource being accessed (for example, **http**), the address of the server, and the location of the file.

The syntax for a URL is as follows: **protocol://host.domain[:port]/ path/filename**.

TIP **You don't usually have to include the protocol when you give a** URL to Internet Explorer. If the URL begins with **www**, **gopher**, or **ftp**, Internet Explorer will add the protocol automatically. Thus, instead of typing **http:\\www.microsoft.com**, you can get away with just typing **www.microsoft.com**.

The Explorer window

The Title Bar shows
the name of the
current Web page.

The address bar
displays the URL of the
current Web page.

Fig. 8.9
Microsoft's Internet
Explorer.

The flag
flies while
you load a
page.

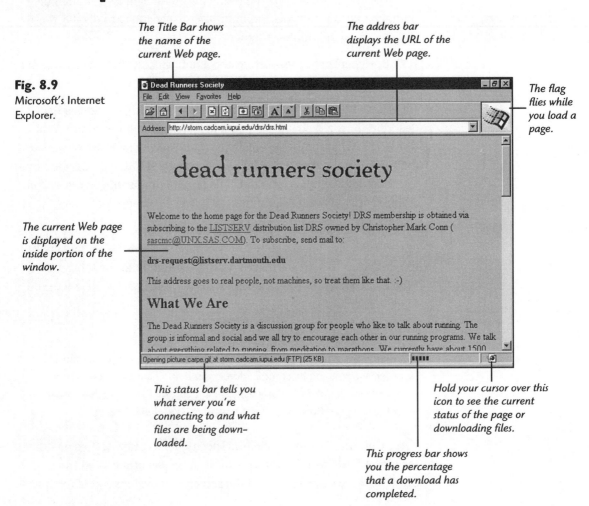

The current Web page
is displayed on the
inside portion of the
window.

This status bar tells you
what server you're
connecting to and what
files are being down-
loaded.

Hold your cursor over this
icon to see the current
status of the page or
downloading files.

This progress bar shows
you the percentage
that a download has
completed.

Table 8.1 Internet Explorer toolbar

Icon	Name	Description
	Open	Type a URL or browse the list of previously opened URLs
	Start Page	Return to the start page
	Back	Display the previous Web page
	Forward	Display the following Web page
	Stop	Stop loading the current Web page
	Refresh	Reload the current Web page from the server
	Add to Favorites	Add the current Web page to the favorites folder
	Open Favorites	Open the favorites folder
	Use Larger Font	Increase the font size one step
	Use Smaller Font	Decrease the font size one step
	Cut	Cut the current selection, within a field, to the clipboard

Table 8.1 Continued

Icon	Name	Description
	Copy	Copy the current selection to the clipboard
	Paste	Paste the contents of the clipboard to the current field

Changing how Internet Explorer displays Web pages

Explorer will allow you to personalize how it displays Web pages. You can control how the links are displayed and how many lines of text will fit in the View Window. If you don't like the default background color, change it. Explorer doesn't care, unless the Web page that you're viewing has a background wallpaper. Here are the items that Explorer lets you change:

- **Font Size.** To change the font size, select View, Fonts from the main menu. You have five sizes to choose from. Select Largest, Large, Medium, Small, or Smallest. Or, you can use the Use Larger Font or Use Smaller Font buttons on the toolbar.

- **Show Pictures.** You can turn off pictures if you want to view only the text of each Web page. This is useful if you're using a very slow dial-up connection to surf the Web. To turn off pictures, select View, Options from the main menu, and Internet Explorer will display the dialog box shown in figure 8.9. Deselect Show Pictures and click on OK to save your changes.

Fig. 8.10

Use the Appearance tab to control how Web pages are displayed by Explorer.

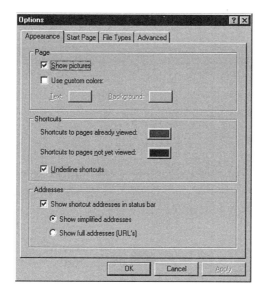

- **Custom Colors.** If you want to use your own colors for the text and background of the Web pages that Internet Explorer displays, select View, Options from the main menu. Then, click on the buttons next to Text and Background to change their color. Click on OK to save your changes.

- **Links.** To change how links are displayed, select View, Options from the main menu and Internet Explorer will display the dialog box shown in figure 8.9. Change the color of your links by clicking on the buttons next to Shortcuts to Pages Already Viewed and Shortcuts to Pages Not Yet Viewed. If you don't want to underline links in a Web page, deselect Underline Shortcuts. Click on OK to save your changes.

- **Addresses.** You don't have to display the URL of each Web page in the status bar. And, if you do, you can control how Internet Explorer displays them. Select View, Options from the main menu. Deselect Show Shortcut Addresses in Status Bar. Then, select either Show Simplified Address or Show Full Addresses. Click on OK to save your changes.

- **Toolbars.** If you're using a 640 × 480 resolution display, you probably don't have a lot of space left to display Web pages in Internet Explorer. To make much more room available for actual Web pages, you can turn off the toolbars. Select <u>V</u>iew from the main menu. If Internet Explorer displays a check mark next to <u>T</u>oolbar, <u>A</u>ddress Bar, or <u>S</u>tatus Bar, these options are turned on. To disable any of these bars, select the appropriate menu option.

TIP   **All of the links Internet Explorer displays won't display in the** color that you select in the Options dialog box. Some Web pages will override your selections with their own colors.

Jumping to a linked Web page

Web pages almost always have links to other Web pages. To jump to a linked Web page, click on the link. The link is highlighted in a different color from the rest of the page and will usually be underlined. Web pages that you have already visited are displayed in yet another color.

The link could also be an image rather than colored text. In either case, the mouse pointer will change to a hand when it is moved over the link, and Internet Explorer will display the name of the link in the status bar. This method of linking Web sites together is the essence of "surfing" the Internet, because it makes jumping from one site to another easy.

Links are not the only way to get to a Web page, though. If you know the URL of the Web page that you want to see, type the URL in the address bar and press Enter. Alternatively, you can click on the Open icon in the toolbar, type the URL, and click on OK to go to that Web page. If you select Open in <u>N</u>ew Window, Internet Explorer will display that Web page in a new Explorer window. You can have more than one copy of Internet Explorer running at the same time.

Make a picture on the page of your Windows 95 background

You have been surfing the Web and you find an interesting picture or image on one of the Web pages that you visited. Internet Explorer makes it really easy to use that image as your Windows 95 wallpaper so that you can see it all the time. Here's how:

1. Load the page with the image in Internet Explorer.

2. Right-click on the image and select Set As Desktop Wallpaper.

3. Minimize Internet Explorer. Then, right-click on your Desktop and select Properties. If you want a single copy of the picture displayed on your desktop, select Center. Or, to have the picture repeated vertically and horizontally until it fills your desktop, select Tile. Then, click on OK to save your changes.

There's a lot more that you can do with wallpaper with Microsoft Plus! installed, too. See chapter 3 for more information.

Copy part of a Web page to other documents

If you are working on a report and want to include some information that you found on a Web page, use the Clipboard to move text and graphics between the page and your document. You can copy the text of the Web page, a picture on the Web page, or the URL of the Web page to the Clipboard. Note that you can't copy both the text and pictures in a Web page at the same time, though.

*   **Copy Text to the Clipboard.** Select the text using the mouse or select Edit, Select All from the main menu. Then, select Edit, Copy or click on the Copy button in the toolbar. This will copy only the text, not the images. Then, paste the text into your document by selecting Edit, Paste from the application's main menu.

*   **Copy an Image to the Clipboard.** Right-click on the image and select Copy Picture. Then, paste the picture into your document by selecting Edit, Paste from the application's main menu.

*   **Copy a URL to the Clipboard.** Right-click on the link and select Copy Shortcut. Then, paste the shortcut into a document by selecting Edit, Paste from the application's main menu.

Saving a Web page to a file

A quick way to save the information in a Web page that you like is to save it to a file. Web pages that you save can be displayed in Internet Explorer without connecting to the Internet. You can also read the page using your favorite text editor such as Notepad. When Internet Explorer is displaying a Web page that you want to save, select File, Save As from the main menu and select a filename. Explorer saves only the text on a page, not the graphics.

 TIP **Use the Save as Type list to save your page as an HTML document** or as Plain Text. If you save the Web page as HTML, you can reload it in Internet Explorer and it will display the same formatting, without the pictures. If you save the Web page as Plain Text, you can easily read it in your favorite editor, but you won't be able to redisplay the page in Internet Explorer.

Printing a Web page

Say that you have stumbled upon just the information for which you've been looking. But it is a massive Web page and you don't have time to look at it online. From the main menu select File, Print. Internet Explorer will print your file—graphics and all.

View the page's HTML source

Are you beginning to wonder how to create your own Web pages? An HTML document is a plain text file that has instructions Internet Explorer uses to format the Web page in the window. If you save an HTML document on your drive, you can use Notepad or any other text editor to see the HTML commands on the page. Figure 8.10 shows how the Compaq Computer Corporation Annual Report looks as an HTML source file. You can also download HTML editors that you can use to view, edit, and create your own HTML documents.

Fig. 8.11
You can use WordPad
to view HTML source
files, too.

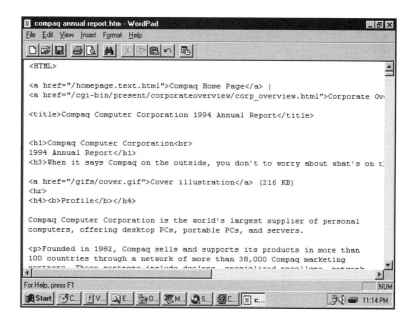

I want to change the start page

When you first install Internet Explorer, it is configured to use MSN Welcome to the Internet as the start page (see chapter 10 to learn about this Web site). This is the first Web page that Internet Explorer loads when you run it each time. You can change the start page to anything you want, though. For example, you may want to start with your own personal home page.

To change the start page, load that Web page in Internet Explorer. Then, select View, Options from the main menu. Click on the Start Page tab and click on Use Current. To reset the Start Page back to the default, click on Use Default.

TIP   **You can easily make your own start page. You can go all the way** and use a Web page authoring tool. Or, you can use your favorite Web page as a starting point and change it to suit your needs in a text editor.

Internet Explorer keeps a history of where you've been

Every time you visit a page on the Web, Internet Explorer puts a shortcut to that Web page in your history folder. The most recent URLs are in the file menu. To go directly to one of those pages, select <u>F</u>ile from the main menu. Then, select one of the entries at the bottom of the menu.

In the history folder, you can see a complete list of all the Web pages that you've visited. To open the history folder, select <u>F</u>ile, <u>M</u>ore History from the main menu. Then, double-click on one of the shortcuts in this folder to go directly to that Web page.

 TIP **You tell Internet Explorer how many Web pages it should keep in** the history folder. Select <u>V</u>iew, <u>O</u>ptions from the main menu. Then, click on the Advanced tab and change the setting under <u>H</u>istory. The default value is 300 and can be as large as 3000.

Jump right to your favorite Web pages

When you stumble onto a Web page that you want to use again, add it to your favorites folder. The favorites folder is a special folder that contains short-cuts to Web pages. The favorites folder makes it easy to keep track of and log into your favorite Web sites.

 TIP **You can save a shortcut to a Web page on your desktop or the** Start menu for quick and easy access. Right-click on a Web page, but not on a link, and select Create Shor<u>t</u>cut. Internet Explorer puts a shortcut to the current page on your desktop. Also, you can drag a link to either your desktop or the Start menu to save a shortcut to that URL in either place.

Internet Explorer adds shortcuts that it finds in your favorites folder to the <u>F</u>avorites menu. You can use the menu to quickly jump to Web pages that you add to the favorites folder. Figure 8.11 shows the <u>F</u>avorites menu.

Fig. 8.12
The Favorites menu lets
you quickly jump to
the coolest web sites.

Adding a shortcut to the favorites folder is easy. First, go to the Web page that you want to add if you're not already there. Then, click on the Add to Favorites button on the toolbar or select Favorites, Add To Favorites from the main menu.

In either case, you will be presented with the Add to Favorites dialog box. You can save the Web page to the current folder or create a new folder for the shortcut. When you're satisfied with your destination, click on the Add button to save the Web page to the selected folder.

TIP **When you've been surfing the Web for a while, your history folder** will be full of shortcuts to the sites that you visited. You can drag the best of these shortcuts into your favorites folder and delete the rest. Open your history folder by selecting File, More History from the main menu. Also, open your favorites folder by selecting Favorites, Open Favorites from the main menu. Then, copy shortcuts from the history folder to the favorites folder.

It's so slow. Can I make it work faster?

If you've got a slower Internet connection, you're probably a bit frustrated with how long it takes to load some Web pages. For example, Web pages with a lot of pictures take a very long time to load on a 2400K modem. Internet Explorer gives you a number of options that can make Web pages load faster. Of course, there is no substitute for a faster modem or an ISDN connection to load Web pages with a lot of pictures much faster.

In this section, you'll learn about three different options to load Web pages faster. You'll learn about using the cache to load Web pages from your hard drive rather than from the server. You'll also learn how to stop a page before it's finished loading, and how to avoid loading pictures altogether.

Use your cache

Internet Explorer keeps a cache on your hard drive of all the pages that you've visited—up to a limit that you specify. You can tell Internet Explorer to load a Web page from the cache rather than from the server, too. This is much faster. To fully use the cache to make Web pages load faster, you need to make it bigger and make sure that Internet Explorer always uses the cache for Web pages that are available there.

 Plain English, please!

> A **cache** (pronounced *cash*) is a place where programs store information that you've recently used or information you may need to use for quicker access. Internet Explorer uses your drive as a cache for Web pages because it's much faster than loading them from the Internet.

- The size of this cache is limited only by the space available on your drive. To configure the size of the cache, select View, Options from the main menu and click on the Advanced Tab. Figure 8.12 shows the options on the Advanced Tab. In the Cache area, move the slider to the right to use more space, and move it to the left to use less space. I don't recommend using more than 20 percent of your drive for the cache, however, as you'll be using valuable drive space for Web pages that you'll probably never visit again.

Fig. 8.13
Click on E<u>m</u>pty to
delete all the Web
pages in your cache.

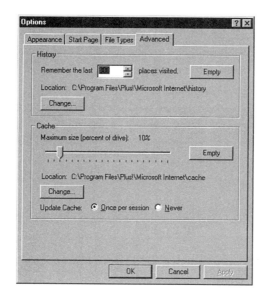

- Click <u>N</u>ever to prevent Internet Explorer from updating pages in the cache. You may want to use this option because many pages will not change very often. If you use <u>N</u>ever, Internet Explorer will always retrieve your page from the cache, if possible. You can force Explorer to update the page only by clicking on the Refresh button found on the toolbar or pressing F5. The default selection here is <u>O</u>nce Per Session. With <u>O</u>nce Per Session, Explorer will always load your page from the server the first time you load that page during the current session.

Stop a page before it's finished loading

You don't have to wait for a page to load completely. That's good, too, because you can read *War and Peace* during the time it takes to load some pages. Rather than brush up on your Russian History, however, you can use the Stop button on the toolbar to tell Internet Explorer that you've seen enough. After you click this button, Internet Explorer displays as much of the page as it had loaded. It represents any pictures that it didn't load with placeholders. Then, it waits for your next command.

TIP **If you want to reload a page that you had previously** stopped, use the Refresh button on the toolbar to instruct Explorer to load the page again.

If you're really desperate, don't display pictures

You might only have a 2400K connection to your Internet provider, but desperately need to connect to the Web. Don't despair! Tell Internet Explorer not to load any pictures—at all. This will make Web pages load significantly faster. Select <u>V</u>iew, <u>O</u>ptions from the main menu and click on the Appearance tab. Make sure that the <u>S</u>how Pictures option is deselected, and click on OK to save your changes. When you use this option, the pictures will be represented by placeholders, just like when you use the Stop button.

Sounds, Graphics, and Video on the Web

● **In this chapter:**

● I want to see multimedia now!

● What types of graphics will I find on the Web?

● Grab some popcorn and watch a movie!

● What is VRML?

● Rolling Stones in real-time

Multimedia has made it to the Web. You can watch video clips, listen to sounds, and view art and graphics from all over the world . . . . ⊳

'm sure you take photographs when you travel on vacation. And you probably remember all the sights and sounds: the music, the language, the landscapes. But you can't take them all back with you—except for those photographs—regardless of the size of your travel budget.

Without a travel budget, the Web lets you experience sights and sounds from all over the world. And, you can keep all of them that you want. This is because multimedia has made it to the Web. You can view videos, listen to sounds, and see pictures from every corner of the world.

In this chapter, you'll learn how to make your computer come alive using the multimedia titles available on the Web. I know that you're itching to see some of those titles—so we'll start there.

What types of multimedia will I find on the Web?

There are a few basic types of multimedia files on the Web. They are graphics, sounds, and videos. Within those basic types, there are different formats, too. For example, video formats include MPEG and AVI. Graphics formats include JPG, GIF, and BMP. I discuss these in more detail later.

 Plain English, please!

MIME (Multipurpose Internet Mail Extensions) is a standard method of representing different types of files on the Internet so that they can be used in a variety of environments. The **MIME type** of a file indicates to Internet Explorer what it should do with the file: play it as a sound, play it as a video, or display it as a picture. MIME types have two parts: type and subtype. For example, the MIME type of an AVI movie is **video/avi**.

Helper Applications are programs that play MIME-encoded files that Internet Explorer doesn't know how to play.

Internet Explorer uses a file's MIME type to determine what to do with it once Explorer has downloaded it. For example, if the MIME type is **video/avi**, Internet Explorer will use a helper application called Media Player to play that file. On the other hand, Internet Explorer can handle most of the MIME types internally. That is, if you click on an **image/gif** file, Internet

Explorer already knows how to display the picture—it doesn't need a helper application.

Graphics

Pictures belong to the **image** MIME type. There are a large number of picture formats on the Web, but here are the ones supported by Internet Explorer:

- **image/gif**. The Graphics Interchange Format was created for use on CompuServe. It has gained a lot of acceptance on the Internet, however, because it compresses an image as much as possible without affecting the image's quality.

- **image/jpeg**. This is a picture format developed by the Joint Photographic Experts Group. This format is extremely compressed. The more JPEG compresses a file, however, the worse the quality of the image. That's why this is also known as a *lossy* image format.

- **image/x-xbitmap**. This is a bitmap format that Internet Explorer internally knows how to display. Because this format doesn't compress images, you won't see it used as frequently as the other formats.

 TIP **There are other image types that Internet Explorer doesn't** directly support. For example, PNG (Portable Network Graphics) is an emerging graphics format that is not supported by Internet Explorer. Keep a look-out for helper applications that will display these other formats as they become available.

An enormous variety of graphics is available on the Web. The easiest way to find what you're looking for is to use one of the Web search tools available with the keywords **image** or **picture** combined with the keywords describing what you had in mind. Figure 9.1 shows an example of a GIF I found using the keywords **image** and **Rembrandt**.

You'll also find a lot of photo albums on the Web. These are Web pages that have a thumbnail version of pictures listed so that you can see more of them faster and at one time. When you find a picture in which you're interested, you click on it to view the entire picture. Again, the easiest way to find photo albums in which you're interested is to use one of the Web search tools available with the keyword **thumbnail** combined with the keywords describing the type of pictures for which you're looking. Figure 9.2 shows a photo album of mountain scenes that I found using the keywords **thumbnail** and **mountains**.

Fig. 9.1
Judas Returning the Thirty Pieces of Silver, by Rembrandt van Rijn. Try searching with the keywords **fine art** to find other images like this.

Fig. 9.2
Click on any one of the pictures to see it in a larger format.

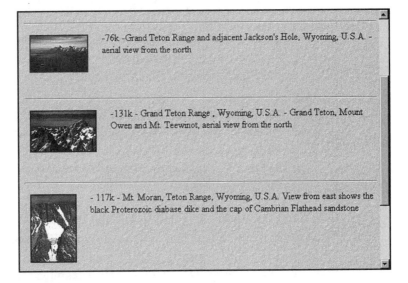

Sounds

You'll find sounds all over the Internet. You'll use them to sample a portion of music tracks, hear popular movie clips, or hear a portion of a speech. Their use is limitless because anyone can put a sound file on the Internet. Though other sound types exist on the Internet, Explorer supports most of the common types. Here are the types that Explorer does support:

- **audio/aiff**. Audio Interchange File Format is not common in Windows. You'll find it frequently on the Web, however.

- **audio/basic**. Likewise, this file format is not common on a Windows computer. It's common on the Internet, though.

- **audio/wav**. Wave Form Audio is the most popular audio format for Windows computers. It has not gained wide popularity on the Internet, however, because it is fairly specific to one platform.

- **audio/x-pn-realaudio**. RealAudio is a real-time format that allows you to hear the audio as it is being transferred to your computer. You can read more about it later in this chapter.

Many sites, such as The Rolling Stones Web site shown in figure 9.3, give you the choice of which audio format to use. If you want to hear the audio immediately, select RealAudio. If you want high-quality sound, however, select one of the other formats.

Fig. 9.3
www.stones.com—
Select one of the titles and you'll be treated to entire tracks of a Rolling Stones live performance.

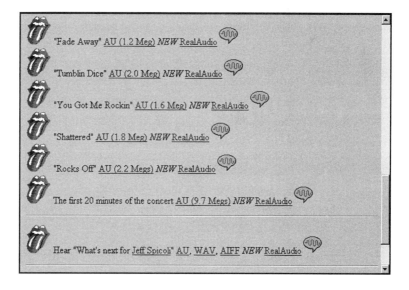

Videos

Videos belong to the **video** MIME type. There are a few popular video formats found on the Web. **video/mpeg**, **video/avi**, and **video/quicktime** are the most common. Internet Explorer supports only the **video/avi** (also known as AVI files in Windows) MIME type by default, however. You'll learn how to install support for **video/mpeg** movies later in this chapter.

AVI stands for Audio Video Interleave. This is the most popular video format for Windows because it is installed with Windows 95. Though not the most popular format on the Internet, if you search the Web for **AVI** and **clip**, you'll find a lot of AVI movies on the Internet. Figure 9.4 shows a still shot of such a video clip.

Fig. 9.4
I found this AVI title of Jay Leno's stand-up routine by searching for **AVI** and **clip.**

A movie of any length requires a large file size. And, if you're trying to view a movie during peak hours, the server may not be able to handle your request very quickly. So, be prepared to take a break while you're downloading the movie onto your hard drive. You can speed up the process by viewing movies during off-peak hours for that server. If you're trying to view a movie title on a server in Australia, you need to consider the time difference when trying to figure out when their peak hours are.

TIP **If you want to keep any of the movies that you've viewed in** Internet Explorer, you'll find them in C:\Program Files\Plus!\Microsoft Internet\cache. This is where Internet Explorer saves files such as movies before it plays them.

 Q&A *All of these videos have to be downloaded before I can watch them. Where can I find video on demand?*

Video on demand is not yet a practical reality on the Internet. There is a lot of effort going into making it possible. For example, go to **www.cardinal.fi/campeius/video.html** or **www.xingtech.com** to get more information about this topic. You'll notice that video on demand requires an Internet connection that is at least 150K/s—more than five times the speed of the modems currently available.

How do I play MPEG movies?

MPEG is the Motion Pictures Expert Group standard for compressing video and audio to make VHS-quality movies feasible on computers. You'll find many more MPEG movies on the Web than QuickTime or AVI.

 TIP **If you want more information about the MPEG standard, search** for **FAQ** and **MPEG** using your favorite Web search tool. Optionally, you can go directly to **www.crs4.it/~luigi/MPEG/mpegfaq.html** to find a compilation of information about the MPEG standard.

When you click on a multimedia file on a Web page, Internet Explorer finds a program on your computer to play it by looking up the file's MIME type and finding a corresponding helper application. Most of the MIME types that you'll find on the Web are supported by Internet Explorer when you install it. .JPG, .WAV, and .AVI are examples.

If you click on a MIME type that Explorer doesn't know how to handle, however, it displays the dialog box shown in figure 9.5. This dialog box gives you the chance to set up a helper application for that particular type of file or save the file on your drive so that you can play it later.

Fig. 9.5
If you already have a program on your computer that can run this type of file, click on Open With to select it.

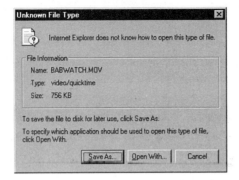

Neither Windows 95 nor Microsoft Plus! comes with an MPEG viewer. So, if you click on one of the many MPEG titles available on the Internet, you'll get that nasty dialog box. I'm going to take care of that right now. Here, you'll find out how to come up with an MPEG viewer and then how to install it so that it works with Explorer.

First, find an MPEG player

MPEG is traditionally implemented with a hardware device for playing videos. A handful of good MPEG players can be found on the Internet,

Why is it so slow?

Multimedia is slow on the Web, and there are many reasons why:

Modem speed. The most important factor is the speed of your modem. Connecting with a 28.8K modem can load files twice as fast as a 14.4K modem. Many multimedia files, such as RealAudio, won't even work correctly with a modem that is slower than 14.4K.

File size. Graphics files are a lot bigger than text files. Some images can be almost one megabyte in size. And videos are even bigger, with some files

well over three megabytes. A three-megabyte file could take an hour or more to download from of the Internet.

Server speed. The fastest modem in the world won't help you a bit if you're always waiting on the server to respond. Two things can affect the speed of a server. First, if the demand for the server is particularly high, the response time will be very low. Second, every server on the Web is not a UNIX SPARC. Many Web servers are on machines that just can't handle the load.

however. Most of them are public domain programs. Here are the two best that I found:

- **VMPEG Lite.** This is the best choice. It installs an MCI driver that allows you to use the Windows 95 Media Player to view MPEG movies. It's also measurably faster than MPeg_Play. You'll find many versions, new and old, on the Internet. Make sure that you get at least version 1.7.

- **MPeg_Play.** This is an alternate MPEG viewer that you'll find on the Internet. It's a bit more difficult to set up, however, than VMPEG Lite, and isn't quite as fast.

Finding either of these MPEG players is easy. Go to your favorite search tool on the Web, such as Lycos or WebCrawler (see chapter 10, "Finding Your Way Around the Web," for more information), and use the keywords **download** and **VMPEG** or **download** and **MPeg_Play**. Alternatively, you can try the site at **gfecnet.gmi.edu/Software/softmult.html**. Click on one of the links in the search results to go to the page with the viewer. Then, click on the appropriate link to download the file.

Internet Explorer will display the dialog box shown in figure 9.6. This dialog box is warning you that you are downloading a file that may contain a virus. Click Save <u>A</u>s and save the file into it's own directory. After Internet Explorer has completely downloaded the file, unzip the file if you downloaded a .ZIP file or run the self-extracting archive if you downloaded a .EXE file and check its contents for viruses with your favorite virus scanner.

Fig. 9.6
Internet Explorer is giving you this warning because of the potential dangers of catching a virus from software that is downloaded from the Internet.

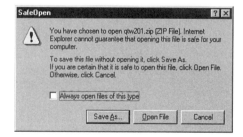

Then, install it in Explorer

Because VMPEG Lite is your best choice, I cover its installation in this section. To install VMPEG Lite, see the README.TXT file included with VMPEG, or use the following steps:

1 Run the VMPEG setup program by double-clicking on SETUP.EXE in the directory where you unzipped VMPEG.

2 Click on Continue.

3 Select Install WinG Runtime Libraries to slightly improve the performance of the MPEG viewer. Then, click on Continue.

4 Type the path to which you want to install the VMPEG program files, and click on Continue.

The VMPEG setup program installs a new MIME type on your computer: **video/mpeg**. This is connected to the Windows 95 Media Player, which knows how to run MPEG files now because VMPEG also installed an MCI driver for MPEG files. Now, when you click on a MPEG file on the Web, Internet Explorer will download the file and play it with Media Player.

 Q&A ***When I click on MPEG movie, it downloads OK. But Media Player loads, and then displays an error message that says it couldn't find the file.***

The version of VMPEG that you downloaded doesn't know what to do with file paths that have spaces embedded in them. Select View, Options from Internet Explorer's main menu. Click on the Advanced tab and click on Change at the bottom of the property sheet. Select a path for your cache that doesn't have any spaces in it.

What is VRML?

There is a lot of exciting technology emerging on the Web. And VRML (Virtual Reality Modeling Language) is at the top of my list. You've probably not given the two-dimensional aspect of the Web much thought. But it's similar to a piece of paper, the one with all the doodling, sitting on your desk. Flat.

HTML is a standard for representing two-dimensional documents on the Web, Likewise, VRML is an emerging standard for modeling three-dimensional objects on the Web.

Installing a VRML viewer

Before you can view a VRML file, though, you need a viewer. InterVista Software's WorldView is a good viewer to get you started. You'll find a copy at **www.webmaster.com/vrml/wvwin32**. Click on Download WorldView and save it to its own directory. Then, use the following steps to install WorldView on your computer:

1 Run the self-extracting archive and install WorldView on your computer as instructed.

2 In Internet Explorer, select <u>V</u>iew, <u>O</u>ptions from the main menu and click on the File Types tab. Internet Explorer displays the dialog box shown in figure 9.7.

Fig. 9.7
This list represents all the file types and their corresponding programs set up on your computer.

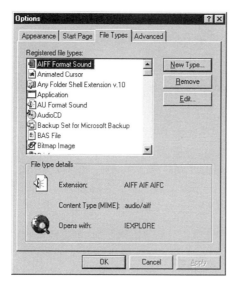

3 Click on <u>N</u>ew Type and Internet Explorer displays the dialog box shown in figure 9.8. Fill in the dialog box as shown in the figure.

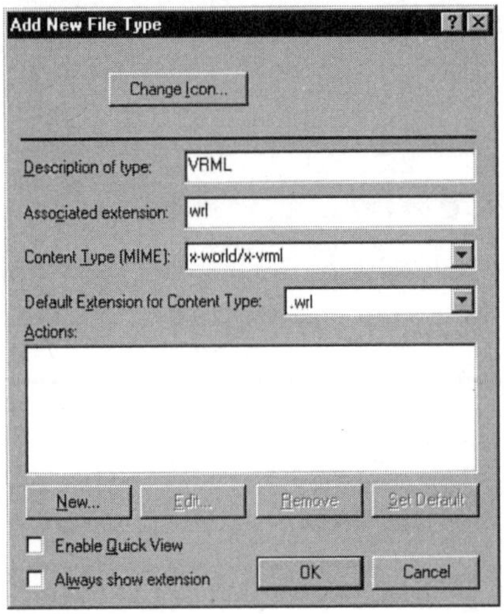

Fig. 9.8
Internet Explorer uses
the information you
provide in this dialog
to match the MIME
type of a file to the
program that is used to
play it.

4 Click on <u>N</u>ew to tell Internet Explorer what program you want it to use
   to play the file. It displays the dialog box shown in figure 9.9.

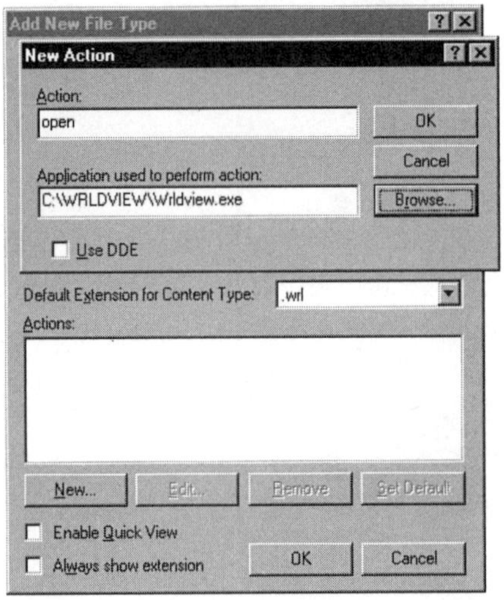

Fig. 9.9
The **open** action for
each file type specifies
which program is used
to open a file.

5 Type **open** in the <u>A</u>ction field. Then, click on B<u>r</u>owse and select the
   path and filename to WRLDVIEW.EXE.

6 Click on OK to save the action. Click on OK to save your new file type.
   Then, click on OK to close the file types dialog box.

Playing a VRML file with WorldView

To play a VRML file on the Web, click on the link. For example, you'll find a lot of good VRML samples at **www.virtpark.com/theme/cgi-bin/serchrnd.html.** Click on one of the links on this page to play a VRML file in WorldView. When you click on a VRML file for the first time, you'll see the dialog box shown in figure 9.10.

Fig. 9.10
This dialog box is Internet Explorer's way of telling you to practice "safe computing."

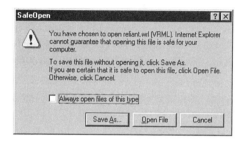

Because it's not likely that you'll catch a virus from playing a VRML, select Always Open Files of This Type and click on Open File. Figure 9.11 shows a VRML file in WorldView.

Fig. 9.11
View the Reliant from different angles.

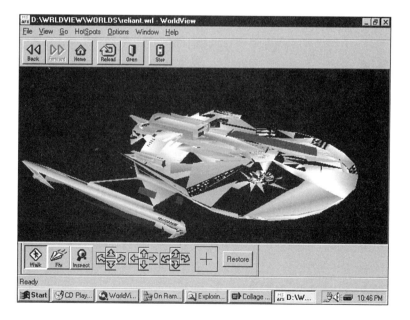

Audio on demand is here—RealAudio

If you're into instant audio gratification, RealAudio is the best way to listen to sounds on the Web. You can listen to music, prerecorded Web radio broadcasts, and other audio files as they are sent to your computer. Contrast this to waiting until the file is completely downloaded before playing it. For example, I tried downloading a 1M sound file from the Web and gave up after waiting an hour. When I clicked on a RealAudio file, however, which was about the same size, it started playing within a few seconds.

Such power doesn't come free. The sound quality of RealAudio is comparable to AM radio. It's a bit fuzzy and you'll hear gaps in the audio. This is budding technology that will improve with time. So, if you're looking for digital music-quality sound, you're better off downloading a .WAV file and playing it on your computer.

On the other hand, RealAudio isn't intended to provide digital audio. Rather, it's intended to allow you to sample sounds or listen to information instead of reading it on a Web page. In fact, some Web sites rely heavily on RealAudio to get their message across. You'll also find a lot of weekly Web radio shows popping up all over the Web.

How do I play RealAudio titles?

Windows 95 comes with the required RealAudio software. You don't have to install a thing. Click on a RealAudio link and the player pops up, as shown in figure 9.12, and starts playing the file. It's easy to spot a RealAudio link on a page because most of them are marked with the RealAudio icon.

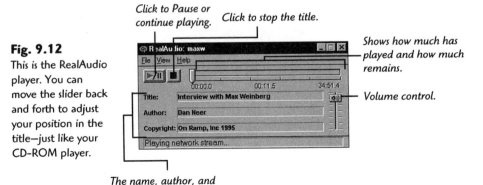

Click to Pause or continue playing.   *Click to stop the title.*

Shows how much has played and how much remains.

Volume control.

Fig. 9.12
This is the RealAudio player. You can move the slider back and forth to adjust your position in the title—just like your CD-ROM player.

The name, author, and copyright for this file.

TIP **After you've started playing a RealAudio file, you can move on to** other Web pages to continue exploring while you listen to the file. In fact, you can close Internet Explorer and the RealAudio file will continue to play.

Point me to some titles that I can listen to now

To satisfy that need for instant audio gratification, here's some more fun sites with RealAudio titles or indexes to other sites that use RealAudio:

- **www.realaudio.com.** This is the home of RealAudio—The Progressive Networks home page. You'll find news and information about RealAudio at this site. In addition, this site contains links to some of the hottest RealAudio pages on the Web.

- **www.realaudio.com/contentp/abc.html.** I've already pointed you to the RealAudio home page, but this page is so good that I didn't want it to get lost. You'll find news updates posted on this page every few hours. Why read the news when you can hear it on the Internet?

- **www.stones.com.** If you're a Rolling Stones fan, you definitely want to visit this site. You can hear entire tracks of albums and live shows. There are also samples of newer cuts.

- **www.rock.net.** This site lives up to its name. You'll find an index of new and old groups to learn about. You can preview their music and look at photographs of the bands.

- **www.radio.cbc.ca.** The CBC Radio site has a large number of Web radio broadcasts for you to hear. It also contains links to many other radio programs that you'll find on the Web.

- **www.mindspring.com/MindSpring/RealAudio.** This page on MindSpring contains an extensive catalog of Web sites that use RealAudio.

Q&A ***When I play a RealAudio title, the sound is very "chunky" and there are a lot of gaps in the audio.***

Are you using a 14.4K or faster modem? If not, you'll need to upgrade your modem to play RealAudio files well. If you have a fast modem and are still hearing gaps in the audio, it may be the result of an overworked server. When a server is overburdened with connections, it can't always send enough audio over the Internet to play a file smoothly.

10

Finding Your Way Around the Web

● **In this chapter:**

- What is a home page?

- The Web is a big place—where do you start?

- You'll find a lot of great places to jump off

- The Web has card catalogs just like the library

The World Wide Web is a big place. But it's not hard to find
interesting and useful information . . . . ❯

Have you ever visited another city—without a map? I have. And I got lost. I found, however, many great restaurants, art galleries, book stores, and clothing stores in the process. Looking back on the whole experience, I prefer to think of it as exploring the city—not getting lost.

The experience of "surfing" the Web is very similar except that, instead of exploring a city, you'll explore a vast universe of information and ideas. You'll find art galleries and book stores on the Web, too. You'll also find free programs, product information, reference material, and even multimedia. But you'll find them all from the comfort of your own home.

Chapter 11, "Really Cool Web Sites," shows some of the best pages on the Web. All of them were found using the tools described in this chapter. You'll quickly discover pages that satisfy your own interest.

Microsoft's home page is a great start

Microsoft anticipated that a lot of people would be getting on the Web for the first time after installing Internet Explorer. So, they made it a bit easier for all the new folks by creating a simple home page on the Internet called Microsoft Welcomes You to the Internet (its URL is **www.home.msn.com**). The first time you start Internet Explorer, it automatically loads this home page, as shown in figure 10.1. If you've already found a page that you'd rather start with, see chapter 8, "Browsing the World Wide Web with Internet Explorer," for more information about how to change your startup page.

 Plain English, please!

A **URL** (uniform resource locator) is a standard way to specify the address of a document on the Web. Incidentally, to show you as much of each Web page as possible, a lot of the screens in this book don't show the address bar. You'll find each page's URL in the figure's caption.

A **home page** is the starting page for a World Wide Web site. Most home pages contain information about the site and links to other Web sites.

Fig. 10.1

www.home.msn.com/
—Watch for announcements from Microsoft at the bottom of this page.

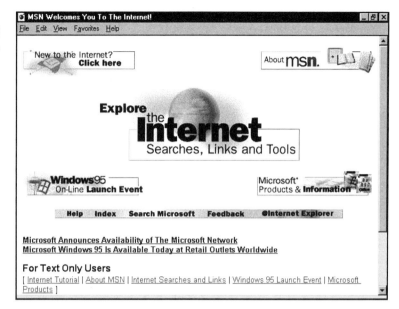

TIP **Many pictures on a Web page have links hidden in them. If you're** not sure, move the mouse pointer over a picture. The pointer changes to a hand if it is over a link.

MSN Welcomes You to the Internet has five major links:

- **New to the Internet? Click Here.** This link loads a tutorial for new Internet users. Here, you'll find good information about using Internet Explorer to surf the Web.

- **About MSN.** Check out The Microsoft Network (MSN). This page tells you about MSN and lets you preview what is happening on MSN today. You'll also find information about the companies providing information and services on MSN.

- **Explore the Internet.** This page, shown in figure 10.2, is a good place to jump into the Internet. Here, you'll find search tools, reference material, and links to many useful Internet Web sites. Click on Internet Searches for access to the Infoseek, Lycos, and Yahoo search tools—all on one page.

Fig. 10.2

You'll find a useful toolbar at the bottom of each Microsoft Web page.

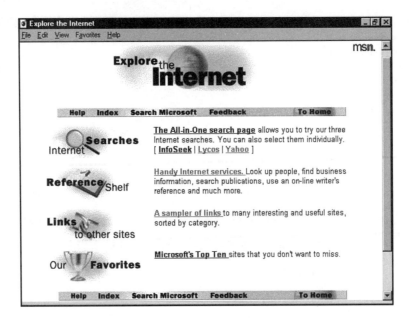

- **Windows 95 On-Line Launch Event.** Do you want to keep up with the latest buzz about Windows 95? Then, click on this link. There are news, free software, technical information, and more available on this page.

- **Microsoft Products & Information.** This link loads the Microsoft On the Web page at **www.microsoft.com**. You'll find anything you want to know about Microsoft and its products on this page. For example, this page has links to technical information for programmers, employment information, and online product support.

The latest and greatest on Net Happenings

Net Happenings got its beginnings as a mailing list. See chapter 12, "Using Exchange to Send and Receive Internet Mail," for more information about subscribing to the Net Happenings mailing list. Any time that something new and exciting happens on the Internet, a message is posted to this mailing list. If you are a subscriber, you'll receive all of the updates. For example, when a new Web page is put on the Web, the creator might send a message to this list that would cause all of the list's subscribers to get the update.

Plain English, please!

When you subscribe to a **mailing list**, you'll receive e-mail from the list owner or other subscribers. The content of the list can vary greatly, but frequently it is newsletters. Chapter 12 describes the different kinds of mailing lists that you'll find on the Internet.

Because of the high demand on the mailing list and the possible aggravation of getting 20 or more e-mails a day, the list owner created the Net Happenings Web page at **www.mid.net/NET**. This page lets you search all of the postings to the mailing list for topics that interest you. You can view postings for a particular day or search all the postings for a particular topic. Figure 10.3 shows the Net Happenings home page.

Fig. 10.3
www.mid.net/NET/
—Are you tired of getting bombarded with e-mail from net-happenings? Try the Net Happenings Web page instead.

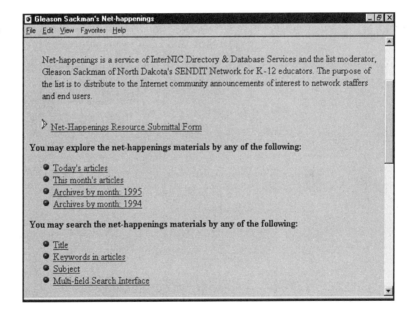

If you want to browse all the postings to Net Happenings, there are four different ways to do it. Here's what they are:

- **Today's Articles** lets you see all of the postings that were added today. You can check in here at the end of each day to see what new and exciting things happened on the Internet.

- **This Month's Articles** allows you to browse articles for the current month. You will need to select a specific day of the month, though. This is useful if you're trying to follow the Internet and missed a few days.

- **Archives by Month: 1995** allows you to browse articles for 1995 by selecting a month and day. Again, this is not very useful unless you have a reason for looking at a particular day of the year.

- **Archives by Month: 1994** lets you browse postings from July through December of 1994 by selecting a month and day. Again, this is not very useful unless you have a reason for looking at a particular day of the year.

Browsing the articles in the archives is useful because you can see what kinds of things are happening on the Internet. This is a great way to keep up-to-date. It's not necessarily the most effective way to search for specific topics, however. For example, you probably won't be able to find any Web pages on cooking if you start looking through all the archives, day by day.

 Plain English, please!

> A **hit** is a single page that was found that matched your criteria. A **FAQ** is a text document or Web page that answers **F**requently **A**sked **Q**uestions about a particular subject. For example, a Web Search FAQ would antici-pate and answer most of your questions about searching on the Web.

You'll have much better luck if you search the archive using the search tools provided. Net Happenings provides many different ways to search for the information you want. Here they are:

- **Title.** Searches for keywords in article titles.

- **Keywords in Articles.** Searches for keywords in article text. This will produce more hits than searching in the title or subject.

- **Subject.** Searches on a subject by selecting a predefined category in a pull-down menu. The categories organize the articles into groups of Web pages, FAQs, Gopher sites, online publications, and so on. If you select FAQ from the list, you'll receive a listing of all the recent FAQ sheets.

- **Multi-field Search Interface.** You can do a combination search on Title, Keywords in Articles, and Subject. This is an advanced search feature that allows you to search for particular keywords within a related group of postings. For example, you can limit your search of cooking to Web sites.

The most effective way to search for a particular topic is the Keywords in Articles search. Here's how:

1 Click on **Keywords in Articles** on the Net Happenings home page. Internet Explorer displays the page shown in figure 10.4.

Fig. 10.4
www.mid.net/NET/
NET_ke_frm.html—
Click on **List of**
Words Indexed to
see an indexed list of
all the words in all the
postings on Net
Happenings.

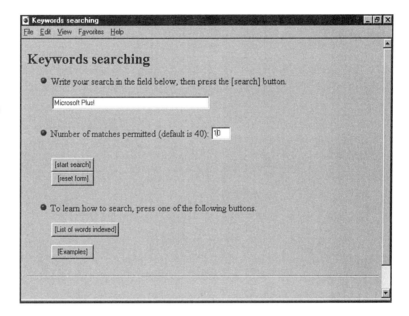

2 Type your keywords in the space provided. Avoid common words such as *the*. You can use as many keywords as you need.

3 Click on Start Search. Internet Explorer will display the search results shown in figure 10.5.

Fig. 10.5
Click on any of the links found to go to that page.

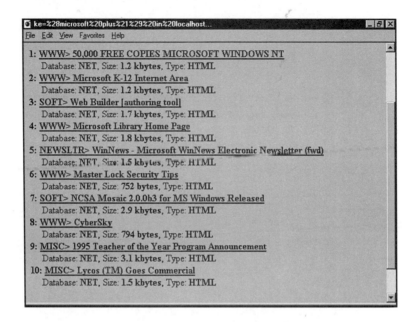

Just touring? GNN has a great collection of links

Sometimes a search just doesn't do the trick. Maybe you don't know what you're searching for. Or, you just want to see what kind of interesting things are out there on the Web. GNN (Global Network Navigator) contains a comprehensive list of Web pages that you can browse.

The GNN home page (**www.gnn.com**), shown in figure 10.6, contains a handful of categories such as Personal Finance and Travel. Click on one of the icons and Internet Explorer will load a page full of related links to other pages and articles. And, while you're at it, go ahead and click on **become a subscriber**. You'll get regular updates from GNN. You'll also be able to purchase products from GNN online.

The GNN home page is a good overview of what's available. But The Whole Internet Catalog is a comprehensive list of pages divided into categories. Click on The Whole Internet Catalog link and Internet Explorer shows the page in figure 10.7. Notice that the larger headings are major categories. Under each major category, you'll find a list of smaller categories. Click on any of the categories to see a list of the links available.

Fig. 10.6
www.gnn.com—Click on the icons under Navigating the Net, Marketplace, and Special GNN Publications to jump to pages with even more links.

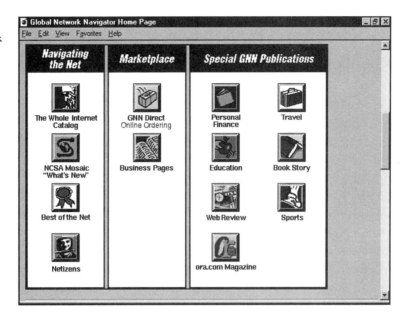

Fig. 10.7
gnn.com/gnn/wic/index.html—The Whole Internet Catalog is one of the most comprehensive collections of Web pages available.

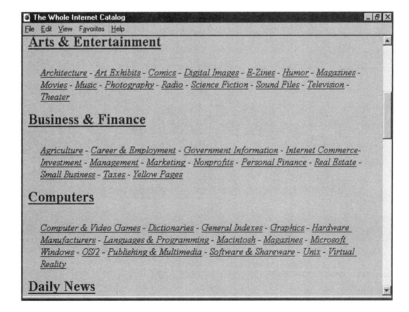

WebCrawler is a card catalog for the Web

If you went to a library that didn't have a card catalog, you'd be lost. How would you find that special book? It would take forever to look at each book on each shelf until you found it. Likewise, finding information on the Web is easier if you use a card catalog such as WebCrawler, as opposed to looking at each page on each Web site.

Pick a topic, any topic

You'll find information on just about any topic that comes to mind using WebCrawler. These examples should give you some idea of how to come up with the keywords for your search.

- **The local weather.** There are plenty of sites offering weather forecasts. The best keywords to use are **weather** and **map**.

- **Your favorite movie.** Information about your favorite movie is easy to find on the Web. You'll find that almost all of the current movie releases have Web pages. The best keywords to use to find a particular movie are the major words in the movie's title and the word **movie**. If you want to find all the sites having movie clips that you can download, try the keywords **movie** and **clip**.

- **Hubble Space Telescope.** The best keywords to find information about the telescope are **NASA** and **Hubble.** You'll find links to sites containing a variety of information about Hubble, and plenty of space pictures, too.

- **Recipes.** You'll find all sorts of cooking recipes on the Web. Many companies post recipes for using their products in new and unique ways. The best keywords are **cooking** and **recipes**.

Surfing the net...from B-2 bombers to Pearl Jam

One of my hobbies is airplanes. So, I did a search on B-2 bombers, and on one of the pages I found a link to the Boeing Corporation. Off I went. While on the Boeing page, I noticed a link to Seattle, which is one of my favorite cities. With just one click of the mouse I was on a "welcome to Seattle" page. Then, I noticed that there was a link for local bands. Click. I ended up at a home page for Pearl Jam, which happens to be my nephew's favorite band. With a click of the mouse, I e-mailed him the lyrics of his favorite Pearl Jam song.

How does WebCrawler work?

WebCrawler differs from other search engines because it proactively searches the Web looking for more pages to index—this type of search tool is sometimes called a **search-bot**. We'll use the Microsoft home page as an example. Once the WebCrawler has a link to this page, it indexes its contents and stores it in the database.

 Plain English, please!

A Web **search engine** or **search tool** is a page that searches the Web for pages that contain the keywords you specify. Some search engines rely on the contributions of its users to find interesting pages, whereas others scour the Web looking for interesting pages on their own.

Then, WebCrawler takes note of the Microsoft home page's links. It loads each of these pages to index their content and search their links. This whole process is repeated over and over—as long as WebCrawler continues to find new Web pages.

 Q&A *How does the WebCrawler avoid bogging down the Web?*

The authors of the WebCrawler are very considerate. They don't search the entire depth of a Web site every time they log on. They also have made sure to scan a site periodically instead of all at once. That way, they aren't putting a huge load on the server they are searching.

You'd be right to suggest that every Web page in the world can't possibly be linked together. This is why some Web pages just don't make it into the WebCrawler database. To solve this problem, the folks at WebCrawler allow individuals to submit URLs to the database for indexing. Then, the process starts again with that page.

If you happen to find a great Web page that isn't listed in WebCrawler, submit it yourself. Click on Submit URLs at the bottom of the WebCrawler page and fill in the form.

Crawling around the Web is easy

WebCrawler is very easy to use. First, make sure that the WebCrawler
Web page is loaded in Internet Explorer. The URL for this page is
webcrawler.com, as shown in figure 10.8.

Fig. 10.8
webcrawler.com—
Click on **Top 25 Sites**
to see the 25 most
frequently referenced
Web sites on the World
Wide Web.

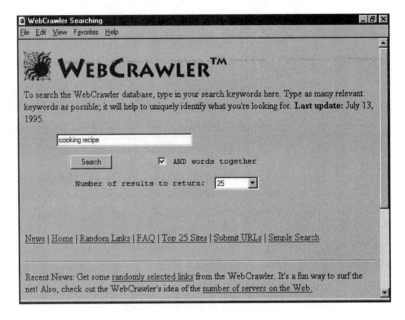

Use the following steps to find the information that you're trying to find:

1 Type your keywords in the space provided. Try to use as many keywords as you can initially. If you don't find any pages, you can remove
the less important keywords and try again.

2 Select AND Words Together if you want WebCrawler to find pages that
have all your keywords, or deselect it if you want WebCrawler to find
pages that match some of your keywords.

3 Select the number of matches that you want WebCrawler to display. You can choose 10, 25, 100, or 500.

4 Click on Search to start your query. When WebCrawler is finished, it will display a page similar to the one shown in figure 10.9.

Fig. 10.9
The numbers to the left of each hit describe how relevant the page is to your query. A page with the number 500 is half as relevant as a page with the number 1000.

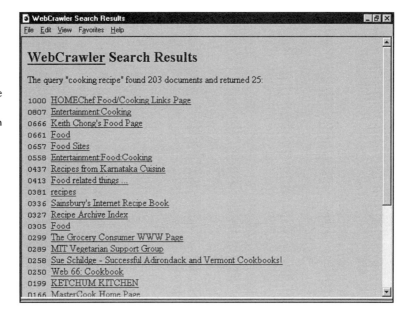

Here are some more search tools for the Web

You've seen WebCrawler. There are many other Web search tools, though. Here's a short list of some of the most popular search tools:

- **Lycos.** The Lycos search tool, found at **www.lycos.com**, searches the Internet for New and changed Web pages. It is a large database that indexes the content of all the Web pages it finds. Figure 10.10 shows the Lycos basic search page.

Fig. 10.10
www.lycos.com—
Click on Search
Options for more
advanced searching.

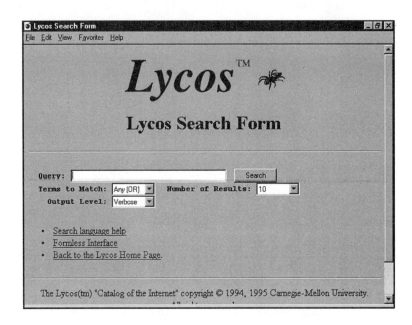

- **World Wide Web Worm.** You'll find this search tool at
  www.cs.colorado.edu/home/mcbryan/WWWW.html. This is another
  comprehensive index of Web sites, which searches in a similar manner
  to WebCrawler. Figure 10.11 shows the Worm. You may find this site to
  be a bit slow, because it is very popular.

Fig. 10.11
**www.cs.colorado.edu/
home/mcbryan/
WWWW.html—**Not
only does the Worm
give you a link to a
matching page, it gives
a link to the page that
cites it, too.

*Select where you
want the Worm
to do its search.*

*Select AND if
you want to
match all your
keywords;
select OR if you
want to match
some of your
keywords.*

*Select how many
matches you want
the Worm to
return.*

*Type your
keywords here.*

*Click here to
start your search.*

- **Yahoo.** Yahoo collects URLs that are contributed by people like you. It is an incredibly comprehensive collection of Web sites that is organized by subject. If you know the type of information you're looking for, but don't exactly know what search words to choose, check Yahoo's variety of categories. The advanced Yahoo search page is at **beta.yahoo.com/ search.htm** and is shown in figure 10.12.

Fig. 10.12
beta.yahoo.com/ search.htm—Yahoo presents its results by category. For example, a search for recipes will result in a list of links under a general cooking category and an ethnic cooking category.

Select AND to match all your keywords; select OR to match some of your keywords.

Type your keywords here.

Click here to start your search.

Select where you want Yahoo to search.

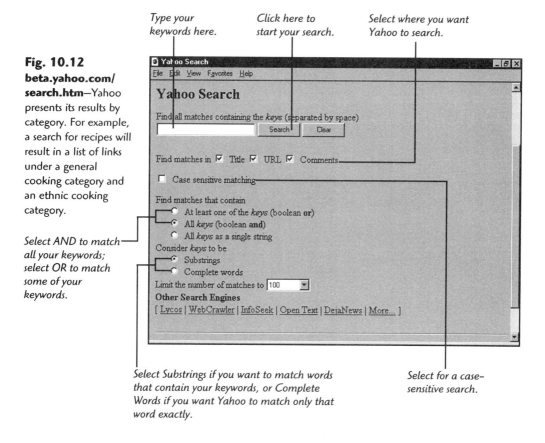

Select Substrings if you want to match words that contain your keywords, or Complete Words if you want Yahoo to match only that word exactly.

Select for a case-sensitive search.

11

Really Cool Web Sites

● In this chapter:

- **Visit the President of the United States**

- **Did my Federal Express package get there?**

- **Where do I find travel information?**

- **I need reference tools**

- **Do companies support their products on the Web?**

- **How about online magazines?**

No matter what your interest, there is something on the Web for you. Point Internet Explorer at some of these pages and have fun . . . . ●▶

Trademark: he World Wide Web is a huge place. There's a lot of information literally at your fingertips. Some of it is serious business. For example, you'll find business travel information, State Department travel advisories, *USA Today*, Dun & Bradstreet, and many more business resources.

Other pages are for fun. You can enjoy online magazines, music, art, games, and more. Also, if you're a student, you'll appreciate being able to look up a word or check out the *Encyclopedia Britannica*.

Is all this stuff really out there? Yes. And this chapter will get you started. I've assembled a large collection of some of the best pages on the Web in this chapter. You'll find a description of each page and its URL. Type the URL (remember, URLs are case sensitive) in Internet Explorer's address bar to go right to each one. And, if you see one you like, add it to your Favorites folder.

Entertainment

Buena Vista MoviePlex Marquee

URL address: **www.disney.com/BVPM/MooVPlex.html**

See previews of Disney movies at this Web site. You can click on a movie title to see a multimedia preview or click on one of the doors to check out the various Disney studios. You'll also find movie trivia at this site.

MovieWEB

URL address: **movieweb.com/movie/movie.html**

You'll find a preview for the season's hottest movies. You'll find the top 25 box office winners for the previous weekend and the top 50 movies for all time. Each movie at this site has its own Web page where you can get pictures, posters, production notes, and trivia about the movie. You can also download videos of the movie trailer.

Fig. 11.1
Click on a movie title to see a multimedia preview. Try the doors, too.

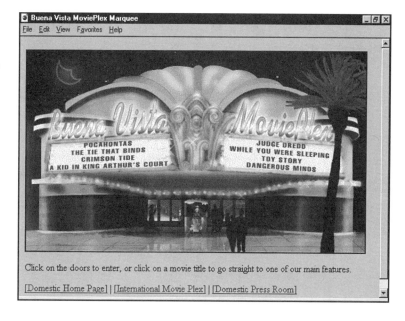

Fig. 11.2
You need a QuickTime player to view the movie clips here. You'll find one at the bottom of the page.

The Internet Movie Database

URL address: **www.msstate.edu/Movies**

The Internet Movie Database allows you to search for movies by title, cast, crew, MPAA rating, genre, country of origin, production company, filming locations, quotes, soundtracks, plot summaries, and year of release. The searches are very flexible.

Fig. 11.3
**www.msstate.edu/
Movies**—Click on the
movie ticket to search
the movie database.

CBS Television Home Page

URL address: **cbs-tv.tiac.net**

At the CBS Web page, you can click on any of the TV screens to find more information about that CBS show or topic. While you're there, check out David Letterman's Top Ten List or order from the CBS catalog. The CBS news page lists descriptions of all the news programming on the network. You can even get up-to-the-minute news. The **Eyewear Gallery** contains pictures and information on the stars of CBS programming. **You're On** lists the schedule for the upcoming evening. You can join the club by clicking on **Eye on Club**—you'll get a discount from the catalog.

Fig. 11.4
The top of the CBS Web page is updated daily with news and information about CBS.

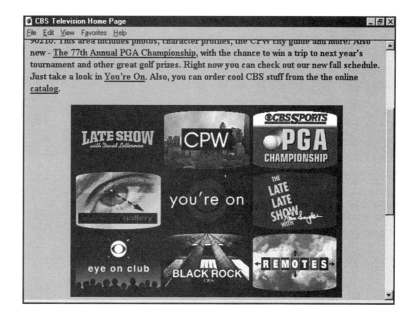

Welcome to MTV.COM

URL address: **mtvoddities.viacom.com**

The MTV home page offers music fans an inside look at some of the network's programming. You can access news and information on the MTV beach house. Check out MTV Animation, which offers multimedia sounds, animation, and pictures.

Paramount Pictures Online Studio

URL address: **www.paramount.com**

Click on one of the movie posters to see video clips and hear audio clips from the movie. This site uses the QuickTime player, though. Click on Media Tools at the bottom of a movie's Web page to get it.

Fig. 11.5
This Web page has a lot of really cool graphics—worth a look.

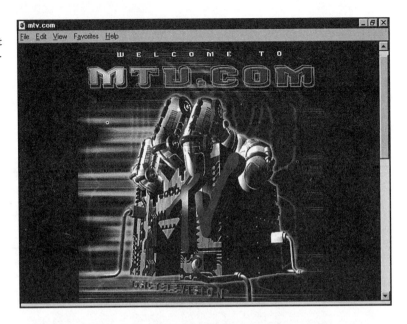

Fig. 11.6
Click on the gate to see what's going on at Paramount.

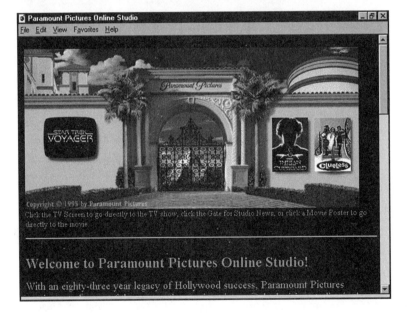

Magazines and newspapers

Web Week Home Page

URL address: **www.mecklerweb.com/mags/ww/wwhome.htm**

Web Week is an exciting weekly newspaper for World Wide Web professionals or people who just want to know what's going on with the Web. You can read the articles or check out the links in the current issue. Other goodies that you'll find include back issues, and information about publishing Web pages for a living.

Fig. 11.7
Click on Search at the bottom of this Web page to search the MecklerWeb site.

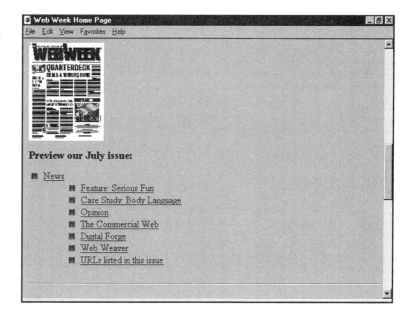

USA Today Online

URL address: **www.usatoday.com**

If you've stayed in many hotels, you probably received a complimentary copy of *USA Today*. Here, you'll find an electronic version. You can easily find stories that interest you, such as news, sports, money, life, and weather. USA Today offers a subscription service that gives you the full content of *USA Today*.

Fig. 11.8
The subscription service requires a special browser, though, which can't be used with Internet Explorer.

Welcome to ZD Net

URL address: **www.ziff.com**

Ziff-Davis publishes some of the best known computer magazines in the world: *PCWeek*, *PC Magazine*, *Windows Sources*, and more. You can view the online version of each of these magazines. Although they don't include the complete content of each magazine, they do contain the highlights. Many of the Ziff-Davis magazines have great FTP sites where you can download software from their magazines.

Welcome to HotWired!

URL address: **www.hotwired.com**

HotWired is a contemporary online community. You can shop, experience multimedia online, exchange information with other HotWired members, and read exciting articles about the Internet. You have to sign up before you can log on. Don't forget your password.

Fig. 11.9
www.ziff.com—
Check out Rumor
Central on the
PCWeek page.

Fig. 11.10
Click on **Join** to
become a HotWired
member.

Welcome to Pathfinder

URL address: **www.pathfinder.com**

Here, you'll find online editions of Time Warner's magazines such as *Time, People, Money, Fortune, Digital Pulse, Sports Illustrated, Life, Entertainment Weekly*, and more. Scroll the page down to see the top headlines for the day, or read the latest news on today's hot topics.

Fig. 11.11
You'll find a large number of Time Warner magazines at the bottom of this Web page.

Reference

Welcome to Britannica Online

URL address: **www.eb.com**

Britannica Online is the online edition of *Encyclopedia Britannica*. This resource contains more than 44 million words and is periodically updated by the encyclopedia's editors. Britannica Online also has links to other related sites and supports multimedia such as graphics, audio, and video. Currently, subscriptions are available only to colleges and universities. Britannica Online anticipates expanding, however.

Fig. 11.12
If you're not a student, you can't do much at this site yet. But it's worth trying out the demo to see what's coming.

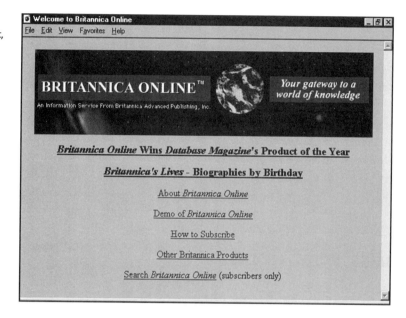

WordNet 1.5 on the Web

URL address: **www.cogsci.princeton.edu/~wn/w3wn.html**

WordNet is a handy online dictionary. Enter a keyword, select the type of search, and click on Search. WordNet will display the information that you requested. You can get definitions, synonyms, antonyms. You can also see how frequently the word is used by the public. This is a must for the frustrated writer.

Fig. 11.13
Put away your
dictionary; WordNet
will look up a word for
you.

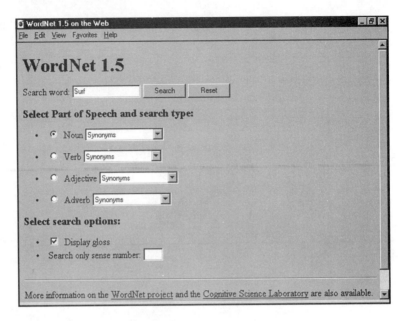

Business resources

FEDEX HOME PAGE

URL address: **www.fedex.com**

You'll never lose a Federal Express package again. Click on **Track A FedEx Package** to find the exact location of your package. And, if it was delivered, you can find out who signed for it.

RSCNet

URL address: **www.rscnet.com**

Get your business on the Web. The resources on this page will help you to effectively advertise your products and services on the World Wide Web. These folks will create a Web marketing plan just for your company.

Fig. 11.14
Click on
**Downloadable
FedEx Software** to
get your own copy of
the company's shipping
and tracking software.

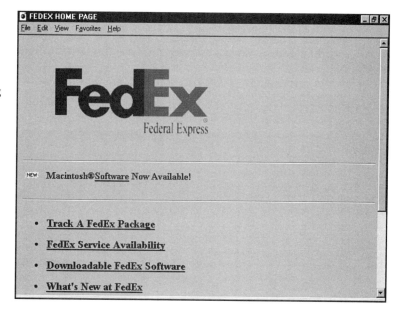

Fig. 11.15
Click on **Request a
Price List** to see how
much professional
assistance will cost you.

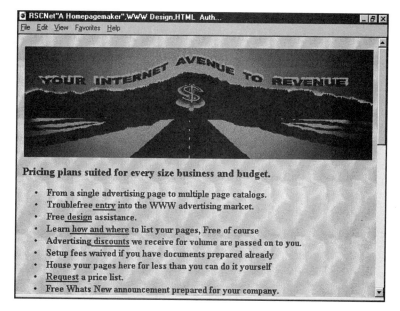

American Airlines Home Page

URL address: **www.amrcorp.com/aa_home/aa_home.htm**

Do you need flight information? Is there an Admirals Club in Dallas? Click on **Index** to see an extensive list of resources available for the business traveler.

Fig. 11.16
See the toolbar at the bottom of this page for Flight Schedules, and AAdvantage member information.

Dun & Bradstreet Information Services

URL address: **www.dbisna.com**

The Dun & Bradstreet page offers business information and insight that you can use. For example, click on **How to Manage Vendors** to see helpful hints for managing vendors. Click on **Strategic Business Planning** for guidelines to business planning. Of course, D&B offers its services to you, too.

AT&T Internet Toll Free 800 Directory

URL address: **www.tollfree.att.net**

Add this page to your favorites folder. You'll never dial 800-555-1212 again. You can browse 800 numbers by category or you can enter keywords to search the directory. Help and advanced search capabilities are available as well.

Fig. 11.17
Click on **D&B Story** to
learn more about Dun
& Bradstreet.

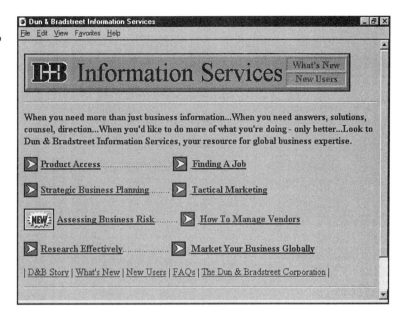

Fig. 11.18
This Web page is a
"must have" in your
favorites folder.

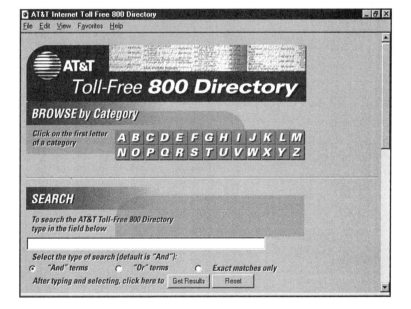

The Information SuperLibrary

URL address: **www.mcp.com**

This book wouldn't be complete without including the Web site for Que
publishing. The Macmillan home page includes links to Que, Sams, Hayden,

New Riders, Brady, and more. You'll find information about each of the books published by these imprints. You'll find sample chapters from many books, too.

Fig. 11.19
Click on **Que's Windows 95 Event Page** to locate books that will help you learn more about Windows 95.

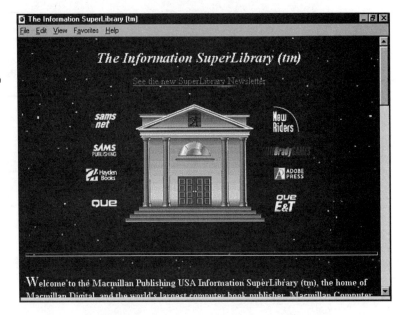

Hardware and software

Compaq Computer Corporation

URL address: **www.compaq.com/homepage.graphic.html**

Here, you'll find product support and information for the full range of Compaq products. Do you need a ROM chip upgrade? You'll find ordering information at this site. Are you fixing to buy a new computer? You'll find complete specifications for every computer model that Compaq sells—right down to the software titles preinstalled on the computer.

Access HP - Welcome to Hewlett-Packard

URL address: **www.hp.com**

If you own an HP printer or computer, you'll definitely want to add this page to your favorites folder. You'll find updated printer drivers and information about the products that HP sells.

Fig. 11.20
Click on Windows 95 to find out more about your Compaq computer and Windows 95.

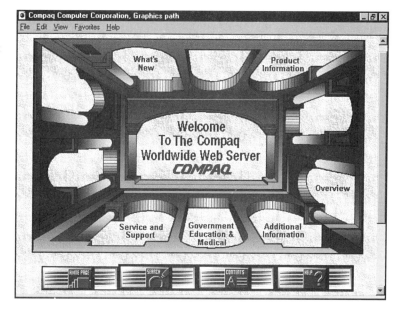

Fig. 11.21
The graphics at this site are great examples for what you can do on the Web—check this one out.

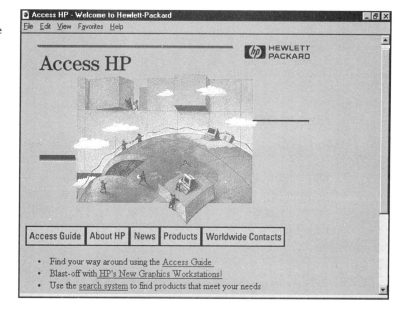

Adobe Systems Incorporated Home Page

URL address: **www.adobe.com**

Read all about Adobe products. For example, you'll find current information about Adobe PostScript, Adobe Acrobat, and other products. Click on **Tips & Techniques** to read tips from Adobe's brightest graphic talent on using Photoshop, Premiere, Illustrator, and Dimensions. Many of these tips are presented as multimedia movies.

Fig. 11.22
Get your own copy of the Acrobat Reader by clicking on **Free Software**.

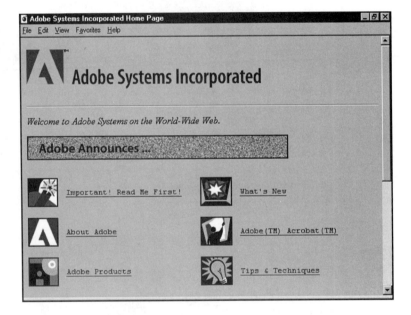

Internet Phone

URL address: **www.vocaltec.com**

Internet Phone lets you have long distance phone conversations over the Internet. For the price of your Internet connection and a small investment in hardware and software, you can cheat the long distance companies out of their long distance fees. Here, you'll find complete product information and a demo of the Internet Phone.

Microsoft Corporation

URL address: **www.microsoft.com**

Of course, no Web page reference would be complete without Microsoft's home page. You'll find an amazing amount of information on this page about Microsoft's products and services, future plans, and even job opportunities. You'll also find an extensive collection of hints and tips for Windows 95 and other Microsoft products. Click on **Microsoft Windows 95** to download a free demo of Windows 95.

Fig. 11.23
AT&T should be worried.

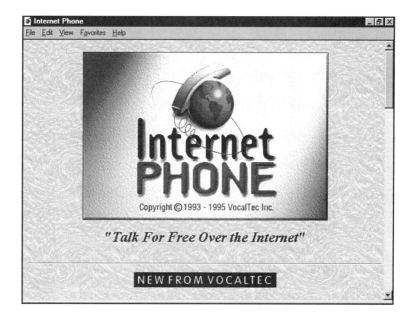

Fig. 11.24
You'll find anything and everything you want to know about Microsoft here.

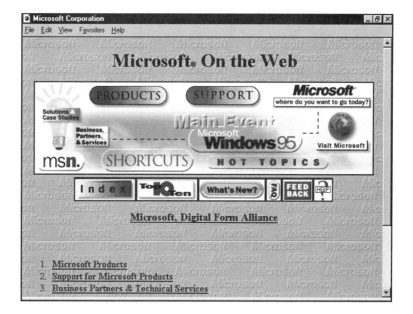

Silicon Graphic's Silicon Surf

URL address: **www.sgi.com**

You'll find a lot of VRML (described in chapter 9) at this site. If you've installed WorldView, you can view a lot of VRML sites here by clicking on **Surf Zone**.

Fig. 11.25
This is a great site to learn what you can do with graphics on the Web.

Advertising and shopping

Shopping 2000 Home Page

URL address: **www.shopping2000.com**

Online shopping has arrived. At Shopping 2000, you can buy music, books, clothing, electronics, flowers, food, wine, and more. You'll find vendors here such as Barnes & Noble, Brita, Hanes, Marshall Fields, and NordicTrack. Many of the advertisements are presented with sounds and multimedia movies. And, you can always view a picture of the product.

1-800 FLOWERS

URL address: **www.800flowers.com**

You didn't forget Mother's Day, did you? Next time, you won't have an excuse. Here, you'll shop their online catalog by occasion, holiday, or gift category. Then, you can place your order. Your mother will love you for it.

Fig. 11.26
Shop in the various departments by clicking on one of the icons in the toolbar.

Fig. 11.27
Click on one of the "scenes" in the middle of this Web page to shop flowers for that occasion.

Mega Internet Shopping List

URL address: **community.net/~csamir/aisshop.html**

This page is the ultimate Internet shopping phone book. You'll find links to virtually every online store on the Internet: malls, specialty shops, and music. Note: be careful about giving your credit card number out over the Internet.

Fig. 11.28
Click on one of the many shopping malls listed on this Web page.

Sports

The NandO Sports Server

URL address: **www.nando.net/SportServer**

You'll never lack for sports news again. The Sports Server provides commentary and analysis on your favorite sports. You'll find information on baseball, basketball, football, and hockey. Check here for you favorite team's schedule and standings.

Golf Digest GolfWeb

URL address: **www.golfweb.com**

Planning a trip to Dallas? Check out the golf courses in the area before you go. In the **ProShop**, you can get detailed product information for clubs, balls, and clothing. You'll also find more information for ordering the products that you find in the catalog. Keeping up with the tour? Check **Tour Action** to see the latest standings in both professional and amateur tours.

Fig. 11.29
Click on **In the PressBox** to meet the people from this site.

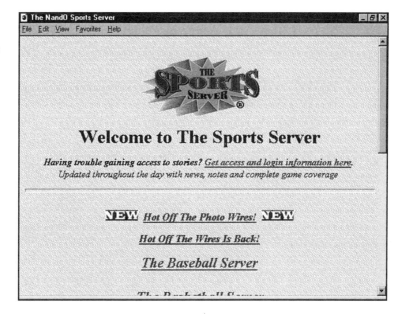

Fig. 11.30
If you're an avid golfer, you need to try this one. Use GolfWeb to find a course in your area.

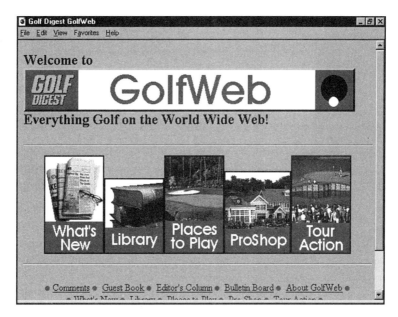

Politics

Welcome to the White House

URL address: **www.whitehouse.gov**

Visit the White House and learn all about how our government works. You'll find information about the first family and tours of the White House. While you're here, check out the President and Vice President's home pages.

Fig. 11.31
Be sure to sign the
Guest Book.

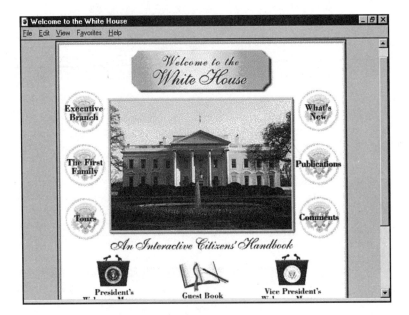

US Congress

URL address: **www.kimsoft.com/uscong.htm**

It just got a whole lot easier to get involved with your government. Come to this page if you want to get the e-mail address of your representative or senator. Also, you'll find extensive government information such as the CIA World Factbook, The State Department, and The National Archives.

Fig. 11.32
You'll find the mailing and e-mail address for each representative and senator.

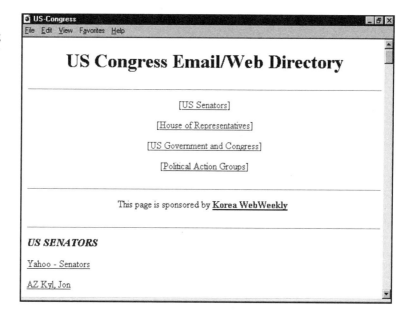

Travel

The Business Traveler Online

URL address: **www.biztravel.com/guide**

The Business Traveler Online is a great source for business services in all your destinations. For example, you can find car, airline, hotel, and restaurant tips for the UK. You'll also find travel tips and even a CIA country report that includes geographical information, disputes, economic, climate, terrain, and more.

Condé Nast Traveler

URL address: **www.cntraveler.com**

Are you looking for that dream vacation? Or, do you like to keep up with travel news? This page is the online version of *Condé Nast Traveler*—the standard travel magazine. You'll find great vacations, a beach finder, and photographs of your favorite destinations.

Fig. 11.33
If you're a vacationer or business traveler, you need to have this site in your favorites folder.

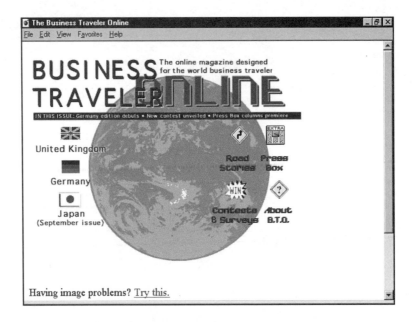

Fig. 11.34
The graphic on this Web site changes every month.

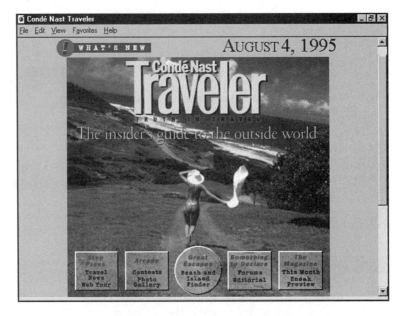

U.S. State Department Travel Warnings

URL address: **www.stolaf.edu/network/travel-advisories.html**

Before you travel aboard, check here for State Department advisories about your destination. For each country, you'll find a description of it along with entry requirements such as visas, medical facilities, crime information, and other vital information such as Embassy locations.

Fig. 11.35
If you want regular information, subscribe to the *travel-advisories* mailing list.

Travel

URL address: **www.iol.ie/gnn/wic/trav.toc.html**

This page provides links to all your travel information needs. You'll find information about vacation destinations, food and lodging, transportation, and more. You'll also find travel tips, links to travel magazines, and links to reference materials such as various flags, tourism offices around the world, and the CIA World Factbook.

Fig. 11.36
This Web site is a great compilation of other travel related Web sites.

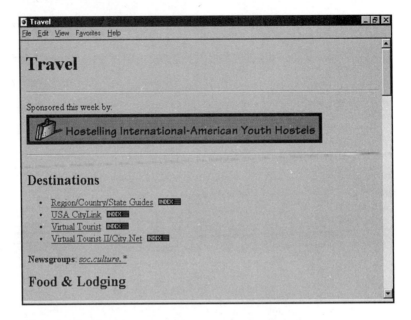

Virtual Tourist World Map

URL address: **wings.buffalo.edu/world/index.html**

This is one of the coolest pages on the Web. Click on a continent on this map and you'll see another map of that continent. Click on a country within that map and you'll see a list of links to various Web sites in that country.

Fig. 11.37
Don't have the budget to travel all over the world? You can do it on the Web.

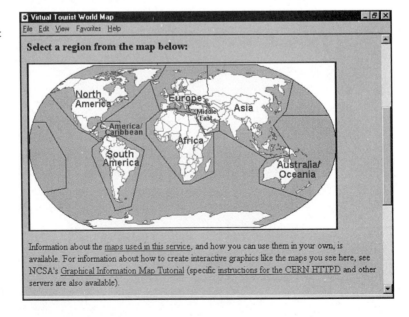

12

Using Exchange to Send and Receive Internet Mail

● **In this chapter:**

- How do you send Internet mail to CompuServe members?

- Free information—sign up for mailing lists

- Why was your e-mail returned?

- How do you convey emotion in an e-mail?

- Set up Exchange to check your mail periodically

- Argh! Mail isn't transmitting to the server

Internet e-mail is quick, reliable, and doesn't require stamps . . . .

The telephone is right there on your desk. So, why would you send an e-mail instead? Here's why:

- It's less expensive. You can communicate a lot of information to people all over the world for the low monthly cost of an Internet account.

- You can send files, such as documents and pictures, with your e-mail. Try that with the phone!

- The person you're calling has to be waiting on the other end of the phone. But if you send an e-mail, the person can pick it up and reply at his or her leisure.

Microsoft Exchange is the Windows 95 e-mail program that enables you to do all this. It's quite flexible. You can install different mail services, allowing you to receive all of your mail in the same place—including your Internet mail. The Internet mail service comes with Microsoft Plus! and is installed when you set up your Internet connection in chapter 7.

In this chapter, I'm assuming that you're loaded with material on how to use Exchange. Therefore, I focus on how to get the most out of Internet mail using Exchange. If you haven't set up Microsoft Exchange yet, however, double-click on the Inbox icon on your desktop. Then, follow the instructions.

First, a word about Internet mail addresses

Before you can send a letter to a friend, you have to know that person's address. Likewise, you have to know the person's Internet mail address before you can send him or her an e-mail.

 Plain English, please!

The process of forwarding Internet e-mail from machine to machine is called **routing**. When you send an e-mail to a friend across the country, the e-mail may be routed through several machines before it reaches its ultimate destination. **99**

An Internet mail address identifies a specific user on a specific machine. For example, the mail address **betty@boop.com** identifies the user **betty** at the machine named **boop.com**. The second part of the name is called the domain and is explained in chapter 7. The first part is the user's actual name on that machine. The Internet is concerned only with routing the e-mail to the **boop.com**. So, it doesn't care much about the name. Once the e-mail is delivered to the machine, it is the machine's responsibility to make sure that the mail gets into **betty**'s mail box.

Where do I get mail addresses?

You'll collect a variety of mail addresses over time: friends, relatives, associates, and other interesting people. You'll also meet people on the Internet who can help you, or people you can help. The addresses will come from different sources, including these:

- **Correspondence.** Most business people who have Internet mail accounts put their mail address on business cards. Some even put their address on business stationary. Also, you'll frequently exchange mail addresses with people you meet at events such as trade shows, user's groups, and seminars.

- **E-mail You Receive.** A good source of mail addresses is the e-mail you receive. Every time that I get an e-mail, I store the return address in my address book. For example, you may give your address to someone you meet at work. When that person sends you an e-mail, stash his or her address in the address book.

- **Usenet.** If you frequent Usenet, you'll run across all sorts of interesting people—some with expertise in areas that interest you. Store their names in your address book. But don't forget to include a comment in the address book describing why these people could be valuable contacts.

- **White Pages.** It's just not possible to provide a telephone book with everyone's e-mail address. Why? Because so many e-mail addresses come and go every day that keeping track of them is impossible. Many white page services have sprung up that come close, however. Chapter 10, "Finding Your Way Around the Web," describes some of the better services that are available on the World Wide Web.

TIP To find an e-mail address by name, try the mail server at MIT. Send an e-mail to **mail-server@rtfm.mit.edu** and put the text **send usenet-addresses/name** in the body of your message. To find my e-mail address, you'd send an e-mail to **mail-server@rtfm.mit.edu** and put the text **send usenet-addresses/Honeycutt** in the body of your message. You'll receive a reply that contains all the users who have posted to a Usenet group using that name.

Here's how to add a new address to your address book

There are two ways to add an e-mail address to your Exchange address book. First, if you read a message in Exchange and want to add the e-mail address of the sender, right-click on the person's name and select <u>A</u>dd to Personal Address Book. Otherwise, you'll need to type your new entry into the book. Here's how:

1 Open the address book by selecting <u>T</u>ools, <u>A</u>ddress Book from the Exchange main menu.

2 Select <u>F</u>ile, New <u>E</u>ntry and the address book will display a list of address types as shown in figure 12.1.

Fig. 12.1
The list displays all the possible addresses for the mail services that are installed in Exchange.

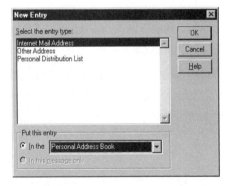

3 Select Internet Mail Address from the list and click on OK. Figure 12.2 shows the mail address property sheet.

4 Type the recipient's name as you want it to appear on the To: line of your e-mail, and also type the e-mail address. Then, click on OK to save your new address.

Fig. 12.2

You can keep more than an Internet Mail address in the address book. You can store the person's address, phone numbers, and notes, too.

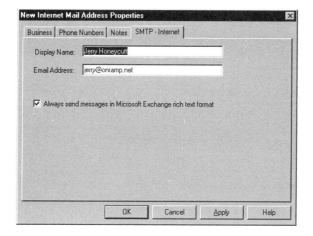

When you want to address an e-mail to that person, click on To and select his or her name from the list.

How do I address an e-mail to a CompuServe user?

Internet mail is only half the story. Far more people have mail boxes than have Internet mail: CompuServe, America Online, Prodigy, Microsoft Network, Bix, and MCIMail users are examples. And you can send e-mail to pretty much all of them—if you know how to address the e-mail correctly. You can't always send file attachments to users on these other networks, however. Check with the person you're mailing to find out whether he or she can get files through Internet mail.

Addressing e-mail to CompuServe users is easy. Their ID is in the form of two sets of numbers separated by a comma, for example: 76477,2751. Replace the comma with a period and attach **@compuserve.com** to the end of the address to send an e-mail to that CompuServe user. Using the previous address, the Internet address would be **76477.2751@compuserve.com**.

Sending an Internet e-mail to America Online and Microsoft Network users is even easier. For America Online users, append **@aol.com** to the end of their America Online ID. For example, **honeycutt@aol.com** would be my address at America Online if I had an account there. For the Microsoft Network, append **@msn.com** to the end of the user's Microsoft Network ID, such as **honeycutt@msn.com**. Table 12.1 shows the domain names for various other networks or services. To address an e-mail to a user on one of these, append the user's ID to the domain name in the table.

Table 12.1   Address for common networks and services

Network	Domain
America Online	aol.com
Applelink	applelin.com
ATTmail	attmail.com
BIX	bix.com
CompuServe	compuserve.com
Delphi	delphi.com
eWorld	online.apple.com
GEnie	genie.geis.com
Microsoft Network	msn.com
Prodigy	prodigy.com

Mailing lists are a great source of information

I'm sure that you've subscribed to a few magazines in your time. Maybe you read a magazine from the doctor's office and decided that you wanted to get it regularly. So, you sent in the subscription card and, shortly thereafter, you began receiving the magazine on a monthly basis.

Mailing lists are similar. They provide an assortment of information about computers, pets, automobiles, politics, and literally any other topic you can think of. There are two kinds of mailing lists:

- **Informative.** These lists are similar to your magazine subscription in that, after you've subscribed, you'll receive a regular e-mail from the list. Some lists send you an update monthly. You'll receive e-mail from other lists on a more frequent basis, however. For example, I sometimes receive 10 e-mails a day from the net-happenings mailing list. But Microsoft WinNews is sent out about once a month. Examples of these lists include newsletters, news clippings, and gossip columns. There are thousands to choose from.

- **Communicative.** These lists allow you and your peers to exchange information with one another. They are similar to bulletin boards except that your message is sent directly to everyone's mailbox who subscribes to the list. For example, if you wanted to update the people on a Windows 95 mailing list about your latest tips and tricks, you would e-mail the list and your tips and tricks would be forwarded to everybody who subscribed. Some mailing lists are moderated. That is, your e-mail's content is scrutinized to make sure that it's appropriate for the list. This doesn't mean, however, that your e-mail would be turned away for bad language or flaming. You're more likely to have an e-mail turned away if you post a message about your dog to a Windows 95 mailing list.

 Plain English, please!

A **bulletin board** is similar to the cork board in your office. Users post messages to a bulletin board and wait for other users to log on, read the message, and reply to it later. The messages are stored on the bulletin board as opposed to being sent via e-mail. Usenet groups are examples of bulletin boards.

A **flame** is an abusive or particularly nasty message sent as an e-mail to an individual or mailing list. Sometimes, flames are sent just to stir up trouble. So, what's the best way to answer a flame? Just don't. The author of the flame was counting on a response from you. The best way to douse the flame, then, is to ignore it altogether.

After you've found a list to which you want to subscribe, you send your subscription request. But this time, you do it with an e-mail instead of a card. After your subscription has been processed, you'll start receiving e-mails from the list on a regular basis.

How do I get on a mailing list?

Just like a magazine subscription, you've got to subscribe to a list to get it. The directions for subscribing to a list are potentially different for every list. When you see information about a list, however, it almost always includes instructions for subscribing to it. Typically, you'll use the following steps for subscribing to a list:

1 Address an e-mail to the list server whose address you got from the advertisement or information about the list.

2 In either the subject line or the body of the message, type **subscribe** *listname your name*. That is, you'll type **subscribe**, followed by the name of the list and your name. You'll be instructed whether to put the text in the subject or in the body of the message. You'll also be instructed as to the exact contents of the text. Note that because your e-mail is never actually handled by human hands, there's no use putting chatty text in the body of your e-mail.

For example, to subscribe to Microsoft WinNews, you'd address your e-mail to **enews99@microsoft.nwnet.com**. In the body of the message, you'd type **subscribe winnews**. Notice that your name is not required here.

My mail box is full! How do I get off this list?

You'll quickly find that your mail box fills up everyday with e-mail from mailing lists. You may tire of the net-happenings mailing list because you'll receive ten or more e-mails everyday from this list. Most mailing lists include instructions for getting off the list at the bottom of each message they send. Lacking instructions, however, you'll usually send an e-mail to the list server with **signoff** *listname* or **unsubscribe** *listname* in the body of your message.

Mailing list servers

There are two primary types of mailing list servers: Listserv and majordomo. If you know what type of list server is used by the list to which you're subscribing, the following information will help you figure out how to send your e-mail.

Server	Address	Message
Listserv	**listserv@***domain*	subscribe *listname your name*
majordomo	**majordomo@***domain*	subscribe *listname your name*

TIP **If you've subscribed to Net Happenings and you're tiring of all the** e-mails, you may want to consider checking out the Net Happenings Web page at **www.mid.net/NET**. It provides the same information without all the e-mails. Also, you can search for specific information using keywords and categories.

Some good mailing lists to get started

To get you going, here are some of the better mailing lists that I've found. You'll run across many more as you explore the Internet.

- **Microsoft WinNews.** This monthly newsletter keeps you up-to-date on the latest happenings at Microsoft. You'll also find tips for using Microsoft products and press releases. To subscribe, send an e-mail to **enews99@microsoft.nwnet.com** with **subscribe winnews** in the body of your message.

- **What's On Tonite.** Tired of paying for the TV Guide? What's On Tonite delivers a complete television schedule for local and cable TV each day. You must subscribe to one of four regions: Eastern, Central, Mountain, or Pacific. To subscribe, send an e-mail to **circulation@paperboy.com** with the text **subscribe *region firstname lastname*** in the body of the message.

- **David Letterman's Top Ten List.** This list speaks for itself. In addition to the previous evening's Top Ten list, it tells you who David's guests are for the next show. To subscribe, send an e-mail to **infobot@infomania.com** with the text **TOPTEN** in the subject line.

- **In, Around, and Online.** This newsletter contains useful information about the Internet and online services. It even contains weekly stock quotes for the major online services. To subscribe, send an e-mail to **listserv@clark.net** with **subscribe online-l *firstname lastname*** in the body of your message.

- **THIS is TRUE.** This weekly newsletter contains clippings from the week's more interesting news. The editor finishes each story with a humorous twist. To subscribe, send an e-mail to **listserv@netcom.com** with **subscribe this-is-true** in the body of your message.

- **Net Happenings.** This mailing list keeps you informed about anything and everything interesting happening on the Internet. Be warned! You'll be deluged with e-mail from this list. It's worth it, though, because you'll get information about other lists and World Wide Web sites everyday. To subscribe, send an e-mail to **listserv@is.internic.net** with **subscribe net-happenings** in the body of your message.

I want to find mailing lists that I'm interested in

Finding a mailing list that fits your interests is easier than you might think. Point Internet Explorer to **www.neosoft.com/internet/paml**. Here, you'll find an incredibly extensive, up-to-date collection of mailing lists. This collection is organized by topic. For example, if you're interested in politics, click on the politics category to see a list of currently available, politically oriented mailing lists with instructions on how to subscribe.

Argh, I sent an e-mail and it was returned

It's frustrating to send a carefully addressed e-mail and have it returned. It's even more frustrating to not understand why it was returned and thus not be able to fix the problem.

There are two primary reasons for an e-mail being returned: the host in the address was unknown or the name in the address was unknown.

 TIP   **Right-click on a received message and select Properties to see all** the dirty details, such as the various machines that have handled the e-mail and the program that was used to create it.

Here's how you'll know whether the host is unknown

Remember how e-mail addresses are formatted? The name is on the left of the @ and the host or domain is on the right side. If you typed an e-mail address with a bad host name in it, you'll get a message back similar to the one shown in figure 12.3. The subject indicates that the host is unknown. The body of the message contains more details about the mail session, which may help you figure out what went wrong.

Fig. 12.3

This e-mail was addressed to a user on an unknown host. The top portion of the e-mail's body shows a transcript of the session that produced the error.

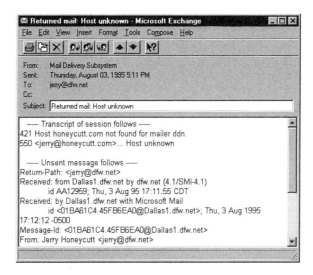

If you did indeed type the wrong domain host, you can resend your message by fixing the address and clicking on the Resend button on the toolbar. Otherwise, you'll need to find the correct address for the person you're trying to e-mail.

Here's how you'll know whether the name is unknown

Again, the left side of the e-mail is the recipient's name. You'll receive an e-mail back like the one shown in figure 12.4 if the message made it to the intended host, but the host couldn't find a user by that name. In this case, the subject line says that the message has a bad user name.

You can try to correct the address and click on Resend if you did indeed type it wrong, or you'll need to get the correct address from the recipient.

Fig. 12.4

This e-mail was addressed to an unknown user on an existing machine. If this e-mail had multiple recipients, the specific address would be shown in the body of the message.

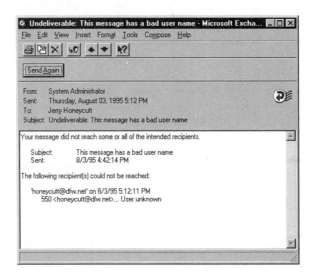

I'm tired of waiting while Exchange checks my mail

If you don't like waiting while Exchange dials the server and downloads your mail, you can have it check your mail periodically. Then, your mail will always be waiting for you when you're ready to read it. For example, you can set Exchange up to download your mail every hour. Your mail is being collected while you're at work or while you're sleeping. Here's how you set up Exchange to retrieve your Internet e-mail periodically:

1 Select Tools, Services from the Exchange main menu.

2 Select Internet Mail from the list and click on Properties. If Internet Mail is not in this list, you'll need to make sure that you've installed it as described in chapter 7, "The Internet—the Easy Way."

3 Click on the Connection tab. Exchange displays the property sheet shown in figure 12.5.

4 Deselect Work Off-line and Use Remote Mail. This allows you to specify a schedule for checking your e-mail.

5 Click on Schedule; Exchange will display the dialog box shown in figure 12.6. Specify the number of minutes between sessions and click on OK.

Fig. 12.5
If you're having problems making your e-mail work, click on Log File, select Troubleshooting from the list, and click on OK.

Choose the dial-up connection to use.

Click to create a new dial-up connection.

Deselect if you want to schedule Exchange to check your e-mail periodically.

Select if you're connecting through a network.

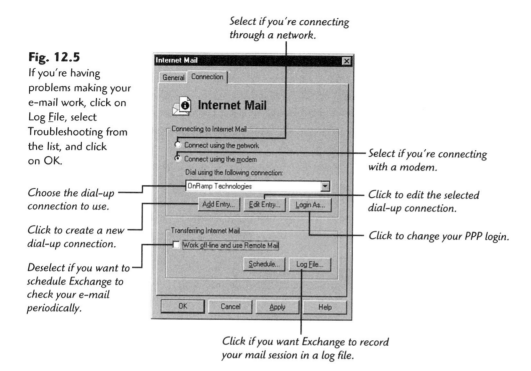

Select if you're connecting with a modem.

Click to edit the selected dial-up connection.

Click to change your PPP login.

Click if you want Exchange to record your mail session in a log file.

Fig. 12.6
You can schedule Exchange to check your mail every few minutes to every few hours. Type **60** to check mail every hour.

6 Click on OK twice to save your changes.

Q&A ***After setting up Exchange to check my e-mail periodically, I get an error that says the modem is in use every time I start Exchange.***

If you have installed fax services, Exchange initializes the modem when it starts. This takes a few seconds and keeps the modem occupied. If you've scheduled Exchange to check your e-mail periodically, it tries to log on to get your mail at the same time that the fax is initializing. You can either disable the fax or just click on OK when you get this error message, and continue working.

Your POP3 and SMTP may be on different servers

When you ran the Internet Setup Wizard as described in chapter 7, the Wizard set up the Internet mail service in Exchange. It made several assumptions, however, that may not work with your Internet service provider. For example, it assumes that your POP3 and SMTP servers are on the same machine. If the provider gave you a different machine address for POP3 than for SMTP, you'll need to configure Internet mail to deliver e-mail to the SMTP mail server. Here's how:

1 Select Tools, Services from the main menu.

2 Select Internet Mail in the list, and select Properties.

3 Click on Advanced Options, type the name of your SMTP mail server, and click on OK to save it. Figure 12.7 shows the General tab of the Internet Mail property sheet.

Fig. 12.7
Configure your e-mail account information on this tab. Click on Message Format to choose whether you'll send e-mail using MIME or UUENCODE.

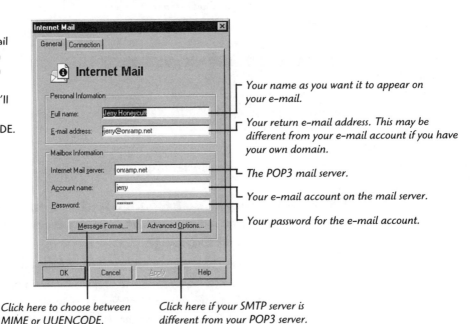

Your name as you want it to appear on your e-mail.

Your return e-mail address. This may be different from your e-mail account if you have your own domain.

The POP3 mail server.

Your e-mail account on the mail server.

Your password for the e-mail account.

Click here to choose between MIME or UUENCODE.

Click here if your SMTP server is different from your POP3 server.

4 Click on OK twice to save your settings. You'll have to restart Exchange before the changes can take effect.

Plain English, please!

MIME and **UUENCODE** are two standards for attaching file attachments to Internet messages. When you attach a file to an Internet e-mail, the files are not sent separately. Instead, they are encoded into a form that can be sent as a text included in the e-mail, and then decoded by the receiver.

POP3 is the mail transfer protocol used to receive e-mail from the host. **SMTP** is the mail transfer protocol used to send e-mail.

Q&A *I sent an Internet e-mail, but it doesn't transfer when I connect to the server.*

Sometimes the outbox gets confused. Change to the Outbox folder, open the e-mail that you're trying to send, and click the Send button on the toolbar. Try retransmitting the message.

I still can't get my e-mail to transfer. Also, I noticed that when I shut down Exchange, the fax icon in the lower-right corner of the display doesn't go away and the fax will no longer automatically answer incoming calls.

Your fax spool files may be corrupt or confused. I'm not exactly sure why this affects your Internet e-mail, but it does. Open the Explorer and delete the contents of C:\WINDOWS\SPOOL\FAX. The next time you start Exchange, you'll get an error message, which you can ignore.

I'm using a service provider but I've got my own domain

If you've registered your own domain with InterNIC, you want people to address their e-mail to you at that domain. Therefore, you want to make sure that your return address is using your domain—not the mail server. Here's how:

1 Select <u>T</u>ools, Ser<u>v</u>ices from the Exchange main menu.

2 Select Internet Mail from the list and click on Properties.

3 Type your return address, using your domain, in E-mail Address.

4 Make sure that Internet Mail Server and Account Name reflect your e-mail address on the mail server.

5 Click on OK twice to save your changes.

> ❝ *Plain English, please!*
>
> **InterNIC** is the closest thing to a regulatory group for the Internet that there is. InterNIC doles out the domain names. It also provides various directory services. For a list of common domains, see chapter 7. You can log on to InterNIC via Telnet at **ds.internic.net** or **rs.internic.net.** ❞

Now, each time that you send an e-mail, it'll be sent through your e-mail account on the service provider. The return address, however, will be set to your domain so that when people reply to your message, they will be replying to your domain. Your service provider will handle routing any messages addressed to your domain to your actual e-mail account.

Special considerations for Internet e-mail in Exchange

You already know how to send e-mail with Exchange. You've probably used the Microsoft Mail, The Microsoft Network, or CompuServe mail services. Although the process of sending an e-mail through the Internet is identical, there are some special considerations:

- **Attachments.** Internet mail supports both the MIME and UUENCODE standards for sending file attachments. Although I recommend that you use MIME because it's better integrated into Windows 95, you need to make sure that people you're sending the e-mail to can decode MIME attachments. Otherwise, they'll receive an e-mail with garbage in it. If in doubt, change your encoding type to UUENCODE by selecting File, Properties from the compose window, clicking on the Internet tab, and selecting Override the Profile Setting. Then, select UUENCODE from the list. You can safely assume that anyone using Microsoft Exchange or Internet in a Box can decode MIME messages.

- **Formatted e-mail.** Microsoft Exchange lets you do all that fancy formatting: bold headings, bulleted lists, and more. But you need to keep in mind that other users may be looking at a mess when they receive your e-mail. That's because their mail program may not support all that fancy formatting. If you know that the recipient is using Exchange or any other MAPI e-mail program, you can safely use the formatting. Otherwise, it's a safe bet to keep your e-mail simple.

- **Receipts.** When you ask for a return receipt at the post office, you're assured that you'll get one back after the package is delivered. When you request a return receipt for an Internet e-mail, however, there is no guarantee that a receipt will be sent—even if the message definitely was read. That's because the individual user's e-mail program has to be kind enough to generate the receipt. If the recipient's e-mail program doesn't, you won't get a receipt. So, don't yell at someone too quickly when you don't get a receipt.

Q&A *When I send an e-mail message to an Internet address, it is sent through Microsoft Network—not my Internet account.*

Select <u>T</u>ools, <u>O</u>ptions from the Exchange main menu. Click on the Delivery tab and notice the bottom list. This list determines the order in which addresses will be processed. If Microsoft Network is above Internet Mail, e-mail that has an Internet address will be sent through the Microsoft Network. Move Internet Mail above Microsoft Network and click on OK.

You can express emotion in an e-mail message

The experts say that 60 percent of all our communication is through body language. So, when you say something to friends, they use your body language to help them interpret what you're saying. For example, if you say "good job" to a colleague with a smile on your face and both hands by your side, she will take that as a compliment. On the other hand, if you say "good job" to that same person without a smile and both hands on your hips, they'll pick it up as sarcasm or insincerity. In either case, your body language says a lot about what you're verbalizing.

Think about e-mail for a moment. When recipients read your message, they can't see your body language. They don't know whether you were smiling, frowning, or crying when you wrote the e-mail. You're communicating only 40 percent of the message. This is why e-mails frequently get misinterpreted. You may have meant to say something sarcastic or humorous, but the reader might not know how to take it without the visual cues.

How do you convey how you feel about what you're writing in an e-mail? Emoticons. **Emoticons** (emotional icons) are graphics that you can use in your e-mail to indicate how you feel about what you've written. You can indicate humor, sarcasm, anger, doubt, or just about any other emotion that you can imagine. For example, if I sent a message that said "I really enjoyed that restaurant last night," how would you interpret that? You'd probably think I really did enjoy it. But what if I wrote "I really enjoyed that restaurant last night :-/" (hint: Look at it sideways)? You'd know I was being sarcastic.

There are as many emoticons as there are ways to put characters together. The most common ones, however, are ":-)" and ":-(". To see an exhaustive list, point the Internet Explorer at **ftp://ftp.utirc.utoronto.ca.** Otherwise, here are some to get you started:

Table 12.2   Emoticons you can use in your e-mail

Emoticon	Description
:(	Frown
:)	Smile
;(	Crying
;)	Up to no good
:|	Expressionless
:@)	Happy as a pig
8)	Bug-eyed
8O	Yelling
:-0	Shocked
:-D	Laughing

Emoticon	Description
:-P	Tongue out
:-(	Unhappy
:'-(	Crying
:-/	Scowling
:-]	Sarcasm
:-|	Expressionless
;-)	Winking
;.(..	Crying
:^)	Happy profile
:^(	Frowning profile
|-(	Tired and grumpy
|-0	Yawning
|-|	Sleeping
|-P	Sleeping with tongue out
8-(	Terrifed
8-)	Wide-eyed
8-|	Concerned
8-||	Angry
8-0	Scared
8-D	Laughing

Part IV: Connecting Remotely with Dial-Up Networking

13

Dial-Up Networking—
Anywhere, Anytime

● **In this chapter:**

- **What is Dial-Up Networking? How does it work?**

- **HyperTerminal vs. Dial-Up Networking**

- **How do I connect to another computer?**

- **Working at home**

Dial-Up Networking is almost as good as being in the office. The hardest part is convincing your boss to let you work at home . . . . ▶

f you have a network at the office, you depend on that network to help you do your job. You probably log on each day to exchange e-mail, print documents, or use other network resources such as hard drives and CD-ROMs.

But what happens when you're at home or on the road? Are you cut off from the office? Can you check your e-mail? You don't have to be cut off while you're away—not with Dial-Up Networking. Dial Up Networking is remote networking software that comes free with Windows 95. It allows you to log onto the network using a phone line and a modem.

What you can do with Dial-Up Networking

Before Dial-Up Networking and the Dial-Up Server came along, networking over the phone line was a daunting task. You had to buy the right equipment. You had to buy the right software. And worse, you had to figure out how to set it all up.

But now you can easily connect to a network over the phone line with everything that is sitting on your desk right now. It's easy to configure, too. Here are some of the things for which you can use Dial-Up Networking:

- **Peer-to-peer.** A peer-to-peer network is a bunch of (two or more) individual computers networked together without a dedicated network server. The computers on the network can share resources such as folders or printers with other computers on the network.

  For example, you may want to copy some files from a friend's computer. You can connect to your friend's computer to create a peer-to-peer network. Then, you can copy the files directly over the dial-up network connection.

- **Networking**. A large office network has a bunch of computers connected to a dedicated server. A dedicated server such as Windows NT or NetWare isn't used for writing memos or playing games. Instead, it just sits there and shares its hard drives, printers, and modems with everyone else on the network. Dedicated servers are usually very fast machines that are designed for this purpose.

You can use Dial-Up Networking to connect your computer to a large network and log on—just as if you were in the office. Then, you can use the network's drives, printers, or any other available resources.

- **The Internet**. Dial-Up Networking is used by Microsoft Plus! to connect your computer to the Internet. I recommend, however, that you use the Internet Setup Wizard as described in chapter 7, "The Internet— the Easy Way."

 Plain English, please!

A **resource** is something on a computer that may be useful to **share** with other users. For example, a disk drive, file, printer, or modem can all be network resources. Before you can use a network resource, someone has to make it available to you. In a peer-to-peer network, that someone is the owner of the machine that has the resource you want. On a larger network, that someone is probably the Network Administrator.

I use HyperTerminal. How is this different from Dial-Up Networking?

HyperTerminal is a terminal emulator that displays text the host sends. You can't use it to access network resources directly. Dial-Up Networking provides a network connection that looks no different from the connection you have at work.

What do I need to use Dial-Up Networking?

Windows 95 provides the Dial-Up Networking software. As a bonus, it's easy to use, too. You'll need a few more things to connect to another computer, however.

- You need a **modem** hooked up to your computer. Make sure that it's configured correctly in the Control Panel. Incidentally, you'll want to use a pretty fast modem because Dial-Up Networking sends and receives a lot of information. The faster the modem, the less time you have to wait while accessing the network.

- You need the **phone number** of the computer that you're calling and a **phone line** with which to call.

- If you'll be calling another desktop computer that is running Windows 95, make sure that it has the **Dial-Up Server** software installed and is accepting phone calls. The other computer must have Microsoft Plus! installed to use Dial-Up Server. You can also use Dial-Up Networking to connect to other computers through an Internet service provider or a Novell network, too.

Dial-Up Networking is easy to understand

Have you ever overheard a conversation between a couple of network "nerds" and wondered what the heck they were talking about? Trust me, it's really not as complicated as it sounds.

Dial-Up Networking lets you connect to a network or single computer just as if you were in the office. The only difference is that you'll do it over the phone line using the Dial-Up Adapter. The Dial-Up Adapter is installed when you optionally install Dial-Up Networking. It makes your modem look like a network adapter that "talks" to the network.

 Plain English, please!

Your computer is called the dial-up **client** and the computer that you're calling is called the dial-up **server.**

You can use your connection to simply access the resources on the dial-up server or you can use it to connect to a larger network. If you're using the dial-up server to connect to a network, the server is also called a **gateway.**

You and your friends speak English when you visit. Why? Because both of you understand English. Likewise, the dial-up client and dial-up server need to speak the same language. This special language is called a **protocol.**

Unlike most of us, the client computer is multilingual. It has to talk to both the dial-up server and the network—both of which use different protocols:

- A **connection protocol** is used by the dial-up client and dial-up server to communicate. There are many connection protocols available, but you'll probably use PPP (point-to-point) because it's the most common and is the default in Dial-Up Networking.

- A **network protocol** is used by the dial-up client and the network to communicate. You'll probably use IPX/SPX to log into a Novell network, NetBEUI to log into a Microsoft Network, or TCP/IP to connect to the Internet.

The difference between the connection protocol and the network protocol is very subtle, but important. An example might help.

When you write a letter to a friend, you enclose the letter in an addressed envelope and send it via the postal service. With Dial-Up Networking, the

More protocols supported by Dial-Up Networking

Dial-Up Networking supports the popular connection protocols described as follows:

PPP is the default connection protocol used by Windows 95. It was designed to simplify the configuration and logon process by automatically handling a lot of the details such as password verification and addressing. You'll probably use this to connect to the Internet or the Dial-Up Server. If you're ever given a choice, use this protocol.

NetWare Connect is provided by Novell and allows you to easily connect directly to a NetWare server. Ask your Network Administrator for more details about setting up a NetWare Connect dial-up server.

Windows for Workgroups is used to connect to Windows for Workgroups Remote Access Server or Windows NT 3.1. Because both Windows for Workgroups and Windows NT 3.1 are retiring, you'll see this connection protocol used less and less.

SLIP is a protocol commonly found on UNIX servers. If you have a choice between SLIP or PPP (you usually do), the better choice is PPP because it's easier to configure.

CSLIP is a compressed version of SLIP.

Also, Dial-Up Networking supports the following popular network protocols:

IPX/SPX is always used by computers on a Novell network. It can also be used with Microsoft and peer-to-peer networks. IPX/SPX is a very efficient network protocol that is widely supported.

NetBEUI is known for its simplicity if not for its speed. It is used primarily for a Microsoft Network or peer-to-peer networking in Windows 95.

TCP/IP was designed to handle the rigors of networking over telephone lines. It is used primarily for wide-area networks (WAN), which are networks that cover a large geographical area. But you'll also see it used in UNIX and frequently with Windows NT. For these reasons, it's also the protocol that you'll use to access the Internet.

form of the letter (for example, the date, inside address, outside address, text, and salutation) is the network protocol because it is the form that both parties are accustomed to. The form of the envelope and how you address it would be the communication protocol because it communicates how and where the letter is to be delivered by the post office.

How do I connect my computer to a dial-up server?

Dial-Up Networking makes it easy to connect your computer to another computer. The computer that you're calling, however, must have Dial-Up Networking installed and the Dial-Up Server installed from Microsoft Plus! with caller access turned on. For more information about the Dial-Up Server, see chapter 15, "Accessing Your Computer Remotely with Dial-Up Server."

Before you get started, you'll need a few things

To keep things simple, I'm assuming that the computer you're calling has the Dial-Up Server installed. You'll need to check or record the following information about the server:

- The **connection protocol** of the dial-up server should be set to Default. This allows the dial-up client and server to decide which protocol is best.

- The **network protocol** depends on the network to which the dial-up server is attached. If you're calling Dial-Up Server on a stand-alone machine, you're probably using NetBEUI as the protocol for peer-to-peer networking. If you're calling a gateway, ask your Network Administrator.

- The **phone number** is the actual phone line connected to the dial-up server. If you're calling a gateway, you'll need to ask the Network Administrator for the phone number.

- The **Password** is set in the Dial-Up Server. This password is used to protect an unwanted caller from getting access to the Dial-Up Server. Check with the person who set up the Dial-Up Server.

Plain English, please!

A **stand-alone** computer is one that is not attached to a network. You can call a stand-alone computer that has the Dial-Up Server to create a peer-to-peer network.

Now that you have the information you need, you can easily set up a new dial-up connection.

Setting up the dial-up connection

Dial-Up
Networking

You'll need to make sure that Dial-Up Networking is installed on your computer. By default, Windows 95 doesn't install it. To make sure, open My Computer and check to see whether there is a Dial-Up Networking icon in the folder. If there isn't, use the following steps to install it:

1 Open the Control Panel and double-click on Add/Remove Programs.

2 Click on the Windows Setup tab.

3 Select Communications in the Components list and click on Details.

4 Select Dial-Up Networking and click on OK.

5 Click on OK again and follow the instructions.

Q&A *My Network Administrator told me that the computer I'm calling is connected to a NetWare network. How do I know that I have everything I need installed?*

When you installed Dial-Up Networking, Windows 95 installed the Microsoft Network Client, NetWare Client, DialUp Adapter, IPX/SPX protocol, and NetBEUI protocol. By default, you have everything you need to access resources on both the dial-up server and the network already installed.

After Windows 95 restarts, you can see the dial-up adapter in the Network properties dialog box by right-clicking on Network Neighborhood and selecting Properties. Your screen should look similar to figure 13.1.

Click to add a network component such as a client, adapter, protocol, or service.

This tab lets you change the name of your computer and the workgroup of which you are a member.

Fig. 13.1

Select Dial-Up Adapter from the list and click on Properties to configure it. If the Dial-Up Adapter doesn't appear in this list, you haven't installed Dial-Up Networking.

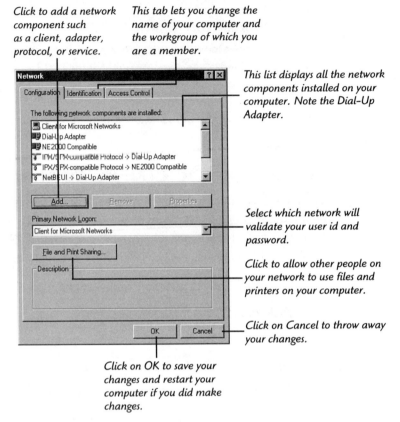

This list displays all the network components installed on your computer. Note the Dial-Up Adapter.

Select which network will validate your user id and password.

Click to allow other people on your network to use files and printers on your computer.

Click on Cancel to throw away your changes.

Click on OK to save your changes and restart your computer if you did make changes.

To create a Dial-Up Networking connection, open the Dial-Up Networking folder in My Computer. Use the following steps to create your connection:

1 If the Make New Connection wizard started when you first opened the folder, click on Next. Otherwise, double-click on the Make New Connection icon to start the wizard. The wizard displays the dialog box shown in figure 13.2. Note that, if you don't have a modem installed, Dial-Up Networking starts the Install New Modem wizard to let you install and configure your modem.

Fig. 13.2
The name for your connection should be descriptive, such as "Office" or "Bill's Computer," to help you distinguish it from other connections in the folder.

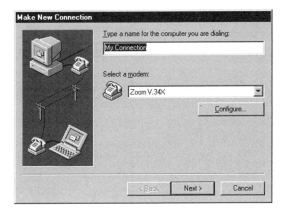

2 Type a descriptive name for your connection and click on Next. The wizard displays the dialog box shown in figure 13.3.

Fig. 13.3
Type the area code and phone number of the dial-up server. If you're calling a network gateway, you'll need to get the number from the Network Administrator.

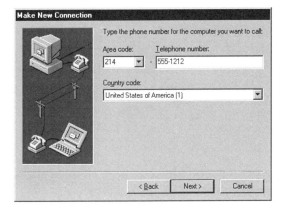

3 Type the area code and phone number of the dial-up server that you're calling, and click on Next.

4 Click on Finish to save your connection.

TIP   **If you're calling a dial-up server and don't need access to the** network to which it's connected, you'll get things done faster if you don't log on to the network. Right-click on the connection and select Properties. Click Server Type on the connection's property sheet and deselect Log On to Network.

By default, your new connection is configured to use all the available connection protocols and network protocols. It's also configured to log you onto the network. Therefore, you don't need to change any properties.

So far, so good! It's time to dial the connection

Now that you have your new connection, it's easy to connect to the dial-up server:

1 Double-click on your new connection. Dial-Up Networking displays the dialog box shown in figure 13.4.

Fig. 13.4
The name and password identify you on the dial-up server. If you are calling a gateway, they aren't used as your network logon.

2 Type a user name to identify yourself to the dial-up server and the dial-up server's password in the space provided.

3 Click on Connect, and Dial-Up Networking will dial the phone and connect you to the dial-up server. While the phone is dialing, you'll see the dialog box shown in figure 13.5, which will display the status, such as dialing or validating password.

Fig. 13.5
This dialog box keeps you up-to-date on the status of your connection. Press Cancel if you want to hang up without connecting to the dial-up server.

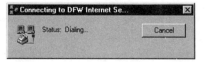

TIP **Select Save Password if you don't want to type your password** every time you log on.

After you're connected, the status dialog box changes to the one shown in figure 13.6. This tells you how long you've been connected and describes the connection protocol that was used for this connection.

Fig. 13.6
You can get more information about your connection by clicking on Details, or you can hang up the connection by clicking on Disconnect.

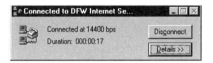

Q&A ***I can connect to the network, but I don't see shared resources on the dial-up server.***

You may not be a member of the same workgroup as the dial-up server. Right-click on Network Neighborhood, select Properties, and click on the Identification tab. The workgroup name should be the same on your computer as it is on the dial-up server. Otherwise, file and printer sharing is not correctly installed on the dial-up server (the other machine). See chapter 15 for instructions on how to set it up, or ask the Network Administrator for help.

Is connecting to the office's NetWare network different?

Dial-Up Networking makes it just as easy to connect your home computer to the office network. It pays off, too. Creating a dial-up connection to the network allows you to use all of those network resources from home. Why in the world would you want to connect to the office network from home? Here are couple of reasons:

- The world is changing. A lot of people are working at home to save the company money and to make life a bit easier for the employees. Dial-Up Networking makes it possible. You may be able to convince your boss to let you work at home for some small concessions. Showing her that you can still function as a part of the team with Dial-Up Networking adds credibility to your story.

- You've probably brought work home with that nagging feeling that you forgot something. Of course, you didn't bring home that file that you need to complete tomorrow's report. You can hop in your car and drive back to the office. Or, you can log on to the network with Dial-Up Networking and copy the file to your computer. It sure beats driving!

 CAUTION   **Talk to your Network Administrator before setting up an office** computer as a network gateway. There may be a policy about such connections because of network security.

Setting up a Dial-Up Networking connection to a network gateway is the same as was described earlier in this chapter in the section, "Setting up the dial-up connection." The network gateway needs to have Dial-Up Networking installed and the Dial-Up Server installed from Microsoft Plus! with caller access turned on. The gateway should be correctly configured to access the network. If you're using your desktop computer as a gateway, you can be pretty sure it is. If in doubt, ask your Network Administrator.

Also, you need to make sure that you have the correct network drivers loaded on the dial-up client—your computer. To verify that you have the correct network drivers loaded, use the following steps:

1 Right-click on Network Neighborhood and select Properties. It displays the dialog box shown earlier in figure 13.1.

2 Check the list to see whether Client for NetWare Networks and the IPX/ SPX Compatible Protocol are in the list. If so, you're in good shape.

3 Otherwise, click on Add to display the dialog box shown in figure 13.7.

Fig. 13.7
From here, you can add a variety of network components. When you add a new network client, the protocols required to use the client are automatically added for you.

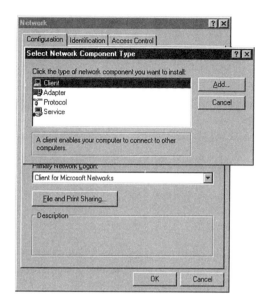

4 Select Client from Click the Type of Network Component You Want to Install and click on <u>A</u>dd.

5 Select Microsoft from the list of manufacturers and select Client for NetWare Networks from the list of network clients.

6 Click on OK twice and follow the instructions.

TIP **Dial-Up Networking won't prompt you for a user name or password** to log into the network unless the user name and password that you typed when you first started Windows 95 doesn't work. So, it's convenient to use the same name and password to log on to Windows 95 as you use to log on to the network.

Q&A ***Our network is a Novell network and I'm calling a gateway. When I connect, I can't see any of the network's resources.***

Make sure that you have the NetWare Client and IPX/SPX protocol installed as described earlier. Also, make sure that you don't have File and Printer Sharing for NetWare Networks installed on the dial-up client. If that doesn't help, click Server <u>T</u>ype in your dial-up connection's property sheet and make sure that <u>I</u>PX/SPX Compatible is selected.

I'm connected; what do I do now?

Your dial-up network connection is no different from a regular network connection. You can browse resources that are available in the Network Neighborhood. To open the Network Neighborhood, double-click on its icon on the desktop.

As a result, a folder opens on the desktop with at least one icon named Entire Network and possible other folders representing other computers and network servers. Double-clicking on any of the icons in the folder opens another folder for that computer or network server.

Eventually, the folder will contain icons that represent resources to which you can connect. For example, to connect to a shared drive, right-click on it and select Map Network Drive. To connect to a shared printer, right-click on it and select Capture Printer Port. Note that you don't have to connect to a network drive to copy or use files on it. You use files directly from a Network Neighborhood folder just like any other folder in Windows 95.

 TIP **If you try to use a shortcut to a network resource when you're not** connected to the network, Windows 95 will ask you whether you want to connect to the network with Dial-Up Networking. Click on Yes to dial-up your network.

14

Using the Scripting Tool

● **In this chapter:**

- **What is a script?**

- **Do I need one?**

- **How do I know what to put in a script?**

- **What kind of commands are available for scripts?**

- **Argh, my script doesn't work!**

Just like a movie script, a dial-up script directs the action . . . . ●▶

At the stop-sign, turn right. Follow the yellow brick road for two miles. Turn left after you've seen the witch. My house will be the one at the end of the road." We've all given instructions like these before—with luck, they made a bit more sense, though.

Unfortunately, giving instructions to your computer isn't so easy. Like some people, you can't count on your computer to apply much common sense to the instructions. The scripting tool provided with Microsoft Plus!, however, makes it a bit easier to provide Dial-Up Networking. See chapter 13, "Dial-Up Networking—Anywhere, Anytime" with instructions about how to log on to a dial-up server.

What is a dial-up script?

A dial-up script is similar to the script that telemarketers use to interrupt your dinner. They write down, on a piece of paper, everything they want to say. They also write down a response to each response that you might say. A brief telemarketing script might look like the following:

Telemarketer: Hello Mr./Ms. J. Doe, my name is Joe Telemarketer with the Microsoft Corporation. I'm calling today to offer you the chance of a lifetime. Have your ever heard of Microsoft?

If J. Doe says "Yes":

Telemarketer: Great!

If J. Doe says "No":

Telemarketer: Microsoft is the dominating force in desktop computing today. Our goal is to have Windows 95 running on every desktop in the world, including yours.

You get the idea. A script for Dial-Up Networking is similar except that the script looks for very specific pieces of text from the server and sends very specific responses in return. For example, a segment of a script to wait for "user id:", respond with your user name, and pause for two seconds looks like the following:

```
waitfor "user id:"
transmit $USERID
delay 2
```

Do I need the scripting tool?

Maybe you don't. If all of your dial-up connections connect and log in to the server correctly, you don't need the scripting tool. Note that you don't need the scripting tool if you're connecting to a computer that is using Dial-Up Server. If you haven't been able log on with a particular connection, however, the scripting tool may help.

Why? Because Dial-Up Networking, by itself, doesn't understand the prompts that the server sends. For example, when you use a Dial-Up Networking connection to connect to the Internet, your user name and password are usually exchanged with the server automatically. But if your Internet provider requires you to type your id and password, you'll have to create a script to wait for the prompts and provide your name and password.

 TIP **Even though you may need a script to connect to your Internet** service provider, you may not need to write it. Ask your provider whether it has a Windows 95 dial-up script that you can use to connect to your provider's server. I bet it does.

To help you determine whether you might need to use the scripting tool, here are some examples of times when you will need it:

- **SLIP connections.** If your Internet service provider provides only SLIP connections, similar to a PPP connection as described earlier, you'll need a script to automatically log on to the server.

- **PPP menus.** Some Internet service providers require you to select PPP from a menu after logging on to the server. You can automate this process using a script.

Automatic verification when you log on

The PPP connection protocol has the capability to automatically log you on to the server without asking for the user id or password. It uses something called Password Authentication Protocol (PAP), which allows the dial-up client to identify itself to the dial-up server as soon as the connection is established. If your server doesn't support PAP, you'll have to create a dial-up script to log on.

- **Authentication.** Some Internet service providers don't support automatic user name and password verification. You can use a script to avoid typing your name and password every time that you log on to the server.

I'm clueless. How do I know what to put in my script?

This is the easy part—you don't have to be the creative sort to figure it out. The content of your script is determined completely by the requirements of the server that you're trying to call. For example, if the server expects you to type your password when it sends "password:", then your script would include the following lines:

```
waitfor "password:"
transmit $PASSWORD
```

There are two ways to determine the requirements for your script: contacting the Network Administrator or recording what you see while you try to connect with the terminal window.

 **Plain English, please!**

> The **terminal window** is an optional window that is displayed right after the dial-up server answers the phone. It allows you to interact with the server during the logon process.

Calling the Network Administrator

The Network Administrator should be able to provide you with instructions for logging in. Try to get them in writing, however. It's easier to write a script based upon their notes rather than what you thought you heard them say.

The Network Administrators notes might look something like this:

1. Dial the phone number.
2. After you connect, press Enter three times.
3. At "user id:", type your id and press Enter.
4. At "password:", type your password and press Enter.
5. At ">", type "PPP" and press Enter.

Your script for this session would look like this (don't worry about what all the commands mean yet; you'll learn about them soon enough):

```
proc main
    transmit "^M^M^M"
    waitfor "user id:"
    transmit $USERID
    transmit "^M"
    waitfor "password:"
    transmit $PASSWORD
    transmit "^M"
    waitfor ">"
    transmit "PPP^M"
endproc
```

Watching the terminal window

A potentially more reliable way to find out what you need to include in your script is to try logging on manually. Then, record notes at each step of the way. First, you'll need to turn on the terminal window for your dial-up connection:

1 Select Programs, Accessories, Dial-Up Networking from the Start menu. Open the Connection properties sheet by right-clicking on it and selecting Properties.

2 Click on Configure to open the modem configuration for this connection.

3 Click on the Options tab. The dialog box should look similar to figure 14.1.

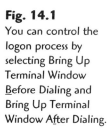

Fig. 14.1
You can control the logon process by selecting Bring Up Terminal Window Before Dialing and Bring Up Terminal Window After Dialing.

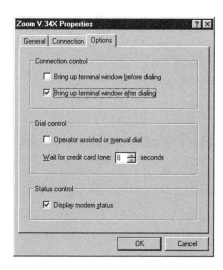

4 Select Bring Up Terminal Window After Dialing, and click on OK.

5 Click on OK to save your changes to the Connection properties.

Use your connection to log onto the server normally. Now you're exposed to all the dirty details. When Dial-Up Networking connects, it won't try to log you on automatically. More than likely, you'll see some sort of banner followed by a prompt for your user id.

Take notes. Write down each prompt that is displayed and the response you typed. When you're completely logged on, click on Continue. Youll know that you're logged on because you'll see a message such as "PPP session" or "Begin Session". This depends completely on the server with which you're connecting.

The notes that I took when logging onto the Internet look like this:

1. Long banner.
2. "DFW login:", typed user id and pressed Enter.
3. "Password:", typed password and pressed Enter.
4. "PPP session", clicked Continue to start session.

The dial-up script came out like this:

```
proc main
    waitfor "DFW login:"
    transmit $USERID
    transmit "^M"
    waitfor "Password:"
    transmit $PASSWORD
    transmit "^M"
endproc
```

TIP Text used with `waitfor` is case sensitive. If you add `waitfor` `"password:"` to your script and the server sends `"PASSWORD:"`, the script won't work.

These scripting commands are all you need

Just about anything you need to do in a dial-up script can be accomplished with the scripting commands available. Before I jump into the commands that are available, I discuss a few rules first.

A script file is nothing more than a text file that you create using Notepad. You must follow these rules, however, when you create your script, or it won't work:

- You can put only one command on each line of the text file.

- The first command in your script must be `proc main`.

- The last command in your script must be `endproc`.

 TIP **To make things really simple for yourself, store your script files in** the Program Files\Accessories directory and make sure that they have the .SCP file extension so that the scripting tool will find them.

Also, many commands allow you to give a string. A string is nothing but a bunch of text inside quotation marks. For example, you use a string with `waitfor` to specify the text for which the script should be waiting. Some text in strings has special meanings. Table 14.1 describes text with special meaning.

Table 14.1   Special text used in strings

Text	Meaning
^a – ^z	ASCII codes 0 through 26, respectively
^M	Carriage return
<cr>	Carriage return
<lf>	Line feed
\quotes	Double quotation
\^	Caret
\<	<
\\	Backslash

For example, the command `transmit "name^M"` sends `name` followed by a carriage return. `waitfor "Signon:<cr><lf>"` waits until it receives `"Signon:"` followed by a carriage return and line feed.

Table 14.2 that follows describes the basic commands available with the Dial-Up Scripting Tool. These commands should handle most of your scripting needs. Each entry in the table has a description and an example.

Table 14.2 Dial-Up Scripting Tool commands

Command	Description/Example
proc <name>	The first command in your script must be `proc main`. The script will start running at the command after this one. For example: ```proc main transmit "example" endproc```
endproc	endproc is typically the last command in your script. When the scripter gets to this command, Dial-Up Networking will start the PPP or SLIP session.
delay <time>	This command causes your script to pause for the given number of seconds. You'll use this command if you need to wait for the server to catch up with the script. For example, the script may spend five seconds displaying a large bit of text. Thus, you'd pause for a few seconds to let it catch up before you try sending it any more text. For example, to delay 2 seconds: ```delay 2```
waitfor <str>	waitfor pauses the script until the string you give is sent by the server. You've already seen examples of using this to wait for the server to prompt you for a password before sending it. For example: ```waitfor "Password:" transmit $PASSWORD```
transmit <str>	This commands sends the string that you give to the server. The string can be any text, but is more likely to be $USERID or $PASSWORD (note that neither is enclosed in quotation marks). $USERID and $PASSWORD are placeholders for the user id and password that you type when you double-click on a connection. For example: ```transit "Jerry"```
	```transmit $USERID```
halt	halt causes the script to stop running. The terminal window is displayed to let you continue logging on to the server manually. For example: ```halt```

TIP **The script file Slip.scp, in your Program Files\Accessories directory,** contains a rather complete script to connect using SLIP. This also is a good example of using some of the more advanced script commands not covered in this chapter.

Now that you've got a script, attach it to your connection

The hard part was figuring out what needs to be in the script and actually writing the script. Before you can try it out, you have to attach it to your Dial-Up Networking connection. To attach your script to a connection, use the following steps:

Dial-Up
Scripting Tool

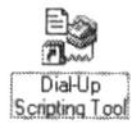

1 Run the Dial-Up Scripting Tool from the Start menu. It's installed in Program Files, Accessories. The Dial-Up Scripting Tool window should look similar to figure 14.2.

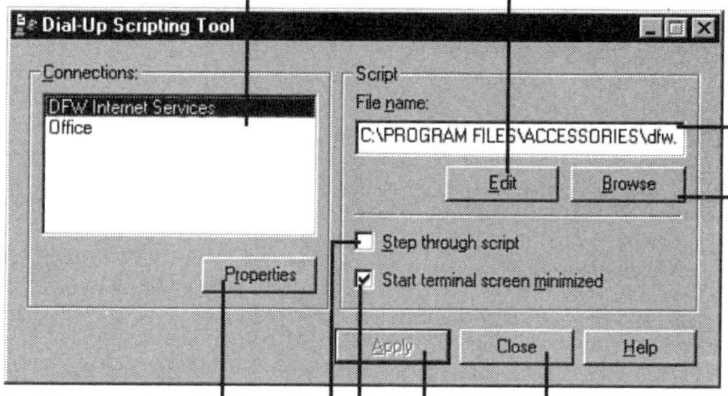
List of available dial-up connections. The current connection is highlighted.
Click to edit the script file or create a new file if one doesn't exist.
Dial-Up Scripting Tool
Connections:
DFW Internet Services
Office
Properties
Script
File name:
C:\PROGRAM FILES\ACCESSORIES\dfw.
Edit
Browse
Step through script
Start terminal screen minimized
Apply
Close
Help
The script file for the currently selected connection.
Click to attach an existing script file to the current connection.
Click to change properties for the currently selected connection.
Click to close the Dial-Up Scripting Tool window. If you haven't saved your changes, you'll be given the chance to do it.
Select to step through the screen one line at a time. This helps find errors in a script.
Click to save the changes that you've made to a connection.
If you want to watch your logon, make sure that this is unselected.

Fig. 14.2
Select a connection. Then, click on Browse to select a script from your disk.

2 In the Connections list, select the Dial-Up Networking connection that you want to change.

3 Click on Browse to select the script that you created from the disk. If you saved it in the Accessories directory and used the .SCP file extension, it will appear in the Open dialog box.

4 Click on Apply to save your changes, and click on Close to close the window.

My script doesn't work. What do I do?

The only way to really tell what is going on in your script is to step through it one line at a time. Fortunately, the Dial-Up Scripting Tool lets you do this. Select the connection that you want to work with in the Dial-Up Scripting Tool. Then, select Step Through Script.

The next time you connect using this script, you'll see a window similar to the one shown in figure 14.3.

Fig. 14.3
The Automated Script Test dialog box allows you to step through your script one line at a time. Now you can see which line isn't working.

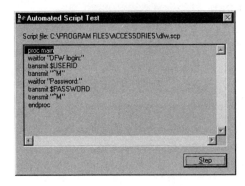

Each time that you click on <u>S</u>tep, you run one line of the script. The results are displayed in the Running dialog box shown in figure 14.4. Now you can easily see whether each line in the script is doing what you expected.

Fig. 14.4

Click on Co<u>n</u>tinue to stop stepping through the script and just run it. Or, you can click on <u>C</u>ancel to stop the script and disconnect from the server.

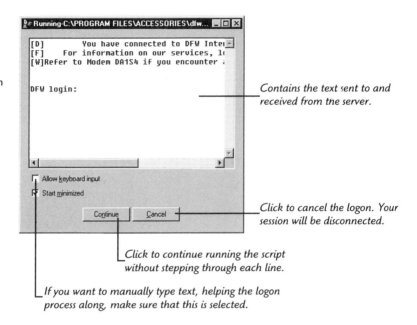

Contains the text sent to and received from tne server.

Click to cancel the logon. Your session will be disconnected.

Click to continue running the script without stepping through each line.

If you want to manually type text, helping the logon process along, make sure that this is selected.

15

Accessing Your Computer Remotely with Dial-Up Server

● **In this chapter:**

- ● **I need remote access to the computer**

- ● **Can I connect to my home computer from work?**

- ● **How do I secure my computer and network?**

- ● **Help! I can't see any resources on the server**

You don't have to be stranded while you're away. The network and all its resources are only a phone call away . . . . ➤

Remote computing is here to stay. Users like yourself are demanding that they be able to stay connected with the office while they're away. They've learned the value of getting their e-mail, an important file, or the latest client information remotely—through the phone lines. And, as you'll see, the value of remote computing is not limited to frequent travelers.

Together, Dial-Up Server and Dial-Up Networking make it possible to stay connected wherever you are. You've got everything on your desktop that you need for remote networking.

What can I do with Dial-Up Server?

The Microsoft Plus! Dial-Up Server has one very specific purpose: to provide dial-up access to your computer. You may find other useful purposes for Dial-Up Server as well. For example:

- **Network access.** If you install Dial-Up Server on a computer that is attached to your network, you can use the Dial-Up Server as a gateway to your network. Thus, you can check your e-mail, retrieve files, or do anything else that you would do if you were there.

66 *Plain English, please!*

Your computer is called the dial-up **client** and the computer that you're calling is called the dial-up **server**.

You can use your connection to simply access the resources on the dial-up server or you can use it to connect to a larger network. If you're using the dial-up server to connect to a network, the server is also called a **gateway.** 99

- **Share files from home.** I frequently find myself needing to share files with friends. But not all of my friends have e-mail handy. I turn on Dial-Up Server, share the resources to which they need access, and wait for their call.

- **Network games.** Many games are designed to run over a network for multiplayer action. Most of them work quite well over a Dial-Up Networking connection. If your game offers an alternative serial line connection, however, you should use it because it will be faster.

Dial-Up Networking is a great match for the Briefcase. For example, copy a file from the network into a briefcase on your notebook computer. When you leave the office and open the briefcase, it will try to connect to the network, using Dial-Up Networking, to update the file. This way, you can get updates to an agenda, schedule, or any file that may be changed while you're away.

The most important thing to remember about Dial-Up Networking is that connecting two computers using Dial-Up Networking creates a peer-to-peer network. Except for the speed of the connection, there is no difference from how you use peer-to-peer networks in the office. Read chapter 13, "Dial-Up Networking—Anywhere, Anytime" for more information about Dial-Up Networking. This is also a good chapter to review before trying to help someone connect to your computer using Dial-Up Server.

❝ Plain English, please!

A **peer-to-peer** network is a bunch of (two or more) individual computers networked together without a dedicated network server. The computers on the network can share resources such as folders or printers with other computers on the network.

Q&A *We've got a lot of remote users. Can we use Dial-Up Server to connect them all to the network?*

The Windows 95 Dial-Up Server supports only one phone call at a time on each computer—regardless of how many modems are installed in your computer. If you need to support a larger number of callers, a better solution is Windows NT RAS, which supports up to 256 simultaneous calls. On a more technical note, Dial-Up Server can't act as an IP router like Windows NT. Thus, a Dial-Up Server connection can't be used as a gateway to the Internet.

Q&A *Once I've connected my computer to another computer that is using Dial-Up Server, can I take the other computer over as I can with some of those remote control programs?*

No. When you've connected your computer to the other computer, you've created a peer-to-peer network. You can access any of the shared resources available on the other computer, but you can't control programs running on it. For example, you can't cause a program to load on the other computer and control how it operates. To learn more about what you can do, once you've connected to another computer, see chapter 13.

What do I need to use Dial-Up Server?

Microsoft Plus! and Windows 95 provide all the software that you need to set your computer up as a Dial-Up Server. You'll need a few more things to start taking calls, however:

- **Modem.** You'll need a modem installed and configured correctly in the Control Panel. Buy the fastest modem you can afford, such as a 28.8K modem.

- **Phone Number.** You'd think this is obvious. In many offices, however, finding out what phone number your computer is connected to can be downright impossible. Most operator services won't tell you the phone number from which you're calling. You can try connecting a single line phone to the line and calling a friend who has Caller ID. But, if you're dialing out through a PBX system, you may not be able to dial in to your computer at all.

- **Network Connection.** If your machine will be a network gateway, you should have properly installed and configured your network connection. Make sure that File and Printer Sharing for Microsoft Networks is enabled, too.

- **Dial-Up Client.** It doesn't do any good to set up the Dial-Up Server if you've got nobody to call you. Dial-Up Server supports Windows 95 Dial-Up Networking, Windows for Workgroups, Windows NT 3.1 RAS, and other clients that support PPP. For more information about PPP and other connection protocols, see chapter 13.

TIP **If you're a network administrator, this tip is for you. You can** disable Dial-Up Server for all or individual users in your organization by using the Policy Editor, which is included on the Windows 95 CD-ROM.

How do I set up Dial-Up Server

Setting up your computer as a dial-up server is easy. But you'll need to make sure that you've installed it first. To make sure that Dial-Up Server is installed, open the Dial-Up Networking folder and select Connections. Dial-Up Server is installed if you see Dial-Up Server at the bottom of the menu. Otherwise, here's how to install it:

1 Open the Control Panel and double-click on Add/Remove Programs.

2 Select Microsoft Plus! for Windows 95 from the list and click on Add/Remove.

3 Select Add/Remove.

4 Select Dial-Up Networking Server, click on Continue, and follow the instructions.

If you want your computer to be a gateway to the network, you'll need to make sure that your computer is configured correctly, has file and printer sharing enabled, and is connected to the network. Then, follow these steps to start accepting calls:

 Plain English, please!

File and Printer Sharing is a networking service that allows a computer on a network to share files and printers with other computers on the network. **"**

Dial-Up
Networking

1 Open the Dial-Up Networking folder. You'll find it in the Start menu under Programs, Accessories.

2 Select Connections, Dial-Up Server from the main menu. You'll see the dialog box in figure 15.1 if your computer is set up for share-level security. Otherwise, you'll see the dialog box in figure 15.2 if your computer is set up for user-level security.

66 *Plain English, please!*

If your machine is configured for **share-level** security, users will be prompted for the password of each resource that they attempt to use. The resource's password is assigned when you create the share. If your machine is using **user-level** security, users will be verified on a server before they can access your computer, and you can assign specific rights to specific users based upon their name. 99

Fig. 15.1
Click on Change Password to secure the Dial-Up Server. This only secures the connection. It doesn't log the user on to the network or provide access to shared resources.

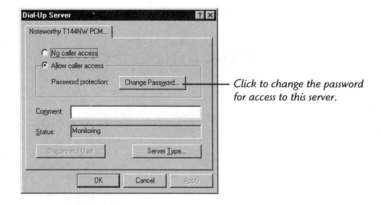

Click to change the password for access to this server.

Click to completely disable caller access to this computer.

Fig. 15.2
Click on Add to add users to the list. When users log on, their name and password are validated on the network server.

Click to add a user to the list.

The status of the call and the current user's name is displayed here.

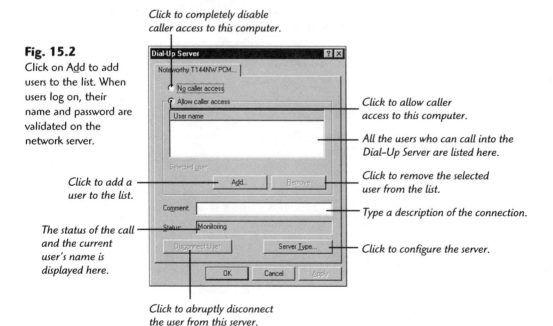

Click to allow caller access to this computer.

All the users who can call into the Dial-Up Server are listed here.

Click to remove the selected user from the list.

Type a description of the connection.

Click to configure the server.

Click to abruptly disconnect the user from this server.

3 Select <u>A</u>llow Caller Access.

4 Configure the password or user list as described in figures 15.1 or 15.2. Then, click on OK to save your changes.

 CAUTION **Don't overlook the password if you're using share-level security.** An empty password opens your machine to anyone who calls it.

Dial-Up Server will answer the call the next time the phone rings. You won't see the Dial-Up Server dialog box, however. If you want to see the status of the connection, such as who is connected, select <u>C</u>onnections, <u>D</u>ial-Up Server from the Dial-Up Networking folder's main menu.

 TIP **Don't forget to leave your Dial-Up Server running. This may sound** very simplistic, but I've gone home a few times only to find I couldn't connect to the office because I powered down my machine before I left.

 Q&A *I can connect to the Dial-Up Server. But, I don't see any of its resources in Network Neighborhood.*

If two computers are connected over a slow network connection—Dial-Up Networking—they may not exchange browsing information correctly. Browsing information represents details about the shared resources available on all the computers in the workgroup. To force the Dial-Up Server to maintain the browsing information, use the following steps:

1 Right-click on Network Neighborhood and select P<u>r</u>operties.

2 Select File and Printer Sharing for Microsoft Networks, and click Properties.

3 Select Browse Master in the <u>P</u>roperty list and select Enabled in the <u>V</u>alue list.

4 Click on OK twice. You may need to reboot both computers for this change to take effect.

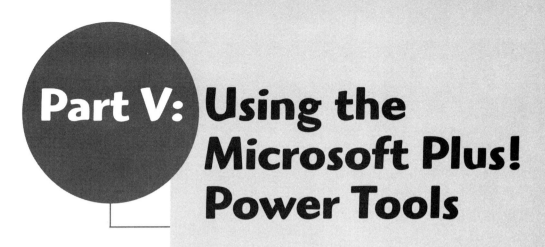

Part V: Using the Microsoft Plus! Power Tools

16

Upgrading to DriveSpace 3

● **In this chapter:**

- **Compressed drives are easy to understand**

- **Why is DriveSpace 3 better than DriveSpace?**

- **Compressing an entire drive**

- **Can I use free space to create another drive?**

- **Where did FAILSAFE.DRV come from?**

- **DriveSpace 3 and the Compression Agent**

- **Compressing a floppy disk**

Get a whole new hard drive—for free! . . . . ➤

've never met a person who had enough drive space. It seems that no matter how big of a hard drive you buy, you'll always find a way to fill it up. When I run out of room in my garage, I start throwing things away. And, when some people run out of drive space, they start throwing files away.

If you're not on a budget, you could purchase a new, larger hard drive. The price of larger drives is coming down more and more every month.

If you're running low on space and purchasing a new hard drive is not possible, you should consider drive compression. Drive compression can give you more space by making the files on your drive take less space. In this chapter, you're going to learn all about drive compression and how to use it to make more space available to fill up.

Read this chapter thoroughly before you compress your drive. Drive compression is a complex tool. If you don't feel comfortable compressing your drive yourself, call a friend to help.

 CAUTION **Before you get started with drive compression, back up the data** on your drive. Otherwise, you may permanently lose your valuable files.

Why is drive compression so special?

Because someone's finally discovered a way to stuff 10 pounds of flour into a 5-pound bag. With drive compression, you can easily stuff 500M of files into a 300M drive. It's like getting another hard drive for free.

 Plain English, please!
M is short for **megabytes**. A 100M drive will hold approximately 100 million characters, or **bytes,** of data. Likewise, **K** is short for **kilobyte,** which is one thousand bytes of data.

If you have an uncompressed, 100M drive in your computer, you can stuff only 100M of files into the drive. If you can compress all of the files on your 100M drive by half, however, you can stuff 200M of files into the drive.

Before learning how to compress your drive, it'll be useful to learn what compression ratios are, how free space is calculated, and how drive compression works.

Compression ratios

A **compression ratio** describes by how much a file is compressed. For example, a file compressed to 2.0:1 is 1/2 its normal size. A file compressed to 1.5:1 is 2/3 its normal size.

All files aren't the same. Different types of files can be compressed to different ratios. Documents, which contain mostly text, can sometimes be compressed 4 to 1. You'll be lucky, however, to compress an executable program 1.5 to 1. That's because a program's file contains binary data, which is harder to compress than the text found in most documents.

 Plain English, please!

> An **executable program** is a file on your hard drive that contains the instructions that the computer uses to perform a particular task. A **data file** contains the information that you store on your computer, such as word processing and spreadsheet files.

Table 16.1 shows the compression types supported by Microsoft Plus! and the average compression ratio that you can expect from each.

 Plain English, please!

> **Compression Agent** is a program that compresses your hard drive while you're not using your computer. It gives you more control over how much of your computer's performance you sacrifice to gain more free space on your hard drive. You'll find detailed coverage of Compression Agent in chapter 17.

Table 16.1 Types of compression in Compression Agent

Type	Average Ratio	Description
UltraPack	2.6:1	The most complete file compression possible; UltraPack is appropriate only for files that are seldom used. It can significantly hinder the speed of a 486 if you compress frequently used files.
HiPack	2:1	HiPack is better than DriveSpace 3's Standard compression because more time is spent compressing the file while you're away from your computer. Infrequently used files, as well as most files on a Pentium computer, use HiPack the best.

continues

Table 16.1   Continued

Type	Average Ratio	Description
Standard	1.8:1	Standard compression is not directly supported by Compression Agent. If DriveSpace 3 is compressing files, any file not compressed by the Compression Agent will be compressed using standard compression.
None	1:1	No compression. Compressing frequently used files can dramatically slow down the speed of those files.

Estimating free space is a bit like doing the laundry

Remember the last time you did the laundry? How did you know how many towels would fit in each load? Experience—you've done the laundry before. You've probably put too many towels in the washer at times, however, and had to remove some. If you don't know exactly how much the towels will squish together, all you can do is estimate and then make adjustments later.

Drive compression works the same way. It only estimates how much space is available on your drive based on its estimate of how much the files will squish together. DriveSpace 3 gets its estimate from how much the files on your hard drive are currently compressed. And, at times, it may get a bit optimistic.

For example, I'll assume that you have a 100M hard drive. (You won't find many 100M hard drives anymore, but this keeps the math simple.) If you've got 100M of files compressed down to 50M on the drive, the average compression ratio for the drive is 2:1 (the left side of the ratio is the total size of the compressed files divided by the size of the drive; the right side of the ratio is always a one). That's pretty good. So, how much free space do you have? You've physically got 50M free on the drive. So, DriveSpace 3 figures that everything else you're going to write to the drive will be compressed 2:1, too. The property sheet for the drive will report about 100M free.

Q&A *My compressed drive reports 100M free. Why can I write only 75M to it?*

The files that you're writing to the drive didn't compress as well as the average ratio DriveSpace 3 had estimated. Consider the example in this section. The files that you're writing to the drive may compress better or worse than the average compression, but seldom will they all be compressed at the average ratio. If the files that you're writing compress only 1.5:1, then there is really 75M of free space on the drive.

I'm pretty sure that the estimated compression ratio that Drivespace 3 is using is incorrect. How do I adjust it?

Select Advanced, Change Ratio. Then, adjust the slider to the left for a smaller compression ratio, or to the right for a bigger compression ratio.

Here's how it works

You'll notice that you don't have to install any special hardware to create a compressed drive. So, where does it go?

When you create a compressed drive, its contents are stored in a compressed volume file on your computer's hard drive. This file is usually called something like DRVSPACE.000. Note that you normally don't see this file, because it's hidden. The CVF may occupy 100M on your hard drive but may contain 200M of compressed files.

 Plain English, please!

A **host** drive is a physical drive in your computer that contains a **compressed volume file** (CVF). Special programs called **device drivers** make the contents of the CVF look like another drive on your computer.

Figure 16.1 shows the relationship between a compressed drive and the CVF with a real example. The host drive is H and the compressed drive is drive C. The CVF called DRVSPACE.000 uses 320M of actual hard drive space on drive H, but the compressed drive C contains 197M of data and potentially 213M of free space.

Fig. 16.1
When you're looking at drive C:, you're really just peering into the contents of the CVF on drive H.

DRVSPACE.000 is using 320 M of space on drive H.

This window shows the contents of the compressed drive C where Windows 95 and my program files are installed. All of this is compressed and stored in the CVF file DRVSPACE.000.

The capacity will change as estimated compression ratio changes and after you run the Compression Agent.

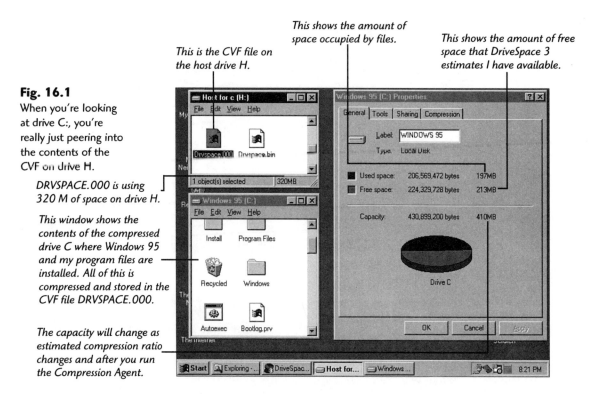

This is the CVF file on the host drive H.

This shows the amount of space occupied by files.

This shows the amount of free space that DriveSpace 3 estimates I have available.

DriveSpace 3 is better than DriveSpace

You've already got the Windows 95 DriveSpace utility. Why should you use Microsoft Plus! DriveSpace 3 instead? Because it's better. DriveSpace has a lot of limitations that were inherited from its predecessor, DoubleSpace. But DriveSpace 3 makes up for it:

- **Bigger drives.** The DriveSpace utility that comes with Windows 95 can compress only hard drives that are smaller than 512M. Larger drives, however, are becoming more popular. DriveSpace 3 will compress a drive that is up to 2G in size.

- **Speed.** DriveSpace 3 is 20 percent faster than DriveSpace. For example, a file that takes 5 seconds to load using DriveSpace may take only 4 seconds using DriveSpace 3. It seems like splitting hairs. But when you load hundreds and hundreds of files each day, as Windows 95 does behind the scenes, you'll notice a significant improvement in how fast your computer operates.

- **Compression methods.** DriveSpace 3 supports more compression methods than DriveSpace. HiPack and Ultrapack compress files more than the standard compression. See table 16.1, earlier in this chapter, for a description of the compression types supported by DriveSpace 3.

- **Feedback.** If you wanted to get information about a compressed drive, where would you look? The property sheet for the drive? DriveSpace 3 adds a tab to the drive's property sheet that displays information about the drive and its compression. Figure 16.2 shows the Compression tab of the property sheet for a compressed drive. Note that there are no entries for UltraPack or HiPack files because the Compression Agent hasn't been run on this computer yet.

Fig. 16.2
The Compression tab on a drive's property sheet shows how much DriveSpace 3 is relying on each compression type.

This column shows the average compression ratio for each compression method.

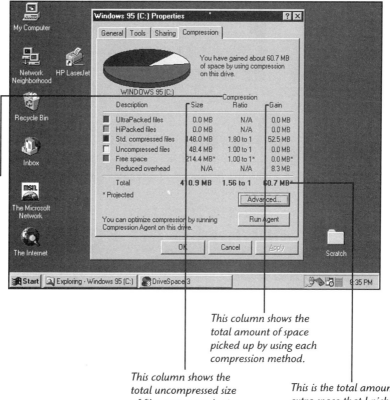

This column shows the total amount of space picked up by using each compression method.

This column shows the total uncompressed size of files compressed using each compression method.

This is the total amount of extra space that I picked up by using DriveSpace 3.

How do I upgrade to DriveSpace 3?

DriveSpace

Upgrading your computer to use DriveSpace 3 is a great choice. It's easy to do, too, and will give you much more drive space. To upgrade a DoubleSpace or DriveSpace compressed drive to DriveSpace 3, use the following steps:

1 Start DriveSpace 3. You'll find it in the Start menu under Programs, Accessories, System Tools.

2 Select the DoubleSpace or DriveSpace drive in Drives On This Computer.

3 Select Drive, Upgrade from the DriveSpace 3 main menu and click on Start to begin.

4 If DriveSpace 3 asks you to insert your Startup disk, insert it into the drive and click on Yes followed by Create Disk.

5 Click on Upgrade Now.

CAUTION If you don't already have a Startup disk, take this opportunity to make one. If for some reason your computer doesn't start, the Startup disk may be the only way to access your drives.

TIP You can't directly upgrade a floppy disk to DriveSpace 3. Instead, copy its contents to your hard drive, delete the CVF file from the floppy, recompress the floppy using DriveSpace 3, and copy the contents back to the floppy.

I want to compress an entire drive

CAUTION Don't start the compression process if you'll need your computer soon. The compression process can take several hours and your computer won't be available. You can't abandon the process once it begins.

Compressing your entire drive is the preferred way to increase your hard drive capacity. It takes longer and slows your computer down a bit more, however, than creating a new compressed drive from the free space on an existing drive. Because you'll be using the entire drive for your CVF, you'll have more space available than if you compressed only the free space available on the drive. Here's what happens:

- A CVF file is created on the host drive that occupies almost the entire drive.

- If you're compressing your boot drive, enough system files are left on the host drive to allow the computer to start up and read the compressed drive.

- All of the files that were originally on your host drive are compressed and moved over to the compressed drive.

- Windows 95 thoughtfully hides the host drive from view after it is compressed. You won't see it in Internet Explorer.

❝ *Plain English, please!*

A **boot** drive is the drive on which Windows 95 is installed. It is almost always drive C. ❞

TIP **If you read files from your floppies more often than you write** files, you may be able to improve the performance of a floppy disk by compressing it, because decompressing data in memory is significantly faster than reading it from the floppy.

To compress a drive on your computer, use the following steps:

DriveSpace

1 Start DriveSpace 3. You'll find it in the Start menu under Programs, Accessories, System Tools. Figure 16.3 shows the DriveSpace 3 main window.

Fig. 16.3
DriveSpace 3 displays a list of compressed drives, uncompressed drives, and hosts on your computer.

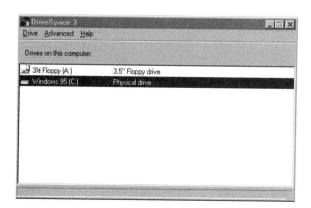

2 Select an uncompressed (physical drive) in Drives On This Computer.

3 Select Drive, Compress from the DriveSpace 3 main menu. DriveSpace 3 displays the dialog box shown in figure 16.4.

Fig. 16.4
DriveSpace 3 shows you how much space you'll pick up by compressing this drive. This is only an estimate.

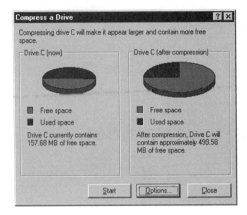

4 Click Start to begin compressing your drive. If you're having second thoughts, click on Close. If you have already clicked Start, you'll have another chance to change your mind after you've created your Startup disk.

5 Click on Yes to update your Startup disk. Insert the appropriate disks when prompted. After you've created your Startup disk, DriveSpace 3 gives you one more chance to change your mind (see figure 16.5).

Fig. 16.5
If you haven't backed up your computer recently, click on Back Up Files to do so now.

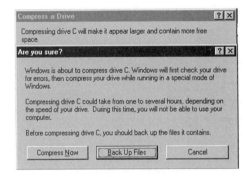

Backing up your computer's hard drive is essential. You'll find the task much easier, though, if you use a tape or zip drive. Both types of drives are available at reasonable prices through your computer retailer.

6 Click on Compress Now. DriveSpace 3 will check your drive for errors before it starts compressing it.

7 If you're compressing a drive that is always in use, such as the drive on which you installed Windows 95, DriveSpace will display the dialog box shown in figure 16.6. Click on Yes to allow it to restart your computer in a special mode that allows it to continue without interruption. When it's finished compressing your drive, it will restart Windows 95. Be patient: This process can take several hours.

Fig. 16.6
DriveSpace 3 may need to restart your computer in a special mode if you're compressing your boot drive.

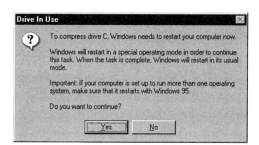

8 If this is the first time that you've compressed a drive, DriveSpace 3 displays the DriveSpace Performance Tuning dialog box after your computer restarts. Click on High Performance (recommended) if you want to use the Compression Agent to compress files while you aren't using your computer; click on More Free Disk Space if you want to get as much free space as possible; or click on Custom if you want to configure DriveSpace 3 yourself.

The compression process was designed to be safe. As a test of faith and courage, I turned my computer off while DriveSpace 3 was compressing my drive. After I restarted it a few hours later, DriveSpace 3 continued compressing my drive as if nothing happened. I lost nothing!

I noticed a new directory on the host drive called FAILSAFE.DRV. Can I remove this directory from my drive?

DriveSpace 3 may have had to restart your computer in a special mode to finish compressing your drive. It will do this if you're compressing a drive that is always changing, such as the drive on which you installed Windows

95. The files required for this special mode are installed in the
FAILSAFE.DRV directory. You can safely remove this entire directory only
after the compression process is completed.

I want to create a new compressed drive with free space on an uncompressed drive

If you don't want to wait on the compression process, you'll want to create a
new compressed drive using the free space available on an uncompressed
drive. Compressing the free space on an existing drive is different from
compressing the entire drive. Here's how:

- The files on the host drive are not compressed.

- You now have two drives in Internet Explorer instead of one. The host
  drive keeps its drive letter and the new compressed drive gets its own
  drive letter.

- The host drive contains less drive space because the compressed drive's
  CVF file is stored in its root directory. Note that you don't have to use
  all of the free space on the drive.

First, create a new compressed drive

Creating a new drive from the free space on an existing drive is easy. Follow
these steps:

DriveSpace

1 Start DriveSpace 3. You'll find it in the Start menu under <u>P</u>rograms,
Accessories, System Tools.

2 Select the physical drive that you want to host your new compressed
drive in Drives On This Computer.

3 Select <u>A</u>dvanced, <u>C</u>reate Empty from the DriveSpace main menu.
DriveSpace 3 displays the dialog box shown in figure 16.7.

Fig. 16.7
You can specify the amount of space to use on the host, size of the compressed drive, or the free space left on the host, and DriveSpace 3 will calculate the other numbers.

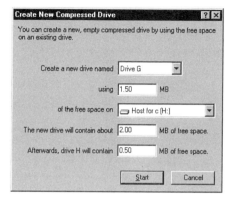

4 Click on <u>S</u>tart to start the compression process.

5 Click on <u>Y</u>es to update your start-up disk. Insert the appropriate disks when prompted.

6 If you're compressing a drive that is always in use, such as the drive on which you installed Windows 95, DriveSpace will display the dialog box shown in figure 16.7 earlier in this chapter. Click on <u>Y</u>es to allow it to restart your computer in a special mode that allows it to continue without interruption. When it's finished compressing your drive, it'll restart Windows 95.

Click on <u>C</u>lose after DriveSpace 3 is finished creating your new compressed drive.

Then, adjust the size as your needs change

If the compressed drive that you created from the free space of another drive runs out of space, you can make it bigger. Your computer will run slower, though, as you rely on the compressed drive more. Also, if your host drive is running low on space, you can make your compressed drive smaller to give space back to the host drive. Here's how:

1 Start DriveSpace 3. You'll find it in the Start menu under <u>P</u>rograms, Accessories, System Tools.

2 Select <u>D</u>rive, <u>A</u>djust Free Space from the DriveSpace 3 main menu. DriveSpace 3 displays the Adjust Free Space dialog box shown in figure 16.8.

Fig. 16.8
As you adjust the slider, the sizes displayed for the compressed and host drives are updated. You can set the size of both drives exactly as you want.

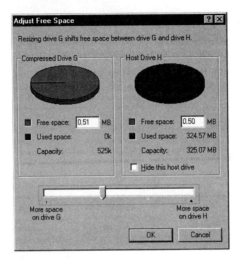

3 Move the slider to the left to give more space to the compressed drive or move the slider to the right to give more space to the host drive.

4 Click on OK when you're finished and DriveSpace 3 will adjust the space for the compressed drive.

I don't want my files compressed anymore

If you're dissatisfied with the performance of your drive compression, you may want to decompress your drive. When you decompress a compressed drive, the files on the compressed drive are copied to the host drive and the CVF is deleted. Then, the host will get its old drive letter back.

For example, assume that you have a compressed drive C, and the host drive is H. If you decompress drive C, its contents are copied to drive H, the CVF file is removed from drive H, and drive H becomes drive C again.

TIP   **Before trying to decompress a compressed drive, make sure that** there is plenty of space available on the host drive; at least 2M and possibly more, depending on how much you've compressed.

To decompress a compressed drive, follow these steps:

1 Start DriveSpace 3. You'll find it in the Start menu under Programs, Accessories, System Tools.

2 Select Drive, Uncompress from the DriveSpace 3 main menu. DriveSpace 3 displays the dialog box shown in figure 16.9.

Fig. 16.9
This dialog shows you the current sizes of both the compressed drive and the host. It also shows you the size of the host after the compressed drive is decompressed.

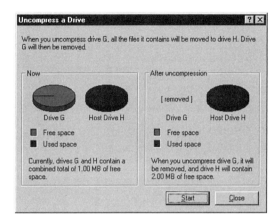

3 Click on Start. DriveSpace 3 starts the decompression process after scanning the drive for errors.

4 Decompressing your drive can take as little as a few minutes for a very small drive to as much as several hours for a larger drive. After DriveSpace 3 is finished, click on Close.

 TIP **Decompressing your hard drive will improve the performance of** your computer. You won't have as much free space available after you do it, however. Also note that if the total size of all your compressed files is larger than the size of your uncompressed hard drive, you won't be able to uncompress your files.

How do I change the compression method?

You can easily change the compression method that DriveSpace 3 uses for your computer. If you chose High Performance the first time that you compressed a drive, however, as described earlier in this chapter, or if you set up drive compression as described in chapter 17, "Getting More Disk Space with Compression Agent," I recommend leaving these settings alone. Otherwise, you may notice a decrease in the performance of your computer. If you want to change the compression method, use the following steps:

DriveSpace

1 Start DriveSpace 3. You'll find it in the Start menu under Programs, Accessories, System Tools.

2 Select Advanced, Settings from the DriveSpace 3 main menu.

3 Choose one of the compression methods shown in table 16.1 from the dialog box shown in figure 16.1.

Fig. 16.10

Change the compression method that DriveSpace 3 is using for your computer. Notice that UltraPack is available only in Compression Agent.

4 Click on OK to save your settings, then close DriveSpace 3.

17

Getting More Disk Space with Compression Agent

● **In this chapter:**

- **This agent cleans up while you're away**

- **Is it going to make my computer slower?**

- **Compression ratios in plain English**

- **Will it work while I'm not using my computer?**

- **Setting up the agent for the best performance**

You can have your cake and eat it, too. Compression Agent gives you more disk space without hurting your computer's performance . . . . ➤

DriveSpace 3, discussed in chapter 16, "Upgrading to DriveSpace 3," is compressing and decompressing files all the time. It doesn't give you much of a choice. The only control you have over it is the type of compression it uses: HiPack or Standard. See table 17.1 later in this chapter for a description of these compression types.

If you use standard compression, the performance of your computer may suffer. And, if you have a 386 or 486 computer, HiPack compression will bring your computer to its knees!

Compression Agent, however, gives you an alternative. It's a little like your mother: coming along behind you to clean up your mess.

Compression Agent cleans up after you're done

Wouldn't it be great if you could write files to your hard drive without compressing them? Then, when you're away from your computer, a really good friend could come along and compress your files for you. Seems like the best of both worlds. It would be even better if your friend would compress files that you don't use much, and leave files that you use frequently alone.

It's not likely that any of your friends will do this for you. Compression Agent will, though. Compression Agent compresses files while you're not using your computer. It also allows you to specify exactly which files get compressed, and how much they get compressed. Files that aren't compressed are faster to load than files that are compressed.

 Q&A *I've got a 540M hard drive and have only used 400M. Do I need disk compression?*

No. The only thing you'll accomplish by using disk compression is slowing down your computer. Consider using compression when you've filled up that hard drive.

Q&A ***Why should I care about performance? Haven't computers become so fast that it doesn't matter anymore?***

No. Every time that hardware manufacturers make bigger, faster machines, software companies make bigger, more powerful programs that require more drive space.

After you have installed and configured Compression Agent, you'll notice significant improvements in the performance of your compressed disks. And, over time, the performance will improve as Compression Agent learns more about how you use the files on your computer. What a friend!

How does Compression Agent know when to work?

The System Agent (see chapter 18) is a Microsoft Plus! tool that allows you to schedule programs to run at specific times. You'll find it next to the clock in the lower-right corner of your desktop. You can schedule Compression Agent to run at times that you choose. For example, you can schedule Compression Agent to run at 2:00 a.m. every Monday morning, 2:00 a.m. every morning (recommended), or 15 minutes after every hour (not recommended because it will frequently interrupt your work). Many other possibilities exist.

Compression Agent stays out of the way, too. You can direct the System Agent to interrupt Compression Agent if you start using your computer while it's compressing files.

You don't want to compress all of your files

When you open a compressed file, Windows 95 has to uncompress it before you can use it. This takes time. Therefore, if you don't compress the files that you use frequently, you can save that time. Likewise, if you do compress the files that you don't use much, you can save a lot of disk space.

Remember the 80/20 rule? It says something like, "You can fool 20 percent of the people 80 percent of the time." An 80/20 rule applies to your files as well: about 20 percent of the files on your hard drive are used 80 percent of the time.

Q&A *I spent a lot of money on all these programs and better be using more than 20 percent of my files. Why would 80 percent of the files on my drive not be used much?*

You probably perform many of the same tasks each day: check your e-mail, write a memo, and play a game. Also, most programs include many files that are never used by the average user. These files are for super-duper functionality that only a few people actually use.

You use some files all the time: WINHELP.EXE, SOL.EXE, PLUS!.BMP, and many programs such as your favorite word processor. You may also use your data files (documents, spreadsheets, e-mail, and so on) frequently. These don't take up a significant amount of hard drive space. So, you can tell Compression Agent not to compress them—saving time. In fact, you can eliminate entire folders, file types, or specific files from the compression process.

Control how much files are compressed

Not only can you control which files are compressed and when they are compressed, you can specify how much they are compressed by choosing a different compression method for different types of files.

Q&A *Why should I care which compression method is used on my files?*

The more a file is compressed, the longer it takes to load. If you fully compress a file that you use often, you'll notice a definite lag in load time.

Compression Agent supports four types of compression: UltraPack, HiPack, Standard, and none. Table 17.1 describes each compression type and gives an average compression ratio. Files can be compressed using different techniques depending on their status. An older file that is compressed using UltraPack may be decompressed to HiPack if it is used again.

 Plain English, please!

A **compression ratio** describes how much a file is compressed. For example, a file compressed to **2.0:1** is 1/2 its normal size. A file compressed to **1.5:1** is 2/3 its normal size. 🟡🟡

Table 17.1   Types of compression in Compression Agent

Type	Average Ratio	Description
UltraPack	2.6:1	The most complete file compression possible. UltraPack is appropriate only for files that are seldom used. It can significantly hinder the speed of a 486 if you compress frequently used files.
HiPack	2:1	HiPack is better than DriveSpace 3's Standard compression because more time is spent compressing the file while you're away from your computer. Infrequently used files, as well as most files on a Pentium computer, use HiPack the best.
Standard	1.8:1	Standard compression is not directly supported by Compression Agent. If DriveSpace 3 is compressing files, any file not compressed by the Compression Agent will be compressed using Standard compression.
None	1:1	No compression. Compressing frequently used files can dramatically slow down the speed of those files.

Windows 95 is terrific about providing a lot of feedback. For example, you can see how much disk space each compression technique is saving in the property sheet for each drive. To display the property sheet for a compressed drive, follow these steps:

1 Right-click on a compressed drive in the Explorer.

2 Select Properties.

3 Click on the Compression tab of the property sheet. The property sheet should look similar to figure 17.1 that follows.

Fig. 17.1
The Compression tab shows you how much of your files are stored using each compression technique. It also shows you the compression ratio and total savings for each technique.

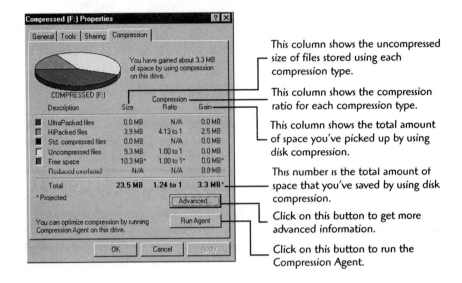

This column shows the uncompressed size of files stored using each compression type.

This column shows the compression ratio for each compression type.

This column shows the total amount of space you've picked up by using disk compression.

This number is the total amount of space that you've saved by using disk compression.

Click on this button to get more advanced information.

Click on this button to run the Compression Agent.

I'm sold. How do I set it up?

You'll want a good compression strategy before you get started. I recommend the following strategy because it provides the most disk space that you can get without severely impacting the performance of your computer:

- Set up DriveSpace 3 to not compress files unless your hard drive is almost full.

- Set up Compression Agent to use UltraPack on files that are more than 30 days old.

- Set up Compression Agent to reduce the amount of compression on files that are used frequently.

- Set up Compression Agent to not compress your documents, spreadsheets, and so on.

- Schedule Compression Agent to run while you're away from your computer. You can schedule it to run at night if you leave your computer on.

TIP **Wait! Disk compression is a fairly complex topic. If you're not** comfortable with following the steps in this section, get a friend to help.

CAUTION **Before setting up compression for the first time, back up your** hard drive to prevent permanent data loss. Although Microsoft has gone to great pains to make disk compression as safe as possible, a few users have lost valuable data.

Turn DriveSpace 3 compression off

Turning DriveSpace 3 compression off allows you to completely control which files are compressed using Compression Agent. To turn DriveSpace 3 compression off, use the following steps:

DriveSpace

1 Select DriveSpace from the Start menu.

2 Select Advanced, Settings from the DriveSpace main menu. DriveSpace will display the dialog box showing in figure 17.2.

Fig. 17.2
Select "No compres-
sion, unless drive is at
least full, then use
standard compression"
to put Compression
Agent in control.

3 Select "No compression, unless drive is at least __ full, then use stan-dard compression." Change the percentage to 90 percent in the field provided. 90 percent is the default for this field.

4 Click on OK and close DriveSpace 3.

Q&A *I can't find DriveSpace or Compression Agent in the Start menu.*

When you install Microsoft Plus!, it puts DriveSpace and Compression Agent in Programs, Accessories, System Tools. You can also start DriveSpace 3 in My Computer. Right-click on a hard drive, select Properties, and click on the Compression tab. If your drive is already compressed, click on Advanced to run DriveSpace 3 or click on Run Agent to start the Compression Agent. If your drive is not compressed, click Compress Drive to start DriveSpace 3 compression for that drive.

Turn UltraPack on for older files

UltraPack is the most compression that you can get for your money. You don't want to use it with frequently used files, however, because it takes too long to read them. Therefore, you'll turn it on only for files older than 30 days. To do this, follow these steps:

Compression
Agent

1 Select Compression Agent from the Start menu.

2 Click on Settings, and Compression Agent will display the dialog box shown in figure 17.3.

File date and time stamping

Each time that a file is accessed on your computer, Windows 95 records the date and time in the file's properties. It also records the date and time of when a file is created or modified. Backup programs typically use the date and time that a file was modified to determine whether a file has been backed up recently. The date and time that the file was last accessed is used by Compression Agent to determine how old a file is. You can see the date that a file was created, modified, or accessed by right-clicking on the file and selecting Properties.

Fig. 17.3
Choose when to use
UltraPack and which
compression method
to use for files not
compressed with
UltraPack.

3 Select "Only files not used within the last __ days" and set the number of days to 30 in the field provided.

TIP **The more days that you specify in "Only files not used within the last___days", the better the performance of a compressed disk.** For example, setting this field to 90 days causes fewer files to be compressed, thus less time is required to load them.

4 Select No, Store Them Uncompressed to have Compression Agent leave frequently used files uncompressed.

Reduce compression on frequently used files

Compression Agent can automatically reduce the compression level on frequently used files. This saves time reading files that you use all the time, such as some system files or documents. To allow Compression Agent to reduce compression on frequently used files, follow these steps:

1 Click Advanced on the Compression Agent Settings dialog box previously opened. Compression Agent displays the dialog box shown in figure 17.4.

Fig. 17.4
Dont allow the agent
to reduce compression
on files if you're
running short of disk
space.

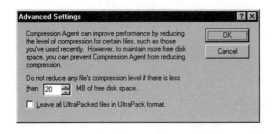

2 Deselect "Leave all UltraPacked files in UltraPack format."

3 Click on OK to close the dialog box.

Don't compress documents, spread-sheets, and so on

You don't want loading documents, spreadsheets, and other frequently used files to take any longer than necessary. In Compression Agent, you can completely turn off compression for specific files, folders, or types of files.

 Plain English, please!

> A files **type** indicates which program was used to create it. For example, an .XLS file is a Microsoft Excel spreadsheet, whereas a .DOC is a Microsoft Word document. **,,**

The best approach is to turn off compression for specific file types so that you don't have to find all the files or folders on your hard drive. To turn off compression for .DOC and .XLS files, use the following steps:

1 Click Exceptions on the Compression Agent Settings dialog box previously opened. Compression Agent displays the Exceptions dialog box shown in figure 17.5.

Fig. 17.5
You can instruct Compression Agent to use a specific compression technique on a file, folder, or type of file.

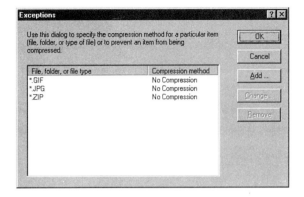

2 Click on <u>A</u>dd to add a file type to the list shown in the figure. Compression Agent displays the Add Exceptions dialog box shown in Figure 17.6.

Fig. 17.6
You add new compression exceptions using the Add Exceptions dialog box.

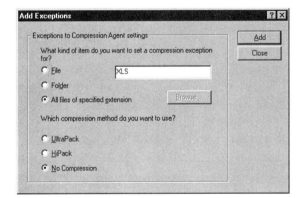

3 Click on All files of a selected <u>t</u>ype.

4 Type **DOC** in the field provided to specify document files.

5 Select <u>N</u>o Compression to disable compression for that file type.

6 Click on <u>A</u>dd to add the exception for .DOC files to the list.

7 Repeat steps 3 through 6 for the .XLS file type.

8 Click on OK to close the Exceptions dialog box.

Compression Agent will try its hardest to compress a file—even if it can't be compressed any more than it already is. Some files, such as .GIF, .JPG, and .ZIP, can't be compressed any more. Disabling compression for these file types keeps DriveSpace 3 from wasting time figuring this out.

❝ *Plain English, please*

.GIF and **.JPG** are picture files that are already compressed. **.ZIP** is an archive that compresses and stores many individual files of any type.

Schedule Compression Agent to run while you're sleeping

When Compression Agent starts compressing files, your system will grind to a halt. You want Compression Agent to run when you aren't using your computer—preferably at night. To schedule Compression Agent to run at 2:00 a.m. every morning, use the following steps:

If you don't want to leave your computer on at night, you can also have Compression Agent run during your lunch hour or while you're in that dreaded, daily staff meeting. Just change the time from 2:00 a.m. to the time of the meeting.

System Agent

1 Start the System Agent by double-clicking on its icon in the bottom right corner of your display.

2 If Compression Agent is already in the System Agents list, double-click on it and go to step 4. Otherwise, select Program, Schedule a New <u>P</u>rogram from the System Agent main menu. System Agent displays the Schedule a New Program dialog box shown in figure 17.7.

Fig. 17.7
Schedule Compression
Agent to run at night.
Click on When to Run
to schedule it.

3 Select Compression Agent from the Program drop-down list and click When to Run. Compression Agent displays the schedule dialog box shown in figure 17.8.

Fig. 17.8
Schedule Compression
agent to run every day
at 2:00 a.m.

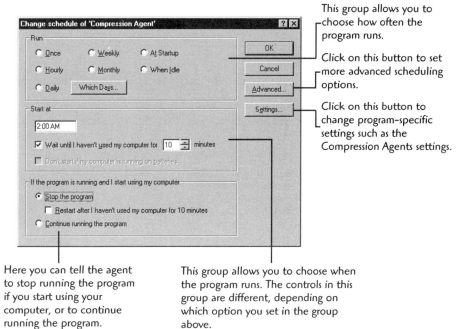

This group allows you to choose how often the program runs.

Click on this button to set more advanced scheduling options.

Click on this button to change program-specific settings such as the Compression Agents settings.

Here you can tell the agent to stop running the program if you start using your computer, or to continue running the program.

This group allows you to choose when the program runs. The controls in this group are different, depending on which option you set in the group above.

4 Select Daily and type **2:00 AM** in the Start At field provided. Click on OK.

Compression Agent will run every night at 2:00 a.m. You can also use a more advanced schedule for Compression Agent. For more information about advanced scheduling with the System Agent, see chapter 18, "Using System Agent to Maintain Your Computer."

 TIP   **If you scheduled Compression Agent to run during lunch, click on** Stop the Program in the Schedule a New Program dialog box. If Compression Agent is still running when you start using your program again, the System Agent will stop it dead in its tracks. Relax. It won't hurt anything.

18

Using System Agent to Maintain Your Computer

● **In this chapter:**

- **Going to sleep? Put your computer to work**

- **How do you check for errors?**

- **How do you run several programs at one time?**

- **How can you schedule other programs?**

A personal assistant saves you time and trouble; System Agent does the same . . . . ▶

Most of us have never had a personal assistant (your spouse doesn't count). But imagine, if you will, a person dedicated to freeing your schedule from mundane tasks that you perform periodically. Would he pick up your cleaning? Take care of your car inspection? Pick up your mail? My personal assistant would proof this book.

Now, think about your computer for a moment. What would you have your personal assistant do? Check your drive for errors? Check to see whether you have enough drive space left? Defragment your drive so that it runs faster? Compress the files on your drive so that you get more space?

If so, you don't need a personal assistant. You need System Agent. You can put programs on System Agent's schedule and it will run them for you. In this chapter, I explore some of the things that you can ask System Agent to do to save you time and trouble.

System Agent has an appointment book

System Agent keeps a schedule just like a personal assistant. If you want to get it to do anything, you'll need to schedule it. Don't believe me? Double-click on the System Agent icon on the lower-right corner of your display—next to the clock, as shown in figure 18.1.

Fig. 18.1
Double-click on the
System Agent to open
its schedule. Right-click
on it to see more
options such as
Suspend System Agent.

Double-click here to
open System Agent.

TIP **If you don't see the System Agent's icon next to the clock, select**
Programs, Accessories, System Tools, System Agent from the Start menu.
Then, click on Yes to turn it on.

System Agent already has four things scheduled

Figure 18.2 shows System Agent's schedule. Wow! You've already got four things scheduled for it to do and you haven't lifted a finger yet. When you installed System Agent, it asked you whether you leave your computer on at night. Then, it scheduled the following four programs accordingly:

- **Low Disk-Space Notification.** Checks your computer's hard drive every 15 minutes for free space.

- **ScanDisk for Windows (Standard Test).** Checks your computer's hard drive for errors every Monday through Friday at 6:00 a.m. It does only a light test so that your computer isn't kept busy for too long.

- **Disk Defragmenter.** Arranges the information on your computer's hard drive so that it loads faster and doesn't take as much drive space. It does this every Monday through Friday at midnight.

- **ScanDisk for Windows (Thorough Test).** Checks your computer's hard drive for errors on the first day of every month at 9:00 p.m. It does an extensive test that will take a while to perform.

Fig. 18.2

This is System Agent's schedule. It already has four things scheduled.

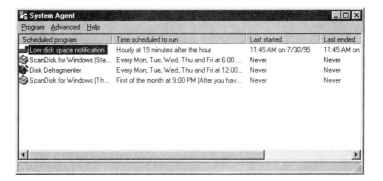

Take a look at the schedule for one of them

To look closer at the schedule for Low Disk-Space Notification, double-click on it in the list to show its properties. Then, click on Change Schedule. You should see the dialog box shown in figure 18.3. This is where you will control the schedule for Low Disk-Space Notification. You can schedule it to run once, hourly, daily, weekly, monthly, when Windows 95 starts, or when you're not using your computer.

Fig. 18.3
You've got complete control over the schedule for Low Disk-Space Notification.

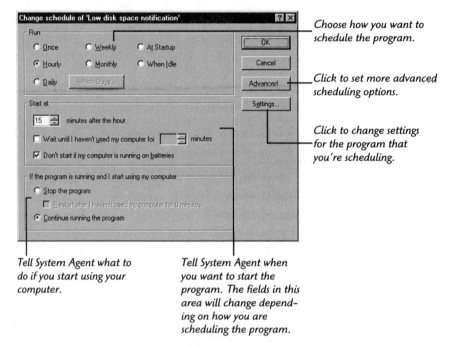

Choose how you want to schedule the program.

Click to set more advanced scheduling options.

Click to change settings for the program that you're scheduling.

Tell System Agent what to do if you start using your computer.

Tell System Agent when you want to start the program. The fields in this area will change depending on how you are scheduling the program.

How do I schedule a program in System Agent?

Before you schedule a program, you'll need to decide a few things first. Here's a list to help you plan:

- What program are you scheduling? You'll need to know its file name.

- How frequently do you want it to run: once, hourly, daily, weekly, monthly, when Windows 95 starts, or when you stop using your computer?

- Do you want it to wait until you're not using your computer? For how long?

- Is your computer a portable? Do you want to keep System Agent from running programs if you're running on battery power?

- What do you want System Agent to do if you start using your computer before the scheduled program is finished running?

Now that you've thought through the issues, you'll follow a two-step process to schedule your program: tell the System Agent what program to run and when to run it.

First, tell System Agent what program to schedule

If you don't have System Agent running on your desktop, double-click on its icon as shown in figure 18.1. Then, use the following steps to tell System Agent what program you want to schedule:

1 Select Program, Schedule a New Program from the System Agent main menu. It displays the dialog box shown in figure 18.4. Alternatively, if you want to change the properties for an existing program, double-click on it in the list to display the same dialog box.

Fig. 18.4
Select a program from the Program list or click on Browse to pick a program from the drive.

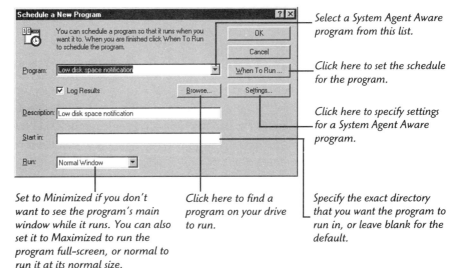

Select a System Agent Aware program from this list.

Click here to set the schedule for the program.

Click here to specify settings for a System Agent Aware program.

Set to Minimized if you don't want to see the program's main window while it runs. You can also set it to Maximized to run the program full–screen, or normal to run it at its normal size.

Click here to find a program on your drive to run.

Specify the exact directory that you want the program to run in, or leave blank for the default.

2 Select a System Agent Aware program in the Program list, or click on Browse to pick a program from your drive. A System Agent Aware program works better because it is designed especially for the System Agent.

Plain English, please!

A program is System Agent Aware if it was created specifically to work with System Agent. Aware programs can be interrupted and restarted by System Agent.

3 Type a descriptive name for the program in Description. Make sure to give it a name that you can pick out of a list.

4 Specify the directory in which you want to start the program.

5 Select Minimized in the Run list if you don't want to see the program's main window while it runs.

6 Click on Settings if you want to set any additional settings for a System Agent Aware program, such as which drive to run.

> **TIP** You can schedule more than one program with a single entry by putting the programs in a Windows 95 batch file. Then, use the batch file as the program name in the properties dialog box. For more information about creating batch files in Windows 95, see *Special Edition Using Windows 95* published by Que.

Then, tell System Agent when to run it

After you've told System Agent what program you want to run, you need to schedule it. Click on When to Run and it displays the familiar dialog box shown in figure 18.3. Incidentally, you can click on When to Run on an existing program's properties dialog box to change its schedule. The top part of the dialog box has many options for the frequency:

- **Once.** The program will run at the day and time that you specify. It will run only once.

- **Hourly.** You can tell System Agent how many minutes past each hour that you want to run the program. This is useful for programs that provide feedback about your computer such as Low Disk-Space Notification.

- **Daily.** The program will run at a specific time on the days of the week that you specify. You might use this for programs that check your computer for errors or to back up your computer.

- **Weekly.** Tell System Agent which day of the week and what time you want the program to run. Drive-intensive programs or programs that take a while to run are good choices for a weekly schedule.

- **Monthly.** You can specify which day of the month and the time of day for the scheduled program to run.

- **At Startup.** Click on this option and System Agent will run the program every time you start your computer. You can use this for reminders or to pop up a to-do list in Notepad every time your computer starts.

- **When Idle.** Tell System Agent to run the program every time you stop using your computer for an amount of time that you specify. I used this while writing this book to back up the chapters, using Microsoft Backup, after I'd left my computer alone for an hour.

When you select one of the preceding options, the middle part (Start At frame) of the dialog box shown in figure 18.3 changes. What it changes to depends on the option. Figure 18.5 shows what the middle part looks like for each frequency that you can select. For example, if you selected Hourly, you'd tell System Agent how many minutes past the hour to start the program in the middle part of the dialog box. If you selected Weekly, you'd tell it exactly what time and which day to start the program in the middle part.

Fig. 18.5

The middle part of the dialog box changes depending on which frequency you choose.

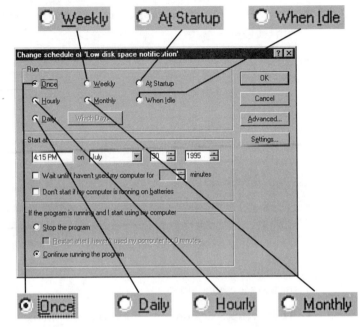

To continue scheduling your program, use the following steps:

1 After selecting a frequency in the top part (Run frame) of the dialog box, specify when you want the program to run in the middle part of the dialog box. If you selected Daily, click on Which Days to specify the exact days in the week to run your program.

2 Click on Wait Until I Haven't Used My Computer if you want the System Agent to wait until you aren't using your computer before starting the program. Fill in the number of minutes it should wait in the space provided.

TIP **You might want to run a particular program every time you stop using your computer for a few minutes.** For example, if you're working on a project, you could set up a System Agent program to copy the project's files every time you pause for five minutes. Select When Idle, select Wait Until I Haven't Used My Computer, and type **5** in the space provided.

3 Select Stop the Program if you want System Agent to stop the program if you start using your computer before the program is finished running. Select Restart After I Haven't Used My Computer if you want System Agent to restart an interrupted program after you leave your computer alone for the given time. Otherwise, select Continue Running the Program.

4 Click on Advanced to set advanced options as shown in figure 18.6. These options change depending on what type of frequency you've selected. These options let you specify how long System Agent keeps trying to run the program before it gives up, and whether System Agent should tell you about programs that it couldn't start. You can also tell System Agent to run a program over and over between the starting and ending time that you specify. In most cases, the default values for the advanced options are acceptable.

5 Click on OK to save your changes.

Fig. 18.6
Advanced options
change just like the
start time shown in
figure 18.5.

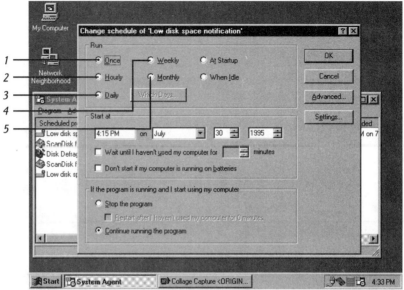

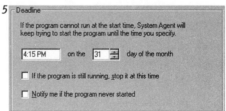

Free programs! System Agent's got 'em

System Agent comes with four programs that you'll find very useful: ScanDisk for Windows, Disk Defragmenter, Compression Agent, and Low Disk-Space Notification. Also, you'll find many software vendors who sell more System Agent Aware programs that you can use.

ScanDisk for Windows checks for errors

ScanDisk

ScanDisk for Windows will check your computer's drives for errors. You can tell it which drives to check, what type of tests to perform, and whether it should fix any errors that it finds. Figure 18.7 shows the settings available when you click on Settings on its property sheet.

Select the Standard test for a quickie, or Thorough for a more exhaustive test, which takes much longer.

Fig. 18.7
Tell ScanDisk which drives to check and what type of test to perform. Schedule this program to do a light test once a day and an exhaustive test once a week.

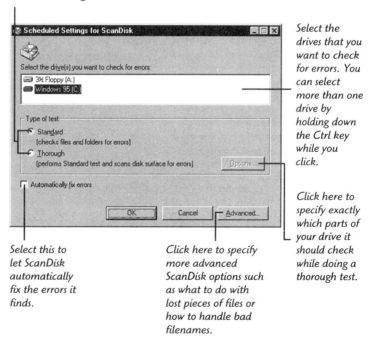

Select the drives that you want to check for errors. You can select more than one drive by holding down the Ctrl key while you click.

Click here to specify exactly which parts of your drive it should check while doing a thorough test.

Select this to let ScanDisk automatically fix the errors it finds.

Click here to specify more advanced ScanDisk options such as what to do with lost pieces of files or how to handle bad filenames.

TIP **If you want to view the actual error log for ScanDisk or any other** System Agent program, select <u>A</u>dvanced, <u>V</u>iew Log from the main menu. It shows the starting and ending time for each program that System Agent runs. Errors are reported after the ending time of each program.

Disk Defragmenter makes your computer faster

Disk
Defragmenter

Files aren't stored all in one piece on your hard drive. They are stored in chunks. Sometimes, these chunks get scattered all over your drive. When this happens, it can take longer to read the file and it could take up more drive space.

 Plain English, please!

Defragmenting is the process of making all of a file's chunks occupy contiguous space on your drive. This makes the files load faster and take up less space. **99**

Disk Defragmenter is a System Agent program that fixes the problem of scattered files. When it runs, it will defragment the files on your drive. Figure 18.8 shows the settings for this program.

Select the drive that you want to defragment here, or select All Hard Drives if you want to defragment all the drives on your computer.

Fig. 18.8
Disk Defragmenter will make your drive run faster and your files take up less space. Schedule this program to run once a day.

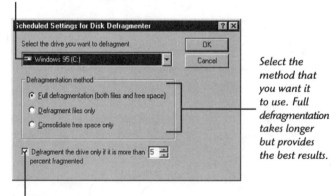

Select the method that you want it to use. Full defragmentation takes longer but provides the best results.

Select this if you want to run Disk Defragmenter only when your drive is really a mess.

Compression Agent gives you more drive space

Compression Agent is a marvelous program that compresses the files on your drive while you're not trying to use it. Files are written to the drive uncompressed while you're using the computer. Then, Compression Agent comes along while you're not looking and compresses the files for you. Chapter 17 provides in-depth information about using Compression Agent.

Low Disk–Space Notification watches your drive

If you're like me, you've never got enough drive space. I can fill up a gigabyte in a week. Low Disk-Space Notification warns you ahead of time that you're about to run out of disk space. Figure 18.9 shows you its settings.

Select the drive that you want to configure in this list.

Fig. 18.9
This program will warn you before you run out of drive space. Schedule this one to run every hour.

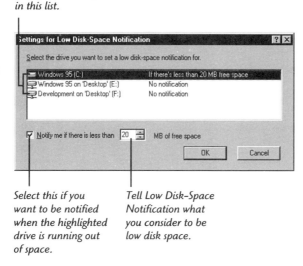

Select this if you want to be notified when the highlighted drive is running out of space.

Tell Low Disk–Space Notification what you consider to be low disk space.

Can I schedule other programs, too?

Yes! Chapter 19, "Using Microsoft Backup with System Agent," shows you how to use Microsoft Backup with System Agent. You can schedule any program that will run in Windows 95. But, there are a few things to think about when scheduling a program:

- The program should be capable of running without intervention from you. In other words, if the program requires a bunch of input from you before it can do its job, it won't be much use trying to schedule it to run in the middle of the night.

- If the program is not System Agent Aware, System Agent may not be able to interrupt it when you start using your computer, and probably can't make it continue where it left off when you've finished.

- If the program is not System Agent Aware, such as Microsoft Backup, its setting will not appear in the program's properties. You'll have to run the program to set its options.

- Some programs accept command-line parameters that cause them to perform a task without intervention. For example, the command `notepad /p readme.txt` would cause Notepad to print the file README.TXT unattended. To find more information about the command lines of different programs, look in the program's documentation.

19

Using Microsoft Backup with System Agent

⬤ **In this chapter:**

- **Back up your important files**

- **How do you back up while you're not using the computer?**

Most people don't back up their important files because it's inconvenient. Use Microsoft Backup with System Agent and you'll never have to think about it again . . . . ⮞

It's pretty easy to lose a file. You could accidentally erase it. There could be an error on your drive. Or, God forbid, a power surge could hit your computer and everything would be gone!

You'd be crushed if you lost the files that were important to you. And it's easy to prevent this by using Microsoft Backup. Would you be more likely to back up if the computer would start it automatically? It works for me! You can use System Agent to schedule a backup, drop a tape in the drive, and forget about it.

Microsoft Backup is a bit quirky

CAUTION   **The online help for Microsoft Backup is not always accurate.** For example, the help says that an incremental backup doesn't include new files, but the context-sensitive help for the Incremental option says they are included. The only way to know for sure is to try it. Incidentally, Microsoft Backup does include files that are added to selected folders!

Microsoft Backup is a bit quirky. You'll notice a few differences between it and backup programs that you've used in the past, such as the backup program included with MS-DOS 6.*x*. Here's a list of some of the differences:

- Microsoft Backup provides a backup type called **incremental**, which is probably what you're used to calling **differential**. This backup type backs up all the files that have changed since the last full backup.

- Microsoft Backup doesn't use the archive file attribute to determine whether a file has changed since the last backup. It compares the modification date of the file to the date of the backup set to determine whether the file has changed.

 Plain English, please!

The **registry** is where Windows 95 keeps information about the hardware and software in your computer. Don't tamper with your registry unless you're a confident Windows 95 user.

- The only way to restore your computer from a tape backup is to use the Full System Backup set, which Microsoft Backup creates in the

Accessories directory. This is the only backup set that will correctly back up and restore your registry.

- To perform an incremental backup, you create a backup file set with the Incremental option set. The first time you use the backup set, all the folders and files that you selected are backed up. The next time that you use the set, only the files that have changed or have been added are backed up. To do a full backup again, you have to delete the fileset and start over.

You might be tempted to create one file set to use for your full backup, and create another file set to use for your incremental backup. This won't work because the incremental file set has no access to the information in the full file set. In fact, the incremental backup will do its own full backup the first time you use it.

 **Plain English, please!**

The **archive** file attribute is a flag stored with a file that indicates whether the file has been changed. Every time the file is changed, Windows 95 turns on this flag. Most backup programs turn this flag off when the file is backed up, and then check it to see whether the file has changed. **"**

Before you begin, plan your backup strategy

Now that you've got a handle on Microsoft Backup, you need to decide how you'll use it. Here are the issues that you need to consider before setting up System Agent to back up your important files:

- **Files.** Which files do you want to back up? You'll want to include all your documents, spreadsheets, pictures, downloaded files, or any other files that you'd miss if your system crashed.

- **Backup type.** If the files that you're backing up take a lot of space on the tape, you may want to consider using the incremental backup option. Make sure that you understand how it works before you set this option. Otherwise, it's a safe bet to stick with the full backup option.

- **Frequency.** How often do you want to back up? If your backup set is pretty small, I recommend that you back up every night—just leave that tape in the drive all the time. If it's a larger backup set or you don't use your computer much throughout the week, you can get by with scheduling your backup once a week.

TIP If you're working on a major project, such as this book, create an incremental backup set for the files in your project. Then, schedule the backup in System Agent to occur every time you stop using your program for a specific period of time, using the When Idle option.

My recommendation is that you select the files that are important to you and back all of them up at the end of every day. Why? Microsoft Backup is a bit confusing and the incremental backup is even more confusing. To make sure that you don't lose an important file, the safest bet is to back up all your files every day. And, by selecting only the files that you can't possibly get back by reinstalling your software, the backup sets won't be too big and you won't lose anything.

Create your backup set in Microsoft Backup

In this section, I'm assuming that you're following my recommendation to back up all your important files every day. To create the backup set you'll use with System Agent, follow these steps:

Backup

1 Start Microsoft Backup from the Start menu. You'll find it in Programs, Accessories, System Tools. If you haven't installed Microsoft Backup, install it now from your Windows 95 CD-ROM or disks. Figure 19.1 shows the Microsoft Backup main window.

Fig. 19.1
Select the folders that
you want to back up
on the left side and
the specific files that
you want to back up
on the right side.

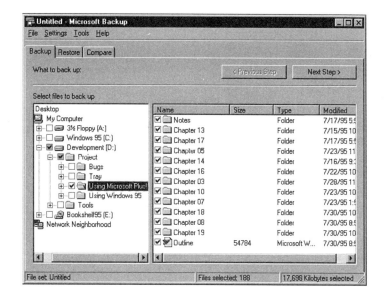

2 Select the folders that you want to back up if you want to include all the files in the folder (including files that are added in the future) and select specific files in the right side if you don't want to include the whole folder.

3 Select Settings, Drag and Drop from the main menu and make sure that Confirm Operation Before Beginning is not selected, as shown in figure 19.2. Then, click on OK.

Fig. 19.2
To work well with
System Agent, backup
should be run
minimized, confirma-
tion should be turned
off, and backup should
quit after it's finished.

4 Click on Next Step. The main window changes as shown in figure 19.3.

Fig. 19.3
Select the tape to
which you want to
back up your files.
Alternatively, you can
back up files to any
path on your com-
puter, but this is not
as safe.

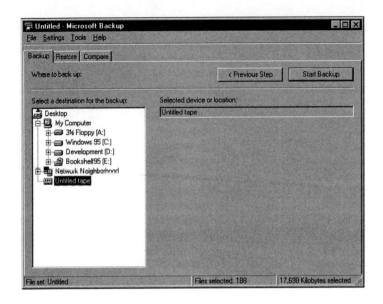

5 Select the tape or file path to which you want to back up your files.

6 Select File, Save As from the main menu and save the backup set to the
   Accessories folder with a meaningful filename, such as "Full Data
   Backup."

7 Close Microsoft Backup.

Then, schedule the backup set in System Agent

Now that you've got a backup set, you need to schedule it in System Agent.
You can read more about System Agent in chapter 18. Here's how you do it:

Sysagent

1 Open System Agent by double-clicking on its icon in the icon tray—
   lower-right corner of your display.

2 Select Program, Schedule a New Program from the main menu. System
   Agent displays the properties dialog box shown in figure 19.4.

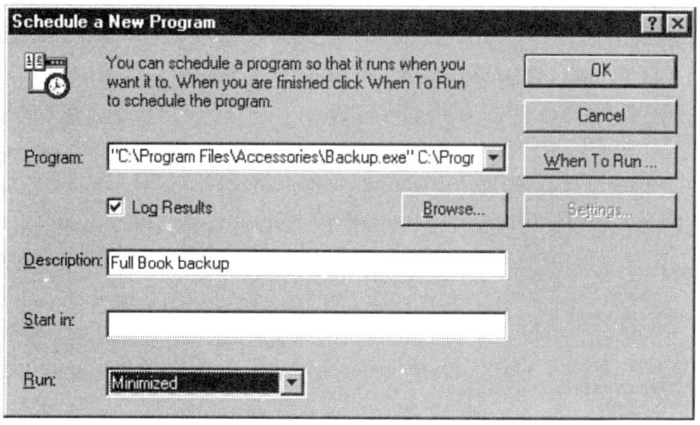

Fig. 19.4

If you're using long filenames, enclose the path to the program in quotation marks, but not the backup set. For example, "C:\Program Files\Accessories\ Backup.exe" C:\Program Files\Accesories\Full Data Backup.set.

3 Type the path to the backup program followed by the path to the backup set in the space provided. Alternatively, click on Browse and select Backup.exe from the appropriate path and type the path to the backup set following it.

4 Select Minimized in the Run list to keep the backup program out of the way while it's running.

5 Click on When to Run. System Agent displays the dialog box shown in figure 19.5.

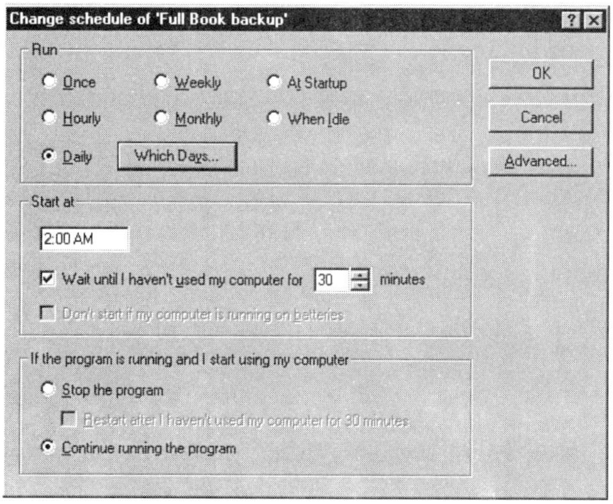

Fig. 19.5

If you want to back up your files every time that you stop using your computer, select When Idle. You can still run other programs during the backup.

6 Select Daily in the top part of the dialog box and type the time that you want to start the program in the space provided.

7 Click on Wait Until I Haven't Used My Computer and enter 30 minutes in the space provided. This tells System Agent to wait 30 minutes after you last used your computer before starting Microsoft Backup.

8 Select Continue Running the Program so that System Agent doesn't try to stop Microsoft Backup if you happen to start using your computer while it's performing the backup.

9 Click on Advanced, and System Agent displays the dialog box shown in figure 19.6.

Fig. 19.6
You can tell System Agent to keep trying to start the backup if it couldn't start it at the specified time.

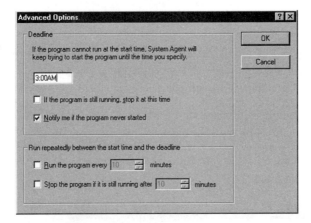

10 Type the latest time that you want System Agent to start the backup if it couldn't start it at the time that you specified.

11 Select Notify Me if the Program Never Started to tell System Agent to alert you if it wasn't ever able to start the backup. This is useful information if you're relying on your backup to keep your files secure.

12 Click on OK to save your advanced options. Then, click on OK again to save your scheduled program.

 TIP **You might consider using a ZIP drive for your backups. They are** becoming very popular because you can store about 10M of files on a single ZIP disk. The disks are very affordable. You'll need about 100 ZIP disks, however, if you're backing up a 1G hard drive. So, consider using them for smaller backups such as backups of your data files.

Action Index

Installing Microsoft Plus!

Surf the World Wide Web

(continues)

Continued

When you need to...	You'll find help here...
Use a different start-up page	127
Save a page in Favorites	127
Use the history for Favorites	127
Send a shortcut in an e-mail	127
Organize Favorites into folders	127
Use shortcut wizard	127
Go directly to a page	127
Return to a previous page	127
Save shortcuts on your desktop	127
Load Web pages faster	127
Stop a page before it's finished	127
Change the history size	127
Refresh a page	127
Turn off pictures	127
Learn about pictures on the Web	149
Learn about sounds on the Web	149
Learn about videos on the Web	149
Save previously viewed videos	149
Play MPEG movies	149
Choose an MPEG player	149
Install an MPEG player	149
Play audio in real-time	149
Surf while using RealAudio	149

When you need to...	You'll find help here...
Learn about Internet Central	165
Find links hidden in pictures	165
Search the Web for a topic	165
Focus a search	165
Keep up with Net Happenings	165
Explore the Web with GNN	165
Search the Web with WebCrawler	165
Learn about good search terms	165
Learn how WebCrawler works	165
Learn about other search tools	165
See a list of great sites	181

The Internet Basics

When you need to...	You'll find help here...
Use built-in Telnet or FTP	113
Learn about TCP/IP, PAP, etc.	113
Learn about HTTP, HTML, URL, etc.	127
Use MSN as your Internet account	113
Use a provider for your account	113
Secure your connection	113
Connect using SLIP or CSLIP	113
Learn why your mail didn't go	209

(continues)

Continued

Changing the way your desktop looks

When you need to...	You'll find help here...
See a window while you move it	31
Smooth the edges of screen fonts	31
Fix smoothing if it doesn't work	31
Fit the wallpaper to the desktop	31
Position the wallpaper exactly	31
Make the desktop icons bigger	31
Use my own desktop icons	31
Find more icons you can use	31
Use icons with more color	31
Use animated mouse pointers	31
Locate the pointers on the drive	31
Learn about desktop themes	47
Apply portions of a theme	47
Use high-color themes	47
Use an entire desktop theme	47
Preview a theme before using it	47
Make your own desktop theme	47
Compare all the desktop themes	61
Use 3.1 programs with themes	47

Playing Space Cadet Pinball

When you need to...	You'll find help here...
Get started quickly	99
Learn about the pinball table	99
Change the keys used to play	99
Play pinball full screen	99
Change the number of players	99
Hear real arcade sound	99
Adjust the sound	99
Learn the basic strategy	99
Learn the intermediate strategy	99
Learn the advanced strategy	99

Using Dial-Up Networking and Server

When you need to...	You'll find help here...
Determine requirements to use	231
Understand Dial-Up Networking	231
Learn about network terms	231
Connect to a dial-up server	231
Connecting to a network gateway	231
See shared resources	231 and 245
Use the right network drivers	231
Prevent logging onto a network	231
Save your logon password	231

When you need to...	You'll find help here...
Connect to Netware	231
Learn about dial-up scripting	245
Decide whether you need scripting	245
Write a dial-up script	245
See the commands available	245
Attach a script to a connection	245
Fix a broken script	245
Use dial-up server and briefcase	257
Determine requirements to use	257
Disable dial-up server w/policies	257
Turn on the dial-up server	257

Manage your computer

When you need to...	You'll find help here...
Protect your hard drive	267
Learn about drive compression	267
Learn about compression ratios	267
See the ratios for your computer	267
Estimate the compression ratio	267
Adjust the ratio	267
Upgrade to DriveSpace 3	267
Upgrade a floppy to DriveSpace 3	267
Compress an entire hard drive	267
Find out about FAILSAFE.DRV	267

(continues)

Continued

Index

**newsgroups (USENET),
115**
newspaper Web sites
USA Today Online,
187-188
Web Week Home Page,
187
**notebook computers,
scheduling programs
on, 22**

**Options dialog box
(Internet Explorer)**
address display
options, 139
Advanced tab
Cache size, 146
History settings, 144
custom colors, 139
File Types tab, 159-160
hiding toolbars, 140
links display options,
139
show pictures option,
138
Start Page tab, 143

P

packets, 117
**PAP (Password
Authentication
Protocol), 117**
**Paramount Pictures
Online Studio Web
site, 185-187**
**passwords (networks),
262-263**
**Pathfinder Web site,
190**
PC Magazine **online,
188**
PCWeek **online, 188**
**peer-to-peer networks,
259**
People **online, 190**
personalizing, *see*
customizing
**phone lines (dial-up
servers), 8**

pictures, *see* **graphics**
pinball game, *see* **Space
Cadet Pinball**
pixels, 40
pointers, mouse
animated, 44-46
Desktop Themes, 49
60's USA, 87-88
custom Themes, 57
Dangerous
Creatures, 62-64
Golden Era, 90-91
Inside Your
Computer, 65-67
Leonardo Da Vinci,
68-70
More Windows,
72-73
Mystery, 75-76
Nature, 78-79
Science, 81-82
Sports, 84-85
Travel, 93-94
Windows 95, 96-97
political Web sites
US Congress, 204-205
White House Web page,
204
**POP3 mail server,
222-223**
**previewing Desktop
Themes, 53-55**
printing Web pages, 142
**Prodigy, Internet mail
addresses to, 213-214**
**product support (World
Wide Web), 130-131**
**Program
Files\Accessories
directory, 251**
**Program menu
commands (System
Agent)**
Schedule a New
Program
Description, 302
Program list, 301
When to Run
options, 302-303

programs
conflicts with Desktop
Themes, 59
icons (Plus! programs),
26
scheduling, 12, 300-301
listing programs to
schedule, 301-302
Microsoft Backup,
316-318
program
requirements,
309-310
run time options,
302-305
shortcuts (Plus!
programs), 26
**Progressive Networks
home page, 163**
property sheets, *see*
**Display Property
sheet**
protocols, 116-117

Q-R

**quicktime movies
(Internet), 154-155**

**ratios, compression,
286**
RealAudio, 153, 162
home page, 163
playing titles, 162-163
**reference Web sites,
131-132**
Britannica Online, 132,
190-191
WordNet 1.5 on the
Web, 191-192
remote access, 8
file sharing, 258
networks, 8-9, 258-260
automatic logon,
9-10
see also Dial-Up
Networking
resolution, 40
**Rolling Stones web site,
153, 163**

PLUG YOURSELF INTO...

MACMILLAN INFORMATION SUPERLIBRARY™

que · SAMS PUBLISHING · Hayden Books · que COLLEGE

NRP · alpha books · Brady · ADOBE PRESS

The Macmillan Information SuperLibrary™

Free information and vast computer resources from the world's leading computer book publisher—online!

FIND THE BOOKS THAT ARE RIGHT FOR YOU!

A complete online catalog, plus sample chapters and tables of contents give you an in-depth look at *all* of our books, including hard-to-find titles. It's the best way to find the books you need!

- STAY INFORMED with the latest computer industry news through our online newsletter, press releases, and customized Information SuperLibrary Reports.

- GET FAST ANSWERS to your questions about MCP books and software.

- VISIT our online bookstore for the latest information and editions!

- COMMUNICATE with our expert authors through e-mail and conferences.

- DOWNLOAD SOFTWARE from the immense MCP library:
    - Source code and files from MCP books
    - The best shareware, freeware, and demos

- DISCOVER HOT SPOTS on other parts of the Internet.

- WIN BOOKS in ongoing contests and giveaways!

TO PLUG INTO MCP: →

GOPHER: gopher.mcp.com

FTP: ftp.mcp.com

WORLD WIDE WEB: http://www.mcp.com

Home Page · What's New · Bookstore · Reference Desk · Software Library · Macmillan Overview · Talk to Us

Complete and Return this Card
for a *FREE* Computer Book Catalog

Thank you for purchasing this book! You have purchased a superior computer book written expressly for your needs. To continue to provide the kind of up-to-date, pertinent coverage you've come to expect from us, we need to hear from you. Please take a minute to complete and return this self-addressed, postage-paid form. In return, we'll send you a free catalog of all our computer books on topics ranging from word processing to programming and the internet.

r. ☐   Mrs. ☐   Ms. ☐   Dr. ☐

me (first) ☐☐☐☐☐☐☐☐☐☐☐☐   (M.I.) ☐   (last) ☐☐☐☐☐☐☐☐☐☐☐☐☐☐☐☐☐

ddress ☐☐☐☐☐☐☐☐☐☐☐☐☐☐☐☐☐☐☐☐☐☐☐☐☐☐☐☐☐☐☐☐☐

☐☐☐☐☐☐☐☐☐☐☐☐☐☐☐☐☐☐☐☐☐☐☐☐☐☐☐☐☐☐☐☐☐

ty ☐☐☐☐☐☐☐☐☐☐☐☐☐☐☐☐☐   State ☐☐   Zip ☐☐☐☐☐ ☐☐☐☐

one ☐☐☐ ☐☐☐ ☐☐☐☐   Fax ☐☐☐ ☐☐☐ ☐☐☐☐

mpany Name ☐☐☐☐☐☐☐☐☐☐☐☐☐☐☐☐☐☐☐☐☐☐☐☐☐☐☐☐☐☐☐

mail address ☐☐☐☐☐☐☐☐☐☐☐☐☐☐☐☐☐☐☐☐☐☐☐☐☐☐☐☐☐☐☐

Please check at least (3) influencing factors for purchasing this book.

ont or back cover information on book .... ☐
ecial approach to the content .... ☐
mpleteness of content... ☐
thor's reputation .... ☐
blisher's reputation .... ☐
ok cover design or layout .... ☐
dex or table of contents of book .... ☐
ice of book .... ☐
ecial effects, graphics, illustrations .... ☐
her (Please specify): _____ ☐

How did you first learn about this book?

w in Macmillan Computer Publishing catalog .... ☐
commended by store personnel .... ☐
w the book on bookshelf at store .... ☐
commended by a friend .... ☐
ceived advertisement in the mail .... ☐
w an advertisement in: _____ ☐
ad book review in: _____ ☐
her (Please specify): _____ ☐

How many computer books have you purchased in the last six months?

is book only .... ☐   3 to 5 books..................... ☐
ooks .... ☐   More than 5 .... ☐

4. Where did you purchase this book?

Bookstore .... ☐
Computer Store .... ☐
Consumer Electronics Store .... ☐
Department Store .... ☐
Office Club .... ☐
Warehouse Club .... ☐
Mail Order .... ☐
Direct from Publisher .... ☐
Internet site .... ☐
Other (Please specify): _____ ☐

5. How long have you been using a computer?

☐ Less than 6 months   ☐ 6 months to a year
☐ 1 to 3 years   ☐ More than 3 years

6. What is your level of experience with personal computers and with the subject of this book?

	With PCs	With subject of book
New	☐	☐
Casual	☐	☐
Accomplished	☐	☐
Expert	☐	☐

Source Code ISBN: 0-7897-0626-1

7. Which of the following best describes your job title?

- Administrative Assistant .... ☐
- Coordinator .... ☐
- Manager/Supervisor .... ☐
- Director .... ☐
- Vice President .... ☐
- President/CEO/COO .... ☐
- Lawyer/Doctor/Medical Professional .... ☐
- Teacher/Educator/Trainer .... ☐
- Engineer/Technician .... ☐
- Consultant .... ☐
- Not employed/Student/Retired .... ☐
- Other (Please specify): _____ ☐

8. Which of the following best describes the area of the company your job title falls under?

- Accounting .... ☐
- Engineering .... ☐
- Manufacturing .... ☐
- Operations .... ☐
- Marketing .... ☐
- Sales .... ☐
- Other (Please specify): _____ ☐

9. What is your age?

- Under 20 .... ☐
- 21-29 .... ☐
- 30-39 .... ☐
- 40-49 .... ☐
- 50-59 .... ☐
- 60-over .... ☐

10. Are you:

- Male .... ☐
- Female .... ☐

11. Which computer publications do you read regularly? (Please list)

_____
_____
_____
_____
_____
_____
_____
_____
_____
_____

Comments: _____
_____
_____

Fold here and scotch-tape to m